ROMANTICISM

Vistas, Instances, Continuities

ROMANTICISM

Vistas, Instances, Continuities

Edited by DAVID THORBURN
and GEOFFREY HARTMAN

CORNELL UNIVERSITY PRESS
Ithaca and London

First published 1973 by Cornell University Press.
Published in the United Kingdom by Cornell University Press Ltd., 2-4 Brook Street, London W1Y 1AA.

International Standard Book Number 0-8014-0791-5 (cloth)
International Standard Book Number 0-8014-9144-4 (paper)
Library of Congress Catalog Card Number 73-8405

Printed in the United States of America by Vail-Ballou Press, Inc.

Contents

Preface

All but two of the essays collected here were originally delivered as lectures in a symposium on Romanticism held at Yale in 1970–71 under the auspices of the English Department. While the essays have been revised for this volume, and two new ones (by Paul de Man and M. G. Cooke) added, the editors hope that the collection retains and even extends the virtues of the lecture series—its range and variety, its commitment to a kind of discourse about literature that is serious and learned but also widely accessible.

The essays wish to honor writers of great influence and also to gauge what changes of critical mood have occurred since these writers came under attack in the 1920's and 1930's by a coalition of modernist poets and conservative thinkers. Though the War on Romanticism is far from over (the claim of "countercultural" writers to be neo-Romantic is fostering new skirmishes and suspicions), it is time to acknowledge that Babbitt's "Rousseau" is as defunct as Eliot's "Shelley" or Yvor Winters's "Emerson." By the shock of juxtaposition—by bringing together, for example, Emerson and Nietzsche, or more expectedly, Wordsworth and Proust—or by a closer, though far from dispassionate, reading of Romantic precursors, new perspectives are born that did not seem attainable a generation ago. Whether the new "Rousseau" or the new "Emerson" will survive longer than the old, posterity will tell; these pages simply register the change. And since contributions were sought from both older and younger scholars, they should also provide a cross section of the views of students of Romanticism who belong to different generations.

It would be misleading to claim, amid such diversity, a narrowly focused agreement concerning the nature of Romanticism; and indeed there are hints of disagreement and even of healthy contention in this book. Moreover, though most contributors do not evade problems of definition, they are often free enough to subordinate the task of periodization to their sense of the importance of an individual author or work. A book on Romanticism should remain a book on literature and changes in interpretation. Yet if we cannot offer the reader still another definition of the Romantic, there remains an essential accord among the critics represented—an accord the more significant because it emerges in a context of such diversity.

The accord is in the nature of an impulse: a revisionist impulse that redeems not only particular Romantic works but the very image of the Romantic writer. That image, no doubt, is not as simplified as it was; there are few today who see the Romantic artist as one who has reduced imagination to feeling and life to gaping at landscapes. Yet it is hard to pride oneself on being modern and then to discover—or uncover—an indebtedness to the Romantics, to writers who could be at once visionary and sceptical. It was much easier to acknowledge the vision and drop out the scepticism, so that of their capable and conscious imagination only the strange intensities or queer affective moments remained. Nearly every essay here provides a corrective to modernist simplifications by restoring continuities that look both backward and forward: there are metaphysical strains in Coleridge as there are powerfully Romantic pressures in such "modern" writers as James and Conrad. Not because they are expansionist but because of the naive and shrunken definitions that have prevailed, these essays insist on a broadened concept of Romanticism. They constitute, collectively, a rejection of older, more restrictive views, in which Romantic writers could be decisively distinguished from (say) Victorian or modern ones, or in which a relatively contained span of years during the earlier nineteenth century could be confidently designated as the Romantic period.

Such an enlarging and complicating of Romantic studies has been a major enterprise of literary scholarship in the past decade or so. Besides offering stimulating approaches to particular writers or to historical and theoretical problems, the present volume tries to acknowledge that enterprise, and to advance it.

DAVID THORBURN
GEOFFREY HARTMAN

New Haven, Connecticut

Acknowledgments

Grateful acknowledgment is extended to the publishers and journals who gave permission to reprint articles, including: the American Philosophical Society, for F. A. Pottle, "Wordsworth in the Present Day," in its *Proceedings*, 116 (December 21, 1972), 443–449; *Partisan Review*, for Peter Brooks, "The Melodramatic Imagination," © 1972 by *Partisan Review*, from its Spring 1972 issue; Routledge & Kegan Paul Ltd., for W. K. Wimsatt, "Organic Form: Some Questions about a Metaphor," from *Organic Form: The Life of an Idea*, ed. G. S. Rousseau (1972); *Studies in Romanticism*, for Geoffrey Hartman, "Reflections on Romanticism in France," from its Fall 1970 issue; and for Paul de Man, "Theory of Metaphor in Rousseau's *Second Discourse*," from its Spring 1973 issue; *Revue d'Histoire Littéraire de la France*, for Victor Brombert, "Esquisse de la prison heureuse," an earlier version of "The Happy Prison," from its March–April 1971 issue; *The Virginia Quarterly Review*, for Harold Bloom, "Emerson: The Glories and the Sorrows of American Romanticism," from its Autumn 1971 issue. We are also grateful for permission to reprint the following poems: J. V. Cunningham, "To The Reader," reprinted from *The Collected Poems and Epigrams of J. V. Cunningham*, © 1971, by permission of the Swallow Press, Chicago; "An Irish Airman Foresees his Death," from *The Collected Poems of W. B. Yeats*, by permission of Mr. M. B. Yeats, The Macmillan Company, Macmillan & Co. Ltd., and the Macmillan Company of Canada Ltd.

I

VISTAS

W. K. WIMSATT

Organic Form: Some
Questions about a Metaphor

The metaphor is ancient, and most of the questions have
been asked before, many times. That I should write an essay
of about twenty pages pretending to say anything worth while
upon such a classic theme requires a courage that I derive
largely from the support of two scholars who have recently
written on it—one, Philip C. Ritterbush, a historian who has
made himself an expert guide in that tropical rainforest of
eighteenth-century romantic nature philosophy and early scientific "representation" of living form, in which some of
our most cherished modern notions about both science and
poetry had their seedbed and first growth; the other, G. N. G.
Orsini, an idealist aesthetician and critic of imposing authority. It is not my aim to expound very much history, either of
science or of aesthetics. I take history as an object that is before us, almost palpably, upon the table, and I choose my
own exhibits. A first one that I call attention to I take from a
play by Molière, *Don Juan, or the Feast with the Statue*. The
agile valet Sganarelle in one of his several running debates
with his atheistic master, bursts into teleology:

Can you perceive all the contrivances of which the human mech-
anism is composed without wondering at the way the parts are
fitted with one another? These nerves, these bones, these veins,

these artieries, these . . . this lung, this heart, this liver, and all
the other organs. . . . My argument is that there is something
mysterious in man which, whatever you may say, none of the
philosophers can explain. Is it not wonderful that I exist and
that I have something in my head which thinks a hundred different things in a moment and does what it wills with my body? I
wish to clap my hands, to raise my arms, to lift my eyes to
heaven, to bow my head, to move my feet, to go to the right, to
the left, forward, backward, to turn. . . . (He falls down whilst
turning.)
Don Juan. Good, so your argument has broken its nose.

(*Don Juan,* III, i)

A centuries-old Aristotelian and scholastic commonplace—
"What a piece of work is a man"—is good enough material
here for a hamstrung sprint of servile boldness, a bumbling
theology. Larger versions of organicism appear in the same
era with a kind of cool solemnity, as in the cosmic unity, the
social and ethical harmonies, which critics nowadays celebrate
and annotate from the whole Western tradition in the *Essay
on Man* of Pope or his *Windsor Forest.*[1]

A quicker pulse, a new accent of excitement, marks, I believe, my second exhibit—if not a subtlety and coolness equal
to that of either Molière or Pope.

> What Beaux and Beauties crowd the gaudy groves,
> And woo and win their vegetable Loves.
>
> . . . . .
>
> The love-sick Violet, and the Primrose pale,
> Bow their sweet heads, and whisper to the gale;
> With secret sighs the Virgin Lily droops,
> And jealous Cowslips hang their tawny cups.
> How the young Rose in beauty's damask pride
> Drinks the warm blushes of his bashful bride.
>
> BOTANIC MUSE! who in this latter age
> Led by your airy hand the Swedish sage,

1. See, for example, Earl R. Wasserman, *The Subtler Language* (Baltimore: Johns Hopkins Univ. Press, 1959), ch. 4.

Bade his keen eye your secret haunts explore
On dewy dell, high wood, and winding shore;
Say on each leaf how tiny Graces dwell;
How laugh the Pleasures in a blossom's bell.
How insect Loves arise on cobweb wings,
Aim their light shafts, and point their little stings.[2]

The author of these heroic couplets, the grandfather of Charles Darwin, tells us in a footnote that he is drawing upon "Linneus, the celebrated Swedish naturalist," and in an advertisement to the volume, he says that "The general design . . . is to inlist Imagination under the banner of Science; and to lead her votaries from the looser analogies, which dress out the imagery of poetry, to the stricter ones, which form the ratiocination of philosophy." The enlistment of the imagination and the looser analogies were a more successful part of the program than the stricter analogies. "Eighteenth-century naturalists," Dr. Philip C. Ritterbush instructs us, "denied or overlooked every distinction between plants and animals that they might have been expected to consider." [3] The frontispiece of a German edition of Alexander von Humboldt's *Journey to the Equatorial Regions of the New World* (1807), transplanted as frontispiece of Ritterbush's *Overtures to Biology* (1964), shows us an Apollonian figure, the spirit of poetry no doubt, unveiling an Asiatic Artemisian statue, appropriate emblem of the mysterious fecundity of nature; the title of Goethe's *Elegie* on the growth of plants (*Die Metamorphose der Pflanzen*, 1799) is inscribed on a tablet lying at the feet of the multimammiferous goddess. Such celebrations were surely not harmful for the development of Romantic nature poetry. At the same time, a degree

2. Erasmus Darwin, *The Botanic Garden* (1789–1791); 4th ed. (London, 1799), Part II, *The Loves of the Plants,* ll. 9–10, 15–20, 31–38. Cf. Philip C. Ritterbush, *Overtures to Biology* (New Haven: Yale Univ. Press, 1964), pp. 162–265.

3. *Overtures*, p. 156.

of confusion in poetic theory may have been a concomitant, even an inspiration, of the poetry. It is perhaps significant that the English Romantic poet who described nature (that is, English landscape) the most often and the most lovingly —Wordsworth, of course—had in his theoretical essays little to say about organic form. Yet, by and large, the prevalence of nature, especially landscape and botanical nature, in English poetry during about two centuries does suggest a kind of latent equation in the poetic mind: Themes or images of organic life in poetry confer upon that poetry the poetic life of organic form. Coleridge, the most important translator of German organic idealism to the English scene, could speak, or seem to speak, both for and against that equation, and in the same essay. "If the artist copies the mere nature, the *natura naturata,* what idle rivalry." [4] On the other hand, it did seem to him that the visible image of nature was in a special way "fitted to the limits of the human mind." Natural forms, in a very natural way, yielded moral reflections; nature was thought, and thought nature. That was the "mystery of genius in the Fine Arts." [5] This might be illustrated by many passages of description and simile in the poetry of both Coleridge and Wordsworth or of Shelley. But, as Bernard Blackstone has pointed out, there is no English Romantic poet better than Keats for showing us the genial swell of organic forms, the unfolded buds, the ripening fruit, the loaded blessing of the vines, the swollen gourd, the plumped hazel shells, and for making such images symbolize a transcendent experience of beauty—even beauty like that of a Grecian Urn. The first volume of Erasmus Darwin's *Botanic Garden* opened with engravings of flowers, and the second

4. *Biographia Literaria,* ed. J. Shawcross (London: Oxford Univ. Press, 1939), II, 257 ("On Poesy or Art").
5. *Biographia Literaria,* II, 253–254, 258.

volume concluded with engravings by William Blake of the Portland vase.[6]

What then of organic form in visual art? The notebooks of Goethe and a crowd of other Nature Philosophers and scientists and their treatises and textbooks are lavish with both pictures and scientific "representations" or modules of organic life. But these no doubt served little enough any aesthetic purpose. The "meticulously veined leaves" painted under the Pre-Raphaelite hand lens of Millais, or Ruskin sprawled out drawing a square foot of meadow grass on a mossy bank,[7] are more valid indexes to our theme, and no less the vegetable curves of Art Nouveau at the end of the century—Hector Guimard's sinuously framing metallic green tendrils and leaves for Paris Métro station portals, for instance, one of which we can see today in New York, in the sculpture garden of the Museum of Modern Art. Let a recent historian of that era in art have the last word about this: "Up from the sidewalk there sprang a profusion of interlacing metal, bouquets of aquatic plants, luminous tulips, gorged with the rich disturbing sap of Paris, its cellars, and subsoil." [8] The date was about 1900, at about the same date the Parisian aesthete Gustave Geffroy wrote the following encomium upon a flower: "*A flower*— . . . Free and growing out of the earth, or captive in a vase, it presents an artist with the perfect example of the universal creative force—in it he may find form, colour and even expression, a mysterious ex-

6. Ritterbush, *The Art of Organic Forms* (Washington, D.C.: Smithsonian Institution Press, 1968), pp. 19–20.

7. *The Art of Organic Forms*, p. 23. René Wellek, (*A History of Modern Criticism,* III [New Haven: Yale Univ. Press, 1963], 140), speculates that Ruskin's liking for organistic theory influenced his distaste for Dutch painting and classical landscapes.

8. Maurice Rheims, *The Age of Art Nouveau,* trans. Patrick Evans (London: Thames and Hudson, 1966), p. 14; cf. p. 95; plate 114.

pression composed of stillness, silence, and the fugitive beauty of things which are born only to die in the same moment." [9]

And this brings us to the art exhibition put on by Dr. Ritterbush at the Museum of Natural History in Washington, D.C., during June and July of 1968—*The Art of Organic Forms:* cells, globules, curves, filaments, membranes, tentacles, emulsions, gelatins, pulsing fluids, capillary action, liquid diffusions, amoeboid shapes, nascent protoplasmic entities,[10] all this and more concentrated in seventy-two paintings, graphics, and sculptures of our own century: Odilon Redon, for instance, *Au fond de la Mer,* c. 1905; Paul Klee, *Male and Female Plants,* 1921; Wasily Kandinsky, *Capricious Forms No. 634,* 1937; Max Ernst, *Prenez garde au microbe de l'amour,* 1949; Pavel Tchelichew, *Itinerary of Light,* 1953. Matta's *Le Vertigo d'Erôs,* 1944, at the Museum of Modern Art, supplies the mysterious greenish ektachrome frontispiece of the *Catalogue* of this remarkable exhibition. The thesis of many of these artists and of their critics, expressed in essays and catalogue notes, is that such submicroscopic life forms symbolize the secret life of the creative human spirit.

We have been skirting a sophism: namely, the notion that the representation of biological forms in a work of verbal or visual art implies something about the presence of organic or artistic form in that work.[11] An idealist historian and philosopher such as G. N. G. Orsini will not wish to linger long in discussion of that issue. Nevertheless, its recurrent presence, even as a hint or as a half-committed fallacy,

9. No doubt to be found somewhere in Geffroy's eight volumes of *La Vie artistique,* 1892–1903. I quote from Martin Battersby, *The World of Art Nouveau* (New York: Funk & Wagnalls, 1968), p. 145. Cf. Rheims, *Art Nouveau,* p. 212.

10. *The Art of Organic Forms,* pp. 83–84.

11. *The Art of Organic Forms,* p. 86.

throughout the now long stretch of the modern organistic era, justifies its being noted and put aside with some deliberateness at the start of a discussion that aims at the center of the critical question of organicism. The issue is perhaps more easily defined in literary art, perhaps more nicely subject to confusion in visual art. Consider the following paradox. If the picture is overt enough, say a Currier and Ives print of watermelon vines, trumpet flowers, and humming birds, it presents organic forms, but I think none of us will be likely to argue that it thereby *has* high artistic form. Move the picture, however, through several shades of abstractionism, say through Art Nouveau sinuosities to pure or supposedly pure nonreferential curves, and then to the golden-section compositional style of Piet Mondrian or the "illusionary modulations," *Despite Straight Lines,* of Josef Albers.[12] We reach a stage where, so far as the picture has content, it is a geometric content. But this too is a geometric form, for geometry is all form. Form and representational content coincide perfectly. So in a sense this must be artistic form, and hence, by idealistic definition, it must be organic form. Yet it is not life form, but rather crystal form, as Dr. Ritterbush would say, or mere lifeless mechanical form, as A. W. Schlegel and Coleridge and many another Romantic would say.[13] So by a line of reasoning that starts with biological imagery we arrive at the conclusion that organic form can occur in visual art only by not occurring at either terminus of a spectrum running from realistic representation to extreme abstraction.

12. Josef Albers, *Despite Straight Lines* (New Haven: Yale Univ. Press, 1961), p. 10.

13. "These results require the use of ruler and drafting pen and establish unmodulated line as a legitimate artistic means. In this way they oppose a belief that the handmade is better than the machine-made, or that mechanical construction is anti-graphic or unable to arouse emotion" (*Ibid.,* p. 16).

If we believe that a poem grows in the mind like a plant (which is what Coleridge and the others did believe, or at least assert), and if we notice that the poem which emerges from the mind does not in fact look very much like a plant, and that furthermore (as we have been saying) the poem may or may not contain vegetable imagery, then as we ponder and expound our doctrine of growth and form, it may well be the perhaps more profound, but certainly less inspectable, part of the doctrine, the accent on the genetic, that we assert with the most energy. And thus it was in fact with Coleridge. A few of his most striking and deliberate statements about organic form occur in his notes for a general lecture on Shakespeare, which editors rightly place in the context of yet other notes for lectures on Shakespeare's power as a poet, his imagination, his judgment so happily wedded with his genius. Here Coleridge executes a double step away from any possible implication that organic form consists in vegetable imagery. He moves the discussion into the fully human and dramatic arena of Shakespeare's plays and his *Venus and Adonis*. At the same time he is recurrently inclined to depart from the poems themselves and to search the organic depths of the mind of the great maker. This is Coleridge's well-known leaning. Wordsworth was content to illustrate the concept of "imagination" in poems and passages of poems, especially in his own. Coleridge, as he himself explains in the *Biographia,* essayed the further radical task of tracing the poetic principle to its seat in the psychology of the poet.

Five properties of plant life (according to the clear exposition by Meyer Abrams) [14] enter into the analogy between plants and poems to be construed from Coleridge's several treatises, notes, letters, and conversations. (Coleridge both draws in part upon a German source, A. W. Schlegel, and in

14. Meyer Abrams, *The Mirror and the Lamp* (London: Oxford Univ. Press, 1953), pp. 170–176.

turn becomes archetypal for a moderate English tradition. Many passages in the first two volumes of René Wellek's *History of Modern Criticism* testify to the preoccupation of the romantic Germans with organic form, and also to their extravagance.[15]) The five properties or principles of organic form, in the order arranged by Abrams, are: 1) the WHOLE, the priority of the whole; without the whole the parts are nothing; 2) GROWTH, the manifestation of growth in the "evolution and extension of the plant"; 3) ASSIMILATION; the plant converts diverse materials into its own substance; 4) INTERNALITY; the plant is the spontaneous source of its own energy; it is not shaped from without; 5) INTERDE- PENDENCE, between parts and parts, and parts and whole; pull off a leaf and it dies. These somewhat overlapping or merging principles are all in effect equivalents of the single principle that we may call "Organic Form." The five, I be- lieve, might be readily synthesized into fewer, or into one; or they might be analyzed into a larger number. They have a close affinity for, or near identity with, a sixth, the favorite Coleridgean concept of the tension and reconciliation of manifold opposites which it is the peculiar power of artistic genius to accomplish.[16] All of these principles as expounded by Coleridge blend a measure of poetic structuralism, or ob- jective doctrine concerning poetic form, with a measure of geneticism, or psychological doctrine, concerning the au- thor's consciousness or unconsciousness. The second prin- ciple, or that of GROWTH, especially invites the genetic

15. See, for instance, II, 48, 358: A. W. Schlegel, in his Berlin Lec- tures, said that Euripides was the "putrefaction of Greek tragic form."

16. René Wellek, "Coleridge's Philosophy and Criticism," in *The English Romantic Poets: A Review of Research,* ed. T. M. Raysor (New York: Modern Language Association of America, 1950), pp. 109, 113, argues the close connection for Coleridge between the organic principle and that of polarity of opposites; he thinks too sharp a distinction be- tween the two is drawn by Gordon McKenzie, *Organic Unity in Cole- ridge* (Berkeley: Univ. of California Press, 1939).

accent. As I have the authority of Orsini on my side, I will not take upon myself the full burden of the argument against what I have fallen into the habit of referring to as the "intentional" or the "genetic" fallacy. "It is only to the finished product," says Orsini, "that we can apply the concept of organic unity." [17] I assent emphatically. Let me add, however, one observation. There is at least one respect in which the physical organism, either growing plant or animal, is immeasurably surpassed by the human poetic consciousness. I mean, in its capacity for self-revision, rearrangement, mending. Plants renew leaves and flowers; animals moult in several ways; a lobster can lose a claw and regrow it; the human body heals cuts and regrows a finger nail. But there is no action of any physical organism that remotely approaches the power of the human mind to revise and recast *itself*, constantly to reaffirm or to cancel its own precedent action, in whole or in part. We confront here self-involution, a spiritual power. (The world soul, says Plotinus, looking to its consequent dreams up the physical universe; looking to its antecedent it reflects the ideas of the nous.) As if a tree could move one of its own branches from the bottom to the top, or on looking itself over could change from an oak to a pine. What we call the "finished product," the poem, is a moment of spiritual activity, hypostatized, remembered, recorded, repeated. The human psyche makes the poem out of itself, or offers a remembered action of itself as the poem. Thus it differs notably from the tree, which does not offer anything, but simply appears, as the necessary product of the process which is itself. The Romantic analogy between vegetable and poetic creation tended to assimilate the poetic to the vegetable by making the poetic as radically spontaneous as possible—that is, indeliberate, unconscious. Some theorists clearly affirmed

17. G. N. G. Orsini, "The Organic Concepts in Aesthetics," *Comparative Literature*, 21 (Winter, 1969), 5.

this. Shakespeare created his Hamlet "as a bird weaves its nest." [18] A poet, urged Schiller, should *be* a plant.[19] An alternative which we have come close to noticing when we alluded to the eighteenth-century nature philosophers, was to draw plant life closer to human consciousness. According to one generous analogical view, plants *were* conscious. Coleridge, as Meyer Abrams has shrewdly pointed out, enjoyed the kind of classical sanity that compelled him to reject both solutions. Shakespeare's judgment was equal to his genius. He never wrote anything without conscious design.[20] On the other hand, "the man would be a dreamer, who otherwise than poetically should speak of roses and lilies as *self-conscious* subjects." [21] The inside history of literature as recorded in the testimonies of authors themselves is full of their awareness that the process by which they have arrived at the mental and verbal act presented as a poem has not necessarily, or even usually, been identical with that act as finally achieved. The moment presented as the poem is a contrived moment. This is so even on the supposition that the author achieves his sonnet in one perfect first draft. For he reviews it and accepts it and puts it out as a poem. No matter how spontaneous and lucky in one sense, in another sense it is also artificial. Few poets have, like the French inspirationalist Charles Peguy, looked on their first impulses

18. Wellek, *History,* III, 166 (Emerson); Cf. II, 290 (Kleist); II, 217 (A. W. Schlegel).

19. Abrams, pp. 168–174; 202–208.

20. Abrams, pp. 364–365. It was still possible for Walter Pater to read the general emphasis of Coleridge's *dicta* on organicism in the opposite way. He thought that Coleridge made the artist "almost a mechanical agent"; poetry "like some blindly organic process of assimilation" ("Coleridge," *Appreciations* [London: Macmillan, 1898], p. 80). And indeed see "On Poesy or Art," *Biographia,* II, 258: "There is in genius itself an unconscious activity; nay, that is the genius in the man of genius."

21. Abrams, 173 and note pp. 364–365.

as so literally inspired that the least revision of a first draft was an aesthetic sin. "A line will take us hours maybe," says Yeats. "Yet if it does not seem a moment's thought, Our stitching and unstitching has been naught." [22] He knew that the hours of stitching and unstitching were a normal part of "Adam's Curse." And with a somewhat different emphasis: "Verse, 'tis true," argues Dryden, "is not the effect of sudden thought; but that hinders not that sudden thought may be represented in verse." "A play is supposed to be the work of a poet." [23]

And so we come to the third of three issues which I am trying to define—not whether the poem presents biological imagery; and not whether the process of its growth in the mind resembles the growth of a tree; but whether the poem itself, the hypostatized verbal and mental act, looks in any way like an animal or a vegetable. In section 65 of the *Critique of Judgment* Kant observes, and few besides Orsini seem to have noticed it,[24] that a work of human art differs from a natural organism in that the latter is self-organizing, that it can repair itself when damaged, and that it reproduces itself. I have already suggested that under its genetic aspect (as the creator's mind in act) the verbal work of art rivals and even surpasses the natural organism in the capacity for self-correction. We have seen that Coleridge, with his strong inclination to the genetic, claimed internality, or self-organization, as one of the characters of the poetic organism. But our theme now is the poem as presented or objectified act—as poetic object. Plato said a composition should have

22. "Adam's Curse," *The Collected Poems of W. B. Yeats* (New York: Macmillan, 1959), p. 78.

23. John Dryden, *Essays*, ed. W. P. Ker (Oxford: Clarendon Press, 1900), I, 102, 114: *Essay of Dramatic Poesy* and *Defence of the Essay*.

24. G. N. G. Orsini, *Coleridge and German Idealism* (Carbondale, Ill.: Southern Illinois Univ. Press, 1969), pp. 160–162.

an organized sequence of parts, and that it ought to be *like* a living being, with foot, body, and head.[25] And Aristotle said that it ought to be a unity, like an organism.[26] But we might ask of Plato: What are the foot, body, and head of a poem? Or of Aristotle: What are the beginning, middle, and end of a squirrel or a tree? Or: Professor Orsini recites for us the rude question of an imagined objector: "What corresponds to the stomach in a tragedy?" Such conceptions, he remarks wisely, are carrying the simile too far. He argues indeed that the simile (or metaphor) of physical organic life is not essential to the concept of aesthetic organic unity.[27] The aesthetic unity is generated by the Kantian *a priori* synthetic idea, the human reason's glorious power of non-empirical creative unifying vision.[28] The art work, says Orsini, has indeed, and literally, an organic form, a synthetic unity in multiplicity. The merely physical organism enjoys this character only by metaphoric extension and hence in a less exact degree.[29] Thus he would reverse the usual direction of the metaphor. One will readily nowadays think of certain senses in which he may be right about the physical organism.

25. Plato, *Phaedrus,* 265.

26. Aristotle, *Poetics,* VIII. 4; XXIII. 1.

27. Orsini, pp. 4–5, 27. Cf. Wellek, *History,* I, 9, 18, 26 (the romantic emphasis upon biology); IV, 70–71 (Brunetière adopting biological evolutionary concepts too literally); Meyer Abrams, "Archetypal Analogues in the Language of Criticism," *University of Toronto Quarterly,* 18 (1949), 313–327; Graham Hough, *An Essay on Criticism* (London: Duckworth, 1966), ch. 22, "Organic Form: A Metaphor."

28. The reference is to Kant's *Logik,* ch. 1, par. 3 (Orsini, pp. 2–3, 4, 17). This kind of unity embraces also mental activities other than the aesthetic—e.g. philosophical, political, scientific, technological (Orsini, p. 26). Though the idealist aesthetician must guard against the sin of "intellectualism" in defining the unifying motifs of aesthetic works (Orsini, pp. 9–10), he is ready to extend the purified concept of "organic" unity into the areas of the highest abstractionism. This, I should say, involves Plotinian and Crocean problems about how to distinguish Art from the whole remaining horizon of being and of human knowing.

29. Orsini, p. 27.

Nowadays a batch of amoebas is chopped up and the parts are reassembled, more or less higgledy-piggledy, as I understand it, and a new set of amoebas emerges— "synthetic." [30] The human body, we read with queasy feelings, fights hard to reject the benevolently transplanted kidney or heart. Yet even this obtuse archaic organism (our body), struggling to carry out the Coleridgean rules, can be coerced for a certain time, even an extended time, into entertaining and being sustained by alien organs. And thus it succeeds in looking a little more than we might previously have thought possible like a machine with interchangeable parts.

The aesthetic organicist, therefore, in his dealing with poems, will no doubt do well to appeal but cautiously to that analogy with the all too ragged physical organism. He may well be content to confine his appeal to a very purified post-Kantian version of the aesthetic properties: the individuality and uniqueness of each aesthetic whole, the priority of the whole to the parts, the congruence and interdependence of parts with parts and of parts with the whole, the uniqueness and irreplaceability of parts and their nonexistence prior to the aesthetic whole or outside it.[31] Surely these are ideas against which no literary critic is likely to rebel— none at least whose knowledge of critical history extends far enough backward for him to appreciate the embarrassments for criticism created by the more extreme versions of legislation according to the classical literary kinds or of evaluation according to the classical ornamental rhetoric, or of explanation according to economic, sociological, or other historical categories, or according to any theological, anthropological, or psychological archetypes. If we had never known any romantic interest in life forms, if we had never heard of organic form, we should today be under the necessity of in-

30. *New York Times,* 13 November 1970, p. 1.
31. Orsini, pp. 17, 10–11.

venting it. We might well be dedicating this very volume to a struggle to invent and proclaim some doctrine of Romantic organicism. Given, however, the very well-established theory as we do know it, and given its several main articles of doctrine, such as we have been reciting, I confess my opinion that both the metaphor and the literal idealist doctrine invite some not unreasonable questions.

If the leaf is detached from the tree, it dies. Still we may press it between the pages of a book and treasure it years later. It has that kind of superiority to certain parts of other and higher organisms, say an ear cut from a vanquished bull by a matador, a human finger cut off and preserved in formaldehyde. The German metaphysical humorist Jean Paul speaks in a typically enough Romantic idiom when in his *Vorschule der Aesthetik* he alludes contemptuously to the traditional right of book-reviewers to pluck the feathers of the "jewelled hummingbird." [32] Jean Paul is confident too that "the spirit of a work like the *Iliad* is manifest both in the whole and in the smallest syllable." [33] "Load every rift with ore," said Keats to Shelley. And even Coleridge, with a hedging glance at a Kantian distinction, uttered this well-known half-betrayal: A poem proposes to itself "such delight from the *whole,* as is compatible with a distinct gratification from each component *part.*" [34] Few of us, I suppose, have had

32. *Vorschule* (1804–1813), Second Preface, par. 11, in *Sämtliche Werke,* ed. Eduard Berend, Part I, vol. XI (Weimar, 1935), 11. I am indebted to the translation by Margaret Cardwell Hale, forthcoming from the Wayne State University Press.

33. Ch. 86, p. 311. The quotation is from Mrs. Hale's close paraphrase of Jean Paul's fragmentary chapter.

34. *Biographia,* II, 10 (ch. 14). He was hedging less carefully when he said that poetry permits a "pleasure from the whole consistent with a consciousness of pleasure from the component parts," and that it communicates "from each part the greatest sum of pleasure compatible with the largest sum of pleasure of the whole" ("Definition of Poetry," *Shakespearian Criticism,* ed. T. M. Raysor, I, 148).

the experience of finding a hummingbird's tail feather. But
I have found many blue jay feathers, and pheasant feathers,
and glossy black crow feathers, all of which I thought were
beautiful and put in my hat or lapel or preserved for a while
at home in a vase. No doubt there is an implicit sustaining
context within which we admire such relics, and the same is
true for certain fragmentary, sketchy, or partly abstracted
representational forms of art—for instance, a single fleeting
leg in a sculpture entitled "Runner" by Leon Underwood.[35]
We admire these in the context of a habitual consciousness
of their relation to the rest of the visible surface of a bird or
a human body. And these surface contexts too have beyond
them an interior context, where interdependence or mutual
need of parts is very great; it is peremptory or absolute.
These we know about, and no doubt the fact has aesthetic
significance. Still we do not need to see these things; we do
not want to see them. The ancient haruspicators were bent
on no aesthetic purpose. Elizabethan or Augustan lovers
might hope to see themselves imaged through a window in
a lady's bosom, or to look more cynically at the "moving toy
shop" of her heart, silks, ribbons, laces, gewgaws.[36] But when
Humbert Humbert in Nabokov's *Lolita* longs in effect to
eviscerate his nymphet, to kiss her insides, heart, liver, lungs,
kidneys, we have already, some chapters before this, begun
to enjoy a dawning comprehension that he is a madman.[37]
I am trying to emphasize one dimension of gross differentia-
tion between physical organism and poetic organism and thus
to reenforce the opinion I have already expressed that it is easy
to push the analogy between them too far. We know there

35. R. H. Wilenski, *The Meaning of Modern Sculpture* (London:
Faber and Faber, 1932), plate 18 (facing p. 133) and p. 160.

36. Murray Krieger, *A Window to Criticism* (Princeton: Princeton
Univ. Press, 1964), Part II; *The Rape of the Lock*, I, 100; and Pope's
Guardian 106.

37. Vladimir Nabokov, *Lolita* (New York: Putnam's, 1955), p. 167.

is not any part, detail, or aspect of a poem which we cannot at least try and wish to see in relation to all the other parts and the whole. The poem is all knowable; it is all knowledge, through and through. It is transnoetic, an act or a possible act of a self-reflexive consciousness. (In this respect, certain other kinds of art, stone statues, for instance, have a status different from that of either a poem or a person. A flaw at the center of the marble does not become known unless the statue is destroyed. Still the statue *is* solid and opaque and is conceived aesthetically in that way. Shelley's remark about the impurity of all the arts other than verbal poetry was more accurate than the more extreme unifying idealisms.) And so we might at first think that the absolute idealist doctrines —no life in the part without the whole, no substitution of one part for another, and the like—if purged of too much contact with the unhappy biological metaphor and applied *literally* (as the idealist says) to poems, might hold up much better. I think this is in fact not true. I am not urging a para-dox, but only one further confrontation with reality. I mean that in some respects the poem as organic unity will come off rather worse without the crutch, or the distraction, of the physical comparison.

The head of many a marble statue has survived truncation —and has been admired for centuries in a garden or a museum. Necessity in the relation of parts to parts and of parts to whole differs very widely with different arts and with different parts. Go into a movie by Antonioni or Fellini just in time to see the last few flickers, and you will likely ex-perience a nearly maximum loss of meaning and aesthetic quality in a part deprived of its whole. Arrive at the begin-ning of the movie, or read the first chapter of almost any novel, and you will likely have the opposite experience. If the high aesthetic doctrine of the whole were true, we would never sit out even a very good movie or a very good play,

never finish reading a novel or a poem. We recognize and
enjoy the trenchancy or the delicacy of Augustan couplet wit
before we finish the first page of any one of the major poems
in that mode. We recognize and reject the sentimental inflation, the witless couplets, of Erasmus Darwin's *Loves of the
Plants* on reading a very few lines. The reader unsophisti-
cated by aesthetic theory has a constant and not always unhappy tendency to escape the tyranny of title pages, chapter,
act, and scene headings, even the tag of the *dramatis persona.*
The wider stretches of poetry are often, like life, a kind of
spread-out and general, or atmospheric, or virtual, context
for local episodes of the most intense aesthetic quality. Many
couplets by Alexander Pope are better poems in their own
right than Ezra Pound's miniature image *In A Station of the
Metro.* Matthew Arnold's "touchstones" do not offer a viable
method of criticism, but his conception of them is far from
absurd. A very different spirit, in a far distant era, the Roman
neoplatonist Plotinus, spoke words of wisdom against the
Stoic notion that symmetry is one of the necessary conditions
of the beautiful. Think, he says, what that doctrine leads us
to. "Only a compound can be beautiful, never anything devoid of parts. . . . Yet beauty in an aggregate demands
beauty in details; it cannot be constructed out of ugliness; its
law must run throughout." [38]
    We are told by the Kantian aesthetician, solemnly, that
the interdependence of parts in the organically unified poem
is so close that to remove any part is to "damage" the whole
(to damage it badly, we suppose), and that no part is replace-
able by any other conceivable part.[39] But how can we ever be

38. *Enneads,* I. vi. 1.
    39. "In the unified object, everything that is necessary is there, and
nothing that is not necessary is there. . . . If a certain yellow patch
were not in a painting, its entire character would be altered, and so
would a play if a particular scene were not in it, in the place where it
is. . . . In a good melody, or in painting, or poem, one could not

sure about either of these propositions? Many poets continue
to revise their poems assiduously, to remove parts, to add
others, to replace others, even to the last gasp of their Deathbed editions. Alexander Pope's intended order of satiric portraits in his moral Epistle *Of the Characters of Women* remains conjectural today. It apparently remained unclear to
him (and to Warburton) what the ideal order was. Some of
the portraits apparently have been lost.[40] Editors, composi-
tors, critics, theatrical producers, and actors make many inspired changes in works, either on purpose or accidentally.
(Richard Burton has turned his back on the audience, lurked
in the shadows, and mumbled the soliloquies of *Hamlet*—in
effect, actor against the play.) Even a dunce, Lewis Theobald,
introduced into Shakespeare an emendation that for two centuries has been gratefully accepted. Startling examples of this
kind, from the annals of textual editing, from critical speculation, from innocent appreciation directed to a corrupt text,
have been assembled in a recent article by James Thorpe,
who was pushing the case for the author against the printer's
devil and his associates.[41] We need have no quarrel with this
cause. We are aiming here, not at genetic or textual problems, but at a confrontation with certain perhaps embarrass-
ing aesthetic dubieties. Five-act plays and epic narratives are
often lumpy—in ways that producers of plays can cope with
but which reading aestheticians may have to blink. The authors are masters of episodes and scenes. Think of the parti-

change a part without damaging (not merely changing) the whole"
(John Hospers, "Problems of Aesthetics," *Encyclopaedia of Philosophy*
[New York: Macmillan, 1967] I, 43–44, quoted by Orsini, pp. 1–5).

40. Frank Brady, "The History and Structure of Pope's *To a Lady,*"
Studies in English Literature 1500–1900, 9 (Summer, 1969), 439–462:
"*To a Lady* is no immutable 'organic' whole."

41. "The Aesthetics of Textual Criticism," *PMLA,* 80 (1965), 465–
482. Cf. Fredson Bowers, "Textual Criticism," *The Aims and Methods
of Scholarship in Modern Languages and Literatures,* ed. James Thorpe
(New York: Modern Language Association of America, 1963), p. 24.

tion of the kingdom by Hotspur, Glendower, and Mortimer
in the First Part of *King Henry IV,* of Justice Shallow's nostalgia for the good old days at Clement's Inn in the Second
Part of the same chronicle play. Think of the closing books
of the *Odyssey.* Think of the Doloneia or nighttime slaughter
of the scout in Book X of the *Iliad*—perhaps genetically in-
trusive, as scholiasts for centuries have suspected—in any
event a hypertrophic development, but a cherished one.[42] A
professor of aesthetics, Catherine Lord, has argued that too
close a degree of organic unity necessarily defeats the epi-
sodic and multifarious nature of such extended literary
works.[43] An advanced speculatist in Renaissance studies,
Harry Berger, notices the "conspicuous irrelevance" of de-
scriptive detail, the "perverse insistence on the digressive elements," with which Spenser roughens and gives character to
the otherwise too smooth and logical lines of allegory in
Book II of *The Faerie Queene.* [44] It is my own heretical belief that a good chess problem, viewed according to the idealist organistic norm, has a more fully determined and hence
more perfect structure than even a sonnet by Shakespeare. A
hallmark of linguistic expression, as linguists are now telling
us, is a certain surplus of information. The *Hopscotch* novel,
with a hundred expendable chapters to be inserted at intervals as the reader wills,[45] and other sorts of open-ended or

42. Cedric Whitman, *Homer and the Heroic Tradition* (Cambridge,
Mass.: Harvard Univ. Press, 1958), pp. 283–284, 353.

43. Catherine Lord, "Organic Unity Reconsidered," *JAAC,* 22
(Spring, 1964), 263–268. Note 17, p. 268, quotes Hans Eichner: ". . .
Shakespeare is the very last dramatist whose plays one would normally
describe as integrated wholes" ("The Meaning of 'Good' in Aesthetic
Judgments," *The British Journal of Aesthetics,* [October, 1963], 316,
n. 3).

44. Harry Berger, *The Allegorical Temper, Vision and Reality in
Book II of Spenser's Faerie Queene* (New Haven: Yale Univ. Press,
1957), chs. 5–7; esp. pp. 122–23, 128.

45. Julio Cortázar, *Hopscotch,* trans. from the Spanish (*Rayuela*) by
Gregory Rabassa (New York: Pantheon Books, 1966).

multiple-choice fictions are now a well-established feature of the literary scene. Such terms as "indeterminacy," "irrelevance," and "nonstructure" and studies devoted to *Strains of Discord* begin to appeal to the critics. We need not be partisans of all these kinds of innovation in order to carry on our dialogue with Coleridge and Professor Orsini.

In saying all this, we are, of course, subscribing without reserve to the Kantian proposition recently cited by E. D. Hirsch [46] that we must confront and interpret the aesthetic object in our best frame of mind. Whatever is ideal (if it is not in fact clearly chimerical) is what in fact the work is and says. This extends (in the absence of other kinds of factual evidence) to textual arguments about intentions. What makes clearly better sense always has the superior claim. Hamlet, as F. W. Bateson has sensibly affirmed, yearned not that "this too, too sullied flesh," but that "this too, too *solid* flesh would melt, thaw, and resolve itself into a dew." [47] The Wife of Bath, as Talbot Donaldson, manifesting both textual erudition and concern for poetic meaning, has been the only editor to conclude, speaks of human organs of generation having been created not by a "perfectly wise wight," but by a "perfectly wise wright"—*a conditore sapientissimo,* as the wife's source St. Jerome had put it. And we are convinced, not because the key word happens to occur in three "bad" manuscripts among the total of fifty-two, but because this is the only reading that makes good sense.[48]

The direction in which my argument has been pointing must be clear. Examples of less than complete organicity such

---

46. Kant, *Critique of Judgment,* 21; E. D. Hirsch, "Literary Evaluation as Knowledge," *Contemporary Literature,* 9 (Summer, 1968), 328.

47. "Modern Bibliography and the Literary Artifact," in *English Studies Today,* ed. G. A. Bonnard (Bern: Francke Verlag, 1961), pp. 67–70.

48. E. Talbot Donaldson, *Speaking of Chaucer* (New York: Norton, 1970), pp. 115, 119–121, 125–128.

as I have cited could be multiplied indefinitely and indefinitely varied. But I seem to hear the neo-Kantian idealist
voices murmuring: "Enough of this. You are talking of im-
perfections. The organicist doctrine applies only to aesthetic
perfection, and perfection in this world is hard to come
by." [49] And I answer: Just so. But I think of passages in Plato
where he seems to be voting in favor of poetry, or at least in
favor of poetic inspiration, if only that inspiration will produce something like the beautiful wisdom of philosophy.
The poets as we know them, Homer and the tragedians, are
a mad gang of corrupters. They are outside the pale. I myself
have been speaking of English poetry as we know it—of
Shakespeare, for instance, or Pope. A doctrine of organicity,
if it means an exceedingly subtle, intimate, manifold (and
hence dramatic and imaginative) "interinanimation" of parts
in a poem, must surely be one of the modern critic's most
carefully defended doctrines. Yet if he faces the facts, he will
at the same time find the organic structure of the poem, perhaps paradoxically, a notably loose, stretchable, and adjust-
able kind of organic form. A "loose" conception of poetic
organicism is, in short, what I am arguing for. The time has
perhaps arrived in the dialectic of literary theory when we
gain little by repeating the organistic formulas. We can perhaps gain more now by trying to test and extend the more
precise schemata that are at our disposal for describing the
organization of poems. Some advances, along with perhaps
some merely ingenious exercises, in modes of grammatical
exegesis are being shown these days by critics of the "structural" inclination, and notably by those of the orientation
toward Paris. Brilliant exercises, for instance, have been
broadcast by Roman Jakobson and a few associates. Sonnets
by Baudelaire, Sidney, Shakespeare, a song by Blake along
with its illumination, verses by two painters, the *douanier*
Rouseau and Paul Klee, are subjected to extremes of analysis

49. Orsini, p. 3.

under the rigorous structural technique, and they yield no doubt some subliminal secrets of "the grammar of poetry and the poetry of grammar." A similarly progressive, a finely tempered and well-assured idiom of analysis is demonstrated in a recent book (1968) by an American scholar, Barbara Herrnstein Smith. The title will suggest something of the special insight: *Poetic Closure: A Study of How Poems End.*[50] Stephen Booth's *Essay on Shakespeare's Sonnets* is an even more recent adventure (1969) which, despite what to my mind is an overemphasis on the reader's "experience" of a sonnet (in addition to the sonnet itself), takes a more or less rewarding interest in such logical and grammatical commonplaces as "Unity and Division, Likeness and Difference," and in such various multiple occurrences of pattern as "Formal, Logical, and Syntactical," "Rhetorical," "Phonetic," and "Lexical." [51]

Taken together, these two books exhibit an ingenious array of structural commentary upon English lyric poems— Elizabethan, Metaphysical and Cavalier, romantic, and postsymbolist. Explication of poems is, to my mind, one of the termini of literary criticism. It should rarely, if ever, be reported or reexplicated in anybody else's essay. It suits my purpose of the moment very well, however, to take some notice of the theoretical or speculative idiom employed by Barbara Herrnstein Smith.

A poem or a piece of music concludes. We tend to speak of conclusions when a sequence of events has a relatively high degree of structure.   [p. 2]

If, on the other hand, there have been no surprises or disappointments, if all our expectations have been gratified, then the poem has been as predictable—and as interesting—as someone's reciting

50. Barbara Herrnstein Smith, *Poetic Closure: A Study of How Poems End* (Chicago: Univ. of Chicago Press, 1968).
51. Stephen Booth, *An Essay on Shakespeare's Sonnets* (New Haven: Yale Univ. Press, 1969).

the alphabet. Art inhabits the country between chaos and cliché.
[p. 14]

We may think of *integrity* as, in one sense, the property of a
system of which the parts are more obviously related to each other
than to anything outside that system.   [pp. 23–24]

Closure . . . may be regarded as a modification of structure that
makes *stasis,* or the absence of further continuation, the most
probable succeeding event. Closure allows the reader to be satisfied by the failure of continuation or, put another way, it creates
in the reader the expectation of nothing.   [p. 34]

. . . this does not mean that our experience of the work ceases
abruptly at the last word. On the contrary, at that point we
should be able to re-experience the entire work, not now as a
succession of events, but as an integral design. The point may be
clarified if we consider that we cannot speak of the "end" of a
painting or a piece of sculpture.   [p. 36]

How shall we describe or locate this unpretentiously lucid
and persuasive idiom of generalization about poems? It is of
course Mrs. Smith's own idiom—an achievement which has
helped to earn her book at least two prizes and a number of
encomiastic reviews. At the same time, we can identify it
with some exactitude, I believe, as a judicious blend of *Ge-
stalt* psychology, which Mrs. Smith acknowledges, and of
Aristotelian common sense, which strangely she is silent
about. We might ascribe this silence to a prudent strategy
by which the author is taking care not to look in the least
oldfashioned. I incline rather to ascribe it to absentminded-
ness—and the fairly close resemblance in some of the phrasing simply to the principle that very good ideas, classically
simple, essential, and true ideas, are likely to crop up spon-
taneously in any age, even in the midst of crowding rival
fantasies and fads. Aristotle, as we have noted, does, in his
account of the literary object, make a momentary appeal to

the analogy of biological organism.[52] But for him it is indeed a momentary analogy and no more. A wholesome lesson that we can derive from this juncture in critical history—both from Aristotle and from Mrs. Smith and others of her like who are these days raising their voices—is that neither the organicism of the extreme biological analogy nor that of the *a priori* or transcendental absolute assertion is likely to encourage superior readings of poetry, but rather that homelier and humbler sort of organicism, in the middle, which I have been trying to describe—empirical, tentative, analytic, psychological, grammatical, lexicographic. This, I believe, was in effect the kind of organicism which was the preoccupation of the American critics who were chronologically "new" a third of a century ago but who were, or are indeed, both as old and as new as mankind's literate ambition to make as much sense as possible of the perennially experienced muddled shape of things.

52. Aristotle, *Poetics,* XXIII. 1.

Reflections on Romanticism in France

There is general agreement that the first important Romantic is Rousseau; and although no agreement exists as to what makes him a Romantic, it is fair to assume the following reason might often be given: for Rousseau nothing is more important than breaking through to individuality, unless it is breaking through individuality. Not that he was free of shiftiness, obliquity and bogus. They show that to know or reveal oneself is not a simple matter; the transparent turns back into the opaque. But there is greatness in the trenchancy of Rousseau's theoretical formulations. He knew what was needed, he knew that it must be based on the individual, and he uncompromisingly stated the fact: "Trouver une forme d' association . . . par laquelle chacun s'unissant à tous, n'obéisse pourtant qu'à lui-meme, et reste aussi libre qu'auparavant" (*Du Contrat social*, Bk. I, ch. 6).

If there is a first Romantic, is there a last? It would be difficult to find him. The reaction, for example, of T. E. Hulme, T. S. Eliot and the New Humanists, appears to us more and more as one within Romanticism. When Eliot declares, in his new poetics, thinking to modify the confessional style, "Poetry . . . is not the expression of personality but an escape from personality," and adds, "But, of course, only those who have personality and emotion know what it means to want to escape from these things," he is a knowing witness to the irreversible self-centeredness of modern writers. The theory of personal and expressive poetry, attributed to the Romantics, and that of impersonality, professed in reaction by a line of poets from Rimbaud through Eliot, respond to the same problem. They value art for its power to recreate ideas into feelings or self-consciousness into organic and communal vision. This is an intrinsic, an ontological task intending to modify man's nature; but also a public effort, aiming at more than a small educated group, so that there is always the danger that visionariness becomes rhetoric—the Romantic megaphone.

Romanticism, in any case, is neither essentially irrational nor unreflective. We recall it was John Stuart Mill who named Wordsworth the poet of unpoetical natures because of the reflective pressure exhibited by his verse. We also remember Keats's judgment, that Wordsworth thought more deeply than Milton, at least more into the heart. These formulas, of course, are deceptive: did not Dante, for instance, think into the heart? Can we nominate him as our first Romantic? And what of Saint Augustine?

It remains true that the Romantics are strangely self-involved. They spell "Art" with a capital "I," to adapt Oscar Wilde on Whistler. Byron's comment on Keats, that in *Endymion* he "viciously sollicited his own imagination" is partly just. Such behavior is the penalty for thinking about one's imagination, about one's relation to it, and having sometimes to prompt the relation. But Byron was wrong in believing that the relation was a private, quasi-incestuous affair. The theme engaged by the great Romantics is that of a general (Keats called it "gregarious") progress of imagination, of which the artist is a mediator. He reveals in what relation he stands to his own mind—which presupposes for mind (or imagination) an existence apart from ego. Authentic self-consciousness includes a strongly objective attitude toward the self: the mind is seen as a *daimon,* not invariably right, perhaps beyond simple categories of right and wrong, but a respondent and secret sharer. Self-consciousness is the feeling of being on the spot, but it is also consciousness of one's consciousness in its various relations.

Poetic and analytic attitudes can keep company, therefore. Yet, as Keats said, the creative must create itself: it is not a matter of listening to the radio of one's mind or leading genius about like a lobster on a string. What Byron observed disdainfully of Keats, that he teased his own imagination, becomes methodical, even programmatic, in the antithetical poetics of Hugo and the synaesthetic experiments of Rimbaud. To keep in touch with imagination is an increasingly heroic task.

Perhaps this desire, so characteristic of the present era, though not unknown in previous ones, to achieve a direct or unmediated relation to oneself, is an illusion. If so, the illusion remains to be explained. It may be an illusion as vital to life as dreaming. At least to life in contemporary society: the dream of a direct communion reacts against the multiplication of secondary objects. Even art feels itself to be *écriture,* signs of signs. "Modern times," Matthew Arnold wrote in 1863,

Modern times find themselves with an immense system of institutions, established facts, accredited dogmas, customs, rules, which have come to them from times not modern. In this system their life has to be carried forward, yet they have a sense that this system is not of their own creation, that it by no means corresponds exactly with the wants of their actual life, that, for them, it is customary, not rational. The awakening of this sense is the awakening of the modern spirit.   ("Heine")

The advance of civilization seems to foster a diversification of knowledge, a pluralism of values, fragmentation, and a sometimes fruitful indifference to the one necessary thing. In these conditions does not emphasis on the self play a functional role? To echo Emerson, who is the modern hero if not the immovably centered man? There is a nostalgia for commitment, and honest commitment goes via one's self, one's body, one's conscience. In some sense, of course, this surfeit of options, of multiplication of properties, frees individuals by diminishing the expectation put on them. They are never in one place and so can never be "on the spot." We have too wide a stake in the world to be messianic: paraphernalia, material or spiritual, are a mode of anti-self-consciousness. Yet it was always the accumulation of relationships, with property or family or history, which sparked an at once explosive and ascetic passion to return to the naked, human source. Affluence fosters the dream of spiritual poverty; and crime, we have learnt, is the result of affluence as well as deprivation, a way of forging one's identity. Two men like myself, says Schiller's Robber Captain, could destroy the whole moral order.

The contemporary situation differs from that of the Romantics only in its apparent irreversibility and uncompromising nature. A hundred and fifty years ago, the sequence of revolutions and restorations seemed to argue that history had a definite structure, yet one which allowed some scope to the individual. Many thought it probable that history alternated according to the Saint-Simonian scheme of "organic" (religious, strongly uplifting) and "critical" (sceptical, full of reasoning and unbelief) ages. They felt they were living in a "critical" age, in a time of unbelief or at its turning. "De quel nom te nommer, heure trouble où nous sommes?" [1]

1. From "Prélude," *Chants du crépuscule* (1835).

Hugo does not know whether this twilight, the "époque en travail" through which he is passing, heralds night or a new dawn. In England it is the early Victorians who share with the French Romantics this concept of an Age of Transition, and the historical self-consciousness it fostered. The crucial question was whether to be of one's time or whether to hasten the turn into the coming (organic-religious) phase. To be of one's time might mean standing against the historical "stream of tendency."

Where are we today? In the West, the critical spirit has absolutized itself except for our belief in the individual. In a technological society, which seduces the individual into what may appear as false modes of participation, into complicities, he has an even greater responsibility to I-Thou relations. At the same time, however, as if there were no contradiction, we insist on the importance of community, on larger than individual or family purposes. Have we advanced significantly beyond Rousseau? Have we not simply discovered more obstacles to the realization of his magic formula? Our dream is still to generate the communal from the individual, or to regenerate it from within self-consciousness. I wish to review some aspects of that problem in the following general sketch of French Romanticism.

1

In 1818, P. S. Ballanche, one of the most interesting social philosophers of the Romantic period, published his *Essay on Social Institutions*. The chapter discussing the influence of the French Revolution on the arts flirts momentarily with the ambition of "une poétique appliquée à l'âge actuel de l'esprit humain"—a poetics in tune with the present era. Accepting the French Revolution as an irreversible event, even as a providential shock to consciousness, Ballanche is disturbed by a paradox strangely similar to Rousseau's "man is born free, and everywhere he is in chains." The French Revolution emancipated human thought yet there are no or few institutions reflecting the fact in 1818. Our thoughts are free, and everywhere they are in chains. The arts are institutions too: is it not time to renew our poetics?

A decade later Hugo would launch his famous slogan, "A peuple nouveau, art nouveau." It comes as no surprise to those who have heard of the Battle of *Hernani* that the French Romantics considered the reform of the arts a political matter, as combat against the "hommes géométriques" (Lamartine's phrase) or the "arid heritage" and "proud sterility" of the *siècle des lumières* which immortalized the masterpieces produced under Louis XIV as if his monarchy were equally absolute in the realm of spirit. Ballanche, an enlightened Catholic, and hardly a Jacobin, went so far to assert that the literature of the period of Louis XIV was beginning to be ancient literature, "de l'archéologie." If the social institutions are outmoded, then the period's literature must be outmoded. His grim consistency has the same reason as Hugo's flamboyance: years after the French Revolution, with so many ideas burgeoning, no new forms and few social reforms seemed forthcoming.

The close association of literary with social reform typical of Romantic statements in the exploding 1820's is due to this disproportion between ideas and realities. The great literary event of 1819, for example, was publication of the poetry of André Chénier who had died in the Revolution. And in 1820, which at least saw Lamartine's *Premières Méditations,* Hugo writes sadly: "No important book yet this year, no strong pronouncement (*parole forte*); nothing that could teach, nothing that could arouse. Is it not time someone appeared out of the crowd, saying, Here I am." Hugo's emphasis on the *parole forte,* on poet as spokesman, is strongly colored by these years of national sterility.

It is uncertain what caused the lateness of French Romanticism as a *movement*—Rousseau, Chateaubriand and Mme.
de Staël were great but single waves.[2] Perhaps the turmoil
and proscriptions of twenty-five years. Or something endemic
to French civilization, which Guizot noticed: whereas English
history, he thought, showed the simultaneous development
of different forces, so that no older principle was totally discarded, and no special interest prevailed absolutely, in France
each political or intellectual principle developed separately
and completely.[3] When Matthew Arnold remarked that most
of the English Romantics, compared to the French or German, were not men of *ideas,* he may have been interpreting
the same phenomenon.

The lateness of Romanticism in France had, in any case,
important consequences for the kind of art produced. A
reservoir of forces had built up: energies to be ignited, voices
to be heard, ideas to be fully expounded. Ballanche points
to the explosive character of the moment when he apologizes
for his "incoherence," which is really a tendency to say everything at once: to give a public, even publicistic, form to post-
Revolutionary thought about social institutions and the historical destiny of France. "We are at a point in history where
all ideas must be expressed, and all important human problems set forth at one and the same time."

French Romanticism, however, is delayed not only with
respect to 1789 but also with respect to other Romanticisms
—to the cultural upheavals in England and Germany. If the
death of Byron in 1824 marks the end of two major phases of

2. It would be more exact to say that Mme. de Stael and Chateaubriand created a *circle* rather than a *movement*. Romanticism in France
is chronologically remarkable by both being very early (Rousseau) and
very late.

3. See M. Guizot, *Histoire de la civilisation en Europe* (Paris: Didier,
1840), "première leçon." The lectures were originally given in 1828-30.

English Romanticism, it but signals the beginning of an accelerating tempo of events in France. That country had to catch up with surrounding nations as well as with its own past. The 1820's were a highpoint of the influx of ideas from Germany begun earlier with Mme. de Staël, while Italy and England also make their presence felt. Michelet's *Journal des idées* has the following entry for May 1825:

Our interest in Socrates' death comes not from the fact of his innocence but because his death expresses the struggle of two moral powers, the subjective (or individual) and the objective (or State). The subjective principle, not having achieved self-consciousness, was then merely something dissident and corrosive which the objective principle, the State, had to purge.[4]

Clearly, Hegel is in the wings. But so, as we read on, are Shakespeare, Milton, Byron and Kant, examined by Michelet for their understanding of history as the story of liberty, of man "condemned" to self-development.

Foreign influences revive, in turn, neglected native resources: ballads, popular themes, literature before the age of Louis XIV. The dozen years from about 1823 to 1835 are a cultural apocalypse. For once a simple listing tells a great deal. During this period Hugo publishes *Han d'Islande* and collections of poetry ranging from the *Odes et Ballades* and *Orientales* to the *Chants du crépuscule;* Fauriel, *Chants populaires de la Grèce moderne;* Loev-Weimar, translations of English and Scotch popular ballads; Lamartine, *Le dernier chant de Childe Harold;* Berlioz, *Harold in Italy* and the *Symphonie fantastique;* Stendhal, *Racine et Shakespeare;* Saint-Beuve, writings on Ronsard and sixteenth-century literature. Guigniaut begins to issue his adaptation of Creuzer's *Symbolik,* which Renan characterized as a "panthéon scientifique

4. Michelet's journal is reprinted in *Écrits de jeunesse*, ed. P. Viallaneix (Paris: Gallimard, 1959).

de tous les dieux de l'humanité." Furthermore, Delacroix
exhibits the *Death of Sardanapalus;* Shakespeare is success-
fully brought to the French stage by Kemble's troupe;
Beethoven is discovered; Nerval translates *Faust* (pt. I).
Again, Delacroix makes his *Faust* lithographs; Berlioz com-
poses music for *Huit scènes de Faust;* there is a translation
of Hoffmann's stories and of De Quincey's *Opium Eater* (the
latter by Musset). Musset and Vigny enter onto the literary
scene; Daumier starts work for the *Caricature;* Hugo's *Cromwell* is followed by *Hernani* and Dumas' *Henri III;* Guizot,
Ampère and Michelet publish their first historical works;
Ballanche brings out *Orphée* and the *Palingénésie sociale.*
Scott's historical novels are translated as they appear. Delacroix sketches his Moroccan journey, Berlioz writes the *Return to Life* in Italy; Stendhal publishes his first great novel;
George Sand's *Lélia* comes out. The Saint-Simonians take
over the *Globe;* Lamennais founds the community at La
Chenaie as well as the short-lived *L'Avenir;* the *Paroles d'un
Croyant* is published; and Balzac is inspired with the idea of
linking his novels into a *Comédie humaine.* "La Boutique/
Romantique," as Musset calls it catchily, is open.

To complete this picture of an *école,* add Paris. It centered
these events and gave them their milieu. Berlin and Vienna
never became this kind of center; and it happened that most
of the great English Romantics lived away from London, in
the countryside or exile. As for Rome, it was no longer in
Rome, as Du Bellay had lamented three centuries before, and
a powerful letter by Lamennais confirms. In Paris, theater,
dinner parties, salons, everything acted as a cynosure. Lamennais was acquainted with Liszt, Liszt with Berlioz, all with
Victor Hugo or Nodier; and at a salon like that of Marie
d'Agoult, one might meet Sainte-Beuve, Heine, Miekewicz,
Baron Eckstein, Balzac, Lamennais, George Sand. Paris was

more than a milieu: it was a microcosm and the heart of a nation.[5]

An art conspicuous, preachy, panoramic, national, was inevitable. It is the art, quite distinctly, of a movement: the artist felt he contained multitudes. We understand Berlioz's *Lélio,* conceived around 1830, which condenses into the figure of the artist the emotional and literary syncretism of its time. Lélio leads us from Goethe's ballad *Der Fischer* through reminiscences of *Hamlet* and *The Tempest* to the song of Neapolitan brigands which marks the high-point of the artist's return to life. "Yes!" (I quote from Lélio's unifying monologue) "Yes! poetical superstitions, a guardian madonna, gorgeous loot heaped up in caves, dishevelled women panting with fright, a concert of cries of horror accompanied by an orchestra of guns, sabres and daggers, blood and lachryma Christi, a bed of lava rocked by earthquakes . . . voilà la vie!"

Romantic agony, you say, *l'esthétique du mal.* True, from Chateaubriand's *Génie du Christianisme* to Baudelaire's *Fleurs du Mal* and Hugo's *Fin de Satan,* the beautiful embraces the blues. It is drawn from passion in its basic sense of love-suffering: amour-passion, heavenly or earthly. "Je viens gémir, luire, éclairer," says the Angel called Liberty to the Satan of Hugo's epic medley. It could be the *devise* of the French Romantics. Victor Cousin, in an elegant commonplace, called the beautiful "la splendeur du bien," but when

5. There are in Ludwig Boerne's *Briefe aus Paris, 1830–31,* amusing descriptions of various salons and festivities. See his letter entries for 5 November 1830 (on Gérard's salon, which included Delphine Gay, Humboldt, Mayer-Beer, David, Vitet and Stendhal), 3 December 1830 (a Romantic evening devoted to listening to a translation of Macbeth), and 8 December 1830 (his reaction to Berlioz's *Symphonie fantastique*). See also, for the salons, Daniel Stern (Mme. d'Agoult), *Mes Souvenirs, 1806–1833* (Paris: Calmann Lévy, 1877), pp. 301 f.

sacred and profane themes commingle in Hugo and Berlioz
it is the radiance of passion.

There is, obviously, as much *feu d'artifice* as fire in all this,
and the uneasy combination of make-believe and sincerity
raises difficult questions. Theatricality, role-playing, infects
everything. "Suis-je Amour ou Phébus? Lusignan ou Biron?"
The tragic note of Nerval's identity crisis blends precariously
with this trill from some gallant aria. Where now is Rousseau's distrust of theater or his critical distinction between
"l'homme de l'homme" and "l'homme de la nature"? Where
anything resembling Wordsworth's insight, after being dis-
appointed in political action, that nature had infinitely more
ways of forming or reforming the individual than society
could muster? There is little real nature-poetry in French
Romanticism; it had to await a later generation, composed of
painters. The point is that French Romanticism is social
through and through, and subjective through and through:
it shifts from subjective to social with *sprezzatura*. For Hugo
an artist is always Man Representative, with "le peuple" as
his constituency; and exile, the isolation of Guernsey, only
intensifies this sentiment. His *Contemplations* (1856) contain, according to the preface, "all the impressions and reflections, all the realities and vague fantastic thoughts, bright
or dark, that conscience recalls and examines, ray by ray,
sigh after sigh. . . ." Each day is a day of destiny for Hugo,
and the critic who objects to such egotism is put down with
"Fool! who think I am not you!"

We are in the midst of the crucial question of Romantic
"subjectivity." Is it, in France, despite the scruples of Rousseau, as unproblematic as it appears? Where are its depths?
When Musset calls his Muse "seul être pudique et chaste"
after the stormy affair with George Sand, do we not groan
without being enlightened? Does not Stendhal have our sympathy for wishing to fight a duel with a friend who defended

Chateaubriand's "la cîme indéterminée des forêts"? There are, it is clear, naive and self-deceptive moments. Michelet, as a very young man, writes his *Mémorial* because, he says, "Rousseau ne sera pas le seul homme que l'on ait connu." This sense of mission, of historical vocation, of being the bearers of an enlightenment that will flood the earth like the knowledge of God, is both exhilarating and absurd.

But our sensibility, of course, has been affected by the post-Romantic reaction: faith in art as spiritual politics only increased the tension between politics and letters and brought on movements which renounced "destiny" and "depth," mythic décor and grandiloquence, the bourgeois-imperial complex and the whole "mensonge romantique." While in a poet like Vigny artistic vocation and the idea of destiny are the central if problematic subjects, with Rimbaud the very word "destiny" seems outmoded. What he calls "la lumière *nature*" replaces the heaven of aims. Rimbaud's life, similarly, in contrast to that of Nerval, refuses to become allegory: Rimbaud rejects all *mythes de profondeur* including that belief in historical destiny which the Romantics kept from the time of Louis XIV but extended to include the masses. The early Rimbaud enjoys (though with a difference) the "opéra fabuleux" of the Romantics, but he soon becomes the Cézanne of French verse, stripping away affluent color and exotic decor, while substituting terse preachment for the *emphase* of Romantic predication:

> Jamais l'espérance
> Pas d'orietur
> Science et patience
> Le supplice est sûr.

Let us return to Hugo's aggressive I-Thou relation, so uncatty compared to Baudelaire's "Hypocrite lecteur, mon semblable, mon frère." His spirited dismissal of the idiot questioner ("Fool! who think I am not you") makes the artist into an idiot creator, which he isn't. Hugo can be stupid at times, as Leconte de Lisle acknowledged, yet his stupidity functions as a force of consciousness that leaps directly from the I to the you, from subjective to social, from self to all. This reflects, too often, a lust for certainty eliminating transitional states—perhaps because Hugo, between 1830 and the *coup d'état* of 1851, had tried to suffer the "clair-obscur" of an Age of Transition. It is remarkable how he returns in the 1850's to the primitivity of white and black, to the apocalyptic distinction between night and redemptive light, or its reversal. The antithetical poetics announced in the preface to *Cromwell* return with a vengeance.

Hugo's problem is that of French Romanticism generally. The way from selfhood to a purified self, or from isolation to a larger, imaginative or communal life, seems more uncertain than in Rousseau. Or, like history itself in the period from Rousseau to Hugo, it is subject to greater vacillation. That pure "feeling of existence" which weighs so lightly on Rousseau ("Entirely inside the present, I remembered nothing; I had no distinct notion of my individuality") and which disperses as if they were mist all factitious mediations ("I perceived the sky, a few stars, and a little verdure. This first sensation was a delicious moment; only through it could I feel myself. In that instance I was born to life") [6] is usually a pregnant and burdensome feeling in Hugo, a "nuée

6. *Les Rêveries du promeneur solitaire.* Deuxième Promenade. Cf. Hazlitt "On the Character of Rousseau" (1817), which delineates the shadow side of this passage from *Les Rêveries:* "The only quality which he possesses in an eminent degree, which alone raised him above ordinary men, and which gave his writings and opinions an influence greater, perhaps, than has been exerted by any individual in modern times was extreme sensibility, or an acute and even morbid feeling of all that related to his own impressions, to the objects and events of his life. He had the most intense consciousness of his own existence."

sombre" rather than a luminous darkness. "La grande plon-geuse" of the imagination dives into this cloud, as the prome-nade becomes a fantastic journey, and revery turns into brooding. Sky and water, memory and vision, God and people converge on the poet as if he were the only thing betwixt and between, the one mediator. He is always on the spot.

Perhaps Hugo did not have enough of what Keats called "negative capability"; perhaps he was too irritable in reach-ing after truth, and taking his objective by emotional or rhetorical storm. But the situation of the artist seemed to demand clairvoyance and social prophecy. The Keatsian way—or impasse—was not possible in so public a time. This burden of leadership is the theme even of a man like Vigny who accepted, disdainfully, his lot. In terms of Romantic aesthetics, what is essential is more than the disappearance of trustworthy mediations between self and world, contin-gency and destiny, natural man and social man, the masses and humanity. It is that while existing or "legitimate" forms are felt to be inauthentic, the idea of exemplary social action and of manifest national destiny is magnified rather than doubted.

No other national literature raised the "social question" more insistently than the French. Saint-Simon, Ballanche, De Maistre, Bonald, Fourier, Lamennais, Michelet and Comte are as essential to an understanding of the period as Berlioz, Hugo and Delacroix. Whatever their political differ-ences, they connect the renovation of society and that of the arts. Whereas Sénancourt (and it is his truth) can never emerge from "le vide de l'autri and "le néant de l'ordre sociale," from 1820 on art is predominantly "aesthetic edu-cation": it strives to occupy its providential place in the mak-ing of men and the development of true social forms.

For most, the new image of man had to arise from the

depth of the subjective spirit. The Romantic artist is haunted by scenes of solitariness: Prometheus on the rock, Christ on the Mount of Olives, or as in Jean Paul's influential *songe,* standing in cosmic silence amid the ruins of the world. What return to life there is comes from a solitude expressive of this abandonment or decay of social supports. The nakedness is not absolute, however: to revive such ancient symbols of loneliness is not to be alone. In these scenes of desolation, we are still accompanied by images which assimilate man's fate as of old. Man is alone, yet alone with thought, with a great conception he has unknowingly, fatefully repeated. I live my life like a novel, Nerval writes in *Aurélia.* His life becomes an allegory: it is greater, more fraternal than he knew. However deep the solitude depicted, art continues to provide a nursery of forms, that reserve of living types which Hugo calls *Adams.*

This reserve, in 1820, contained a very small number of works, mainly from the time of Louis XIV. They had to sustain thoughts of French greatness when that was increasingly in doubt. To deflate these works would impoverish the reserve even more. Obviously new role-models, new spiritual and imaginative possibilities had to be created: the "mal du siècle" showed that while many of the young felt a *career* was still possible (the Napoleonic code provided, after all, for "une carrière ouverte aux talents") a *vocation* was not in sight.[7] Villemain, enlightened apologist for the glories of

7. According to Chateaubriand, in the *Génie du Christianisme,* "Il y a eu dans notre age, à quelques exceptions près, une sorte d'avortement général des talents." In our century Van Wyck Brooks has made the pertinent observation that "Obermann . . . reduced himself to pure virtuality. . . . He demands independence of society and refuses to recognize any middle ground between the strictly individual and the strictly universal. It follows that he cannot accept as his vocation any of those ready-made professions that spring from and support the social order" (*The Malady of the Ideal* [London: A. C. Fifield, 1913]). Senancourt's *Obermann* was published in 1804, republished with an introduc-

tradition, can do no better in 1824 than to echo the Napoleonic code and insist that "La carrière est encore ouverte" in the arena of political and religious oratory. But precisely: a career is not—or no longer—a calling. The distinction was sometimes illusory: Julien Sorel is a careerist in a time when being such is a vocation. As Vigny remarked bitterly: "No young head could think, because made giddy day-in day-out by the canons and bells of the Te Deums" (which marked Napoleon's victories). Only art, however, could now renew the image of a vocation that was more than careerist, or of a heroism tied to inward or social reform rather than political ambition.

Villemain again did not help with his suggestion that the young might develop their imagination by reconstructing the "immortal epoch" of Louis XIV, "the atmosphere of glory and enthusiasm which emanated from a conquering, enlightened and magnanimous king, whose courtiers even were often great men." No wonder Hugo fulminated in his *Jacobin Journal of Ideas* (1819–1820) against this sector of thought, which "does not want the earth to turn or talent to be creative, and which orders the eagles to fly with wax wings." Even Hugo, however, did not degrade the seventeenth century, since no other art was present, and its immense influence revealed the artist's role in shaping the national consciousness. His attack is centered on eighteenth-century negations. He wished to replenish the reserve, to generate or recover forms allowing the I to be Other and raise itself to a more comprehensive vision of national destiny. "La tragédie court les rues," Ducis had said during the Revolution; but it is not till Hugo and Balzac that the giant forms of art frequent the streets again, and street-forms the world of art.

---

tion by Sainte-Beuve in 1833, and again, with an introduction by George Sand, in 1840.

2

The reserve of which we have spoken is composed of acknowledged works of art which guarantee, even when they
do not directly influence, the paper in circulation. Many
draw on that reserve without knowing it, but in times of
crisis it is a conscious and challenged possession. Something
like a museum, something like a pantheon, it gathers together those structured spiritual forces that have guided men
in the past. To young artists it may be a burden or else a
bait: an angel they must wrestle, a double or secret sharer
which haunts them.

The French Romantics augmented this reserve by bringing from the basement neglected works—of "impure" taste,
religious or popular character or foreign extraction. But the
crisis, the felt spiritual need, was too deep for representative
measures. The gap between canonical and non-canonical art
had become so great that only a new idea of their interrela-
tion could suffice. While the notion of living "without reserve" did not catch on because of the quest for role-models
(Romanticism conceiving itself, on the whole, as a modern
or more broadly based Classicism), we do find the beginnings
of the anthropological view that art comprises more than
canonized masterpieces. An unstructured or semi-structured
reserve—customs, ceremonies, oral traditions, artifacts of all
sorts—receives consideration. Realia of this kind are Balzac's
gold: he gloats over them like another Grandet.

How radically, on this point, Voltaire differs from the
Romantics! For Voltaire, the philosopher of history interested in ancient customs is a man in danger of methodizing
madness ("mettre de la raison dans la folie"). Reason is
reason and folly is folly; and history, on the whole, is a ship
of fools rather than an ark of salvation. But the Romantics
view formal history on a large scale as an epic in prose, while
historical fiction triumphs in all the genres. Ballanche, who

creates a new myth of redemption drawing on Vico's analysis of Roman law, writes his *Orphée* as "l'historie condensée de quinze siècles du genre humain," and remarks of Bossuet's *Discours sur l'histoire universelle* that it is "a magnificent literary conception, a kind of epic embracing all times and places." A "légende des siècles," in effect, two centuries before Hugo.

To oversee history is an old ambition. But now history includes so much more. More races, cultures, life-styles. The perspective has widened, both horizontally and in depth. History is no longer sublime in the old sense—restricted to a progress, triumphal or tragic, of semidivine persons. Herder's influence grows in the 1820s and brings with it an existential query. How is the acculturated person, standing genuinely within his time, to sight all this and gather it into a synoptic frame? The situation is, once more, mythogenetic: the comprehensive forms or guiding myths must come from the depth of the individual mind. Wanted: a hero of consciousness.

Even if history exhibits a divine plot (as most continued to believe, following in this Bossuet or Vico), the gods themselves have departed. The hero must fathom alone his way through history. Actually, Ballanche remarked, there were two divine departures. With the advent of Christianity, "the gods departed but their images stayed. Now another voice is heard in the literary world: the *images* of the gods are departing." We approach the last act in a divine strip-tease of the imagination. As the historical consciousness grows, a multitude of fallen gods come to light. Surrounded by ancient images of the divine, the Romantic is more alone than ever.

The hero of consciousness, therefore, is a solitary haunted by vast conceptions in which he cannot participate. This is the dilemma, basically, of Faust and Ahasuerus, two figures that come to the fore in the Romantic period. There are

many others, of course. As heroes they are often more pursued than pursuing—by gods they defy or disbelieve. They
must be redeemed in various ways: some by "negative capability," some by a more positive power of assimilation. The
latter way is stressed in French Romanticism. So Ballanche
flirts suggestively with a feminine figure, the sibyl. He asserts
that France had its sibyl once in Joan of Arc: a woman of the
people, almost anonymous, through whom the whole nation
found its expression. "A people feels the need for territorial
unity, for unity of language and unity in its traditions. This
feeling focuses on a person who has great assimilative powers;
it identifies with her; it becomes her very self. Repressed by
acts of violence, that need flees from spirit to spirit until it
finds shelter in une *organisation de sibylle*."

I am unable to translate this final phrase, which points to
something less crude than Hugo's Adams and archetypes. It
may express that subtler, more diffused power of shaping or
unifying which art exhibits intrinsically. Finally, of course,
the hero of consciousness is the mythogenetic artist rather
than any one of his creations. History's host, he must live
among "departing images." Their burden is better than
sheer self. What is he without them except a porous mind?
And how could the new myth, the new order, come from
nothing?

Let me, to conclude, give one example of the sibylline or
assimilative labor of the French Romantics. In November of
1825 Michelet settled on the project of writing "un discours
étincelant sur l'unité du genre humain." This project took
him, in a sense, all his life, although the first fruits were his
essay on universal history published in 1831. He was not
thinking, however, of a essay in the months immediately
preceding November 1825. A different form was struggling
for expression:

Dialogues des morts intitulés: Les Amours. J'étais enterré depuis peu, et je commençais à reconnaître avec effroi mon nouveau gîte. C'était au mois de février. . . . La nuit venue, je m'étais assis sur la balustrade dont on a entouré mon monument, lorsque j'entends une voix, si basse et douce qu'une ombre seule pouvait l'entendre: *Ami, tu n'es pas seul.* . . . La description des amours et des assemblées des morts au printemps, leur attente du jugement, etc.[8]

This is June 1825, and by September the conception has developed:

une histoire dramatique du dogme de la fatalité. . . . Ce serait un ouvrage tout dramatique dans le style. On parlerait successivement de la croyance de chaque époque, comme d'une croyance vraie. On emploierait quelquefois les idées de Lucien, mais sérieusement. Voici les chapitres ou époques: Le Destin, Jupiter grec, Jupiter Capitolin, Jéhova, Jésus-Christ, Jésus et les saints. . . . L'ouvrage serait présenté comme celui d'un rêveur du Moyen Age qui regarderait comme vrai tout ce qu'a jamais cru la majorité du monde civilisé.[9]

Michelet's first problem is that of intellectual perspective. He thinks of history as the story of liberty, not of fatality,

---

8. Dialogues of the Dead entitled: Love-Stories. Recently buried, I was beginning to recognize with fright my new lodgings. It was the month of February. . . . Night had fallen, and I was sitting on the railing that circled my tombstone when I heard a voice, so low and soft that only a shade could have heard it: *Friend, you are not alone.* . . . a description of the love-making and assemblies of the dead in springtime, their waiting for judgment, etc. (From *Journal des idées,* accessible in *Écrits de jeunesse,* ed. P. Viallaneix).

9. A dramatization of the dogma of fatalism. . . . It would be a work thoroughly dramatic in its style. The idea would be to talk successively of the belief of each epoch as if it were a true belief. The ideas of Lucian would occasionally be used, but seriously. Here are the chapters or epochs: Destiny, Greek Jupiter, Capitoline Jupiter, Jehovah, Jesus Christ, Jesus and the Saints. . . . The work would be presented as emanating from a Medieval Dreamer who accepted as true everything the majority of civilized people in the world had ever believed.

yet he knows how extensive and real the reign of the "dead"
has been. What point of view can convey this twofold consciousness? There is, further, the formal problem of what
convention might best express a modern, synchronic perspective. The choice seems to lie between something over-
credible, like the medieval dream-vision, and something
over-sceptical, like Lucian's *Dialogues of the Dead*. Beyond
all this, however, lies a perplexity of the heart, a hint of the
deep, emotional side of Michelet's undertaking. *Ami, tu n'es
pas seul.* This history seeks to embrace all humankind. The
consolation is unmistakable even though the imaginary situation could have taken a demonic turn: into history as nightmare, *Walpurgisnacht* or dance of death. The universal historian risks this danger rather than yielding to solipsism.

Like Ballanche, Michelet was unable to discover an up-to-
date poetics. His vast prose effort walks among the dead—the
ancient credibilities—with too confident a step. Another
abortive, if highly expressive, attempt at a synoptic rendering of departing myths is made by Edgar Quinet. Also deeply
influenced by Herder, Quinet clarifies the horror of unbelief
which drove Nerval to the delusions of *Aurélia*. (I was mad,
Blake has Cowper say, as a refuge from unbelief, and you
are as mad as any of us.) In Quinet's *Ahasvérus* (1833) the
splendid machinery of romance, the historical tableaux, the
cosmological dream-visions are illuminations set off in a
ruin. The author summons pageant after pageant to delay the
fatal sentence spoken by Eternity: "Ni être ni néant, je ne
veux plus que moi." With that the visionary clock runs down
and leaves nothing but ego behind. Quinet's tired theological
insight hides a ruinous solipsism: "I don't want being, I
don't want nothingness; I want myself." If we strip the mind
of myth and metaphysics—those historical errors—what remains but the naked self?

Why continue the story? Each artist faces the problem

anew. From 1830 to the 1850s there is intensification rather than advance. In the *Légende des siècles,* which remains a sequence of diachronic highpoints, Hugo does not progress beyond the poetics of the preface to *Cromwell:* "Croiser dans le même tableau le drame de la vie et le drame de la conscience." It is clearly not the "épopée idéale, à la fois successive et spontanée" which Ballanche programmed in the *Vision d'Hébal* (1831). The *Fin de Satan* is perhaps more remarkable, but Hugo's conception of Satan, peculiar and powerful as it is, is also embarrassingly intimate. Satan's desire is so vast that it feeds the fear of isolation. The implacable solitary becomes a love-monster:

> c'est là l'inoui, l'horrible, le divin
> De se dresser, d'ouvrir des ailes insensées,
> De s'attacher, sanglant, à toutes les pensées
> Qu'on peut saisir, avec des cris, avec des pleurs,
> De sonder les terreurs, de sonder les douleurs.

Desire may be infinite, but art is limited. Later writers, especially the symbolists, resist Romantic pressures to convert the palace of art into a brothel of forms. A pantheon is not a pandemonium, and poetry is not opera. Art cannot long subsist on the energy of nostalgia, on the remembrance of obsolete myths and lapsed fidelities. It seemed more honest to render consciousness as such: believing less the more it knows, the fuller the emptier, and basically unconsummated. Is not soul as soul always immersed in departing images? "Ces nymphes, je les veux perpétuer." Here is the constant to which historical periods, faith or roles are the variables.

Nerval is an important transitional figure because he creates a new poetry by incorporating rather than rejecting Romantic assumptions. For Nerval, all art, but especially theater, remains linked to vast presuppositions of a magical or metaphysical nature. So Goethe's mythopoeia in the *Second Faust* is analysed in terms of a metaphysics of the

imagination. Nerval will not allow Goethe the wide whimsy
of art, or a more radical autonomy. Blending, as in ancient
systems, ideas on the abode of the dead with cosmological
speculation, he imagines that the world we live in, the
"monde matériel," is shadowed about by concentric circles
of centuries which have shed their materiality and are pure
"intelligences." The phantoms Faust draws into his world
come from that planetary sphere, where all things exist in a
state of "divine synchronism":

Elles co-existent toutes, comme les personnages divers d'un drame
qui ne s'est pas encoure dénoué, et qui pourtant est accom-
pli dans la pensée de son auteur; ce sont les coulisses de la
vie où Goethe nous transporte ainsi. Hélène et Paris, les ombres
que cherche Faust, sont quelque part errant dans le *spectre* immense que leur siècle a laissé dans l'espace; elles marchent sous
les portiques splendides et sous les ombrages frais qu'elles rêvent
encore, et se meuvent gravement, en *ruminant* leur vie passée.
C'est ainsi que Faust les rencontre et, par l'aspiration immense
de son âme à demi dégagée de la terre, il parvient à les attirer
hors de leur cercle d'existence et à les amener dans le sien.[10]

The intellectual detritus carried along is part of the problem. But we recognize the need of the Romantics for an airy
Hades of this kind, for a reserve of ideal or imaginative
forms. The status of these forms is what we find difficult.
What being do they have? They are not ideas merely, not

10. All coexist, like various characters in a play that hasn't reached
its resolution yet is already complete in its author's mind; Goethe trans-
ports us thus into the wings of life. Helen and Paris, the phantoms
sought by Faust, are wandering somewhere in the immense *shadow* their
era has left in space; they stroll under the fine arcades and among the
fresh, shady walks of which they still dream; they move about gravely,
ruminating their past life. Faust encounters them thus; and, by the
immense aspiration of his half unearthly soul, succeeds in drawing them
away from their circle of life and bringing them into his. (From Nerval's
introduction to his translation of Goethe, *Les Deux Faust de Goethe,*
ed. F. Baldensperger [Paris: Librairie ancienne Honoré Champion,
1932], p. 233).

even Platonic ideas, and to say they have the being of art-
forms begs the question. Nerval thinks of them as existing
in the "coulisses de la vie"— in the wings, between acts,
waiting to go on stage. Mythology would call them daemons:
inhabitants of the middle air, neither all divine nor all human, and desirous of a more individuated existence.

When Nerval's prince recites, "Je suis le ténébreux, le
veuf, l'inconsolé," we do not think of daemons or middle
beings or the limbo of art. We do not even think, necessarily,
of an actor stepping from the wings. Suggestive as it is, this
poetry carries its burdens lightly. Its metaphysics are held, so
to say, in reserve. Yet is not the "ténébreux" one of those
"ombres . . . quelque part errant dans le *spectre* immense
que leur siècle a laissé dans l'espace"? The artist, another
Faust, draws him out of the shadows into life, *his* life. Behind the *Chimères* is that "histoire universelle . . . synchro-
nisme divin" which haunted so many Romantics. Nerval's
phantoms rarely console, however. An ontological uncertainty remains which is of the essence of art and its paradigms.
The "ténébreux" may be an archetype drawn by the artist
into his life, but he could also be the LaBrunie who has remained a mere dream of himself, powerless to leave the
limbo of his "musée imaginaire." The shadow is all there is.
Nerval's "ombre" remains inconsolable and his message is
the obverse of that heard by Michelet—*Ami, tu es seul.*

VICTOR BROMBERT

The Happy Prison:
A Recurring Romantic Metaphor

> Et le bonheur est une forte prison.
> —Paul Claudel

What causes King Lear's elation, toward the end of the play, at the thought of going to prison? "Come, let's away to prison"—he seems almost impatient to be locked up. How is one to explain this impatience and hint of joy? Is it battle fatigue (he has indeed incurred the worst!); is it mental derangement, is it despair? All is lost, to be sure—but Cordelia has been found. In twelve intensely suggestive lines, Shakespeare indicates the reasons for this unexpected delight. For father and daughter, prison will be an enchanted cage. Indeed like "birds i' the cage" they will be able to sing their poem of love, forgiveness and innocence:

> So we'll live,
> And pray, and sing, and tell old tales, and laugh
> At gilded butterflies.

In this cage they will feel freed from life's snares and servitudes; they will—so the old king dreams—be endowed with a superior vision and glimpse the mystery of things "as if [they] were God's spies." In short, prison is here conceived as the locus of spiritual freedom and revelation.

A very similar joy is experienced in Stendhal's *Charter-*

house of Parma, though by a young man and in a different register, namely by the hero Fabrice del Dongo, as he is locked up in the cell of the Farnese tower and discovers to his surprise the lyric potential of incarceration. He who feared the Spielberg fortress, as a symbol of reactionary despotism, now allows himself to be charmed by the "douceurs de la prison": the altitude, the splendid view, Clelia Conti's birds (they too are locked up in their "lovely cages": cages within a cage)—all contribute to bringing about a secret joy that Fabrice can only translate into an interrogation: "Is this truly a prison? is this what I feared so much?" Here, too, imprisonment implies a purification and the experience of freedom. In his "solitude aérienne" Fabrice feels far removed from the worldly pettiness of Parma. Fortress of dreams and amorous contemplation, the Farnese tower stands in Stendhal's metaphoric landscape very clearly on the side of happiness, and from this happiness Fabrice has no desire to escape.

Examples of the happy prison abound in Romantic literature. I am referring less to a period concept than to a form of imagination which expands beyond a given historical period. The illustrations taken from Shakespeare and Stendhal suggest a double tradition, of a theme and of metaphor. The image of immurement is essentially ambivalent in the western tradition: the walls of the cell punish the culprit and victimize the innocent; but they also protect poetic meditation and religious fervor. The prisoner's cell and the monastic cell look strangely alike. There exists no doubt a nostalgia for enclosure, as well as a prison wish. "The sweet prison cells" ("les douces cellules de la prison"), writes Jean Genêt, for whom incarceration appears as a guarantee of peace, security, stripping of all vain lendings—in other words a return to the self.[1] The released prisoner's agoraphobia is a well-known motif: it is the fear of the threatening outside.

1. Jean Genêt, *Journal du voleur* (Paris: Gallimard, 1949), p. 272.

Psychology and psychoanalysis have much to say on this subject. Bertram D. Lewin, in *The Psychoanalysis of Elation* (New York: Norton, 1950), suggests that the idea of the closed space corresponds not to an anxiety fantasy but to one of safety, of being in hiding. Poets, novelists, intuited as much: Balzac in one of his most astonishing melodramatic and symbolic scenes, shows us the great criminal and escape-artist Vautrin newly locked up in the prison of the Conciergerie, inspecting his cell to make sure that not a single hole might allow for the intrusion of a foreign glance. He carefully probes all the walls and then paradoxically concludes, in the heart of his dark jail, "Je suis en sûreté"—"I am safe!"

This is not to deny that real and metaphoric jails serve the theme of terror and oppression, that images of labyrinths, undergrounds, traps, buried secrets, crushing covers and asphyxiating encirclements have haunted the Romantic imagination, providing a symbolic décor for a tragic awareness. The motif of the gloomy prison becomes especially insistent toward the end of the 18th century—no doubt, in large part, for political and philosophical reasons. The symbolic value attributed to the Bastille and other political or state prisons viewed as tyrannical constructs, the nightmarish architectural perspectives in the famous "Prigioni" etchings of Piranese, the cruel fantasies of the Marquis de Sade conceived in prison and projected into further enclosed spaces, the setting of the Gothic novels in dungeons, vaults and oubliettes—all this tells us a great deal about the structures of the Romantic imagination, and the favored dialectical tensions between oppression and the dream of freedom, between fatality and revolt, between the finite and infinity.

But one need only evoke Pascal to realize that the metaphoric correspondence between imprisonment and the human condition is not a new idea. The notions that the soul is tragically encaged in the body, that the body is tragically exiled in the world's prison, are commonplaces in the Gnostic, Christian, and Neo-Platonic tradition. The Pythagorian pun on the terms *soma-sema* (body-tomb) is well-known. If writers, after the classical age, insist particularly on the prison image, this is no doubt bound up with a poetization of suffering and of a tragic condemnation. Thus Alfred de Vigny, filled with his readings of Pascal, denounces all vain hope: "Dans cette prison nommée la vie, d'où nous partons les uns après les autres pour aller à la mort" ("In this jail called life . . .").[2] But inversely—and this seems revealing—the documentary and humanitarian texts describing prison conditions in the pre-Romantic and Romantic periods, even when avowedly rationalistic and documentary, tend to poetize imprisonment. Beccaria, denouncing the "fredda atrocità" of jails in *Dei Delitti e delle pene,* evokes the tragedy of time, the oppressive and erosive workings of the imagination. Texts such as *Des Lettres de cachet et des Prisons d'état* by Mirabeau, or *La Bastille dévoilée* and *Mémoires historiques et authentiques sur la Bastille,* as well as the famous *Mémoires* of the state prisoners Linguet and Latude, all have in common mythopoeic tendencies; their denunciation is also a metaphoric amplification: the poetry of silence and allusions to Dante's *Inferno* go together with mythological images of Cerberus, Charon, of the Hydra, of caverns, of Tartarus.

The confrontation with anguish and nothingness in a prison setting is a recurrent motif, fully and almost abusively exploited by Romantic as well as by Existentialist writers. Hugo, Stendhal, Dostoevsky, Sartre, Camus—to name but a few—have thus dramatized the tête-à-tête with ultimate fear. The alienation is seen as twofold, social as well as visceral.

2. Alfred de Vigny, *Oeuvres complètes* (Paris: Gallimard [Pléiade], 1948), II, 945.

Leonid Andreev, in *The Seven Who Were Hanged,* admirably conveys the situation of the condemned prisoner as he views his cigarette and cigarette-holding hand with surprise and terror. Few images, it would seem, lend themselves more readily to a suggestion of absurdity or negativity than that of the cell. What better illustration than the admirable ninth stanza of *The Prisoner of Chillon* where Byron, by means of a series of negative constructions (no thought, no feeling, not night, not day, not even dungeon-light) suggests the loss of consciousness within the context of stagnant atemporality! All he apprehends is

> vacancy absorbing space,
> And fixedness—without a place.

As for spatial despair, it has been analyzed by Jung and others concerned with extra-terrestrial projections and cosmic dreams. The entire work of Victor Hugo is an illustration of the desire and hope for a breakthrough. The recurrent image of the wall, the enigma of this wall and of the massive jail door, function in his case as part of a vast soteriological scheme. On the one hand there is the desperate observation

> Nous sommes au cachot, la porte est inflexible.

But the answer is always ready. To the cry "Ouvrez les soupiraux" corresponds the clinking of the mysterious keys.

> On entend le trousseau des clefs mystérieuses
> Sonner confusément.[3]

Finally, among the images of the tragic prison most favored by the Romantics there are those which *interiorize* the experience of claustration, and in particular the image of the skull or the brain. Victor Hugo, once again, provides rich illustration. The "noir cerveau" of Piranesi in the poem *The*

3. Victor Hugo, "Pleurs dans la nuit," *Les Contemplations* (Paris: Garnier, 1957), p. 253.

Magi prepares for the metaphor of the brain-jail ("crâne-cachot") where the infamous spider suspends its web. There is an obvious association between Hugo's walled-in images of the brain and Baudelaire's brain-as-rotten-ceiling: same spider web, same blind animal, same lack of light. But there is one significant difference—and on that difference hinges the very ambivalence of the prison metaphor. For Baudelaire, the unfathomable sadness of all vaults implies ideas of asphyxia and lethal oppression; the refuge in solipsism involves the terror of being buried alive. For Hugo, on the other hand, man's captive mind will hear the jingling of the mysterious keys, the doors—all doors—will open, not only jails but Hell itself will be abolished, a universal liberation will come about. What is involved is the very activity of the poet as a liberating, almost divine force—for what the brain of the poet holds locked up preciously is nothing less than the infinite dimension of poetry and the secret of the world. "Un poète est un monde enfermé dans un homme." [4]

The ambivalence of the metaphor may help explain the Romantic fascination with the image of the sequestered poet, and in particular the fortune of a legend: that of the mad, enchained bard, Torquato Tasso. For in its larger mythic dimension, the carceral imagery implies the presence of a threshold, the possibility of a passage, an initiation—a passage from the inside to the beyond, from isolation to communion, from punishment and suffering to redemption, from sadness to that profound and mysterious joy which Hugo von Hoffmansthal, in *Die Frau ohne Schatten,* associates with the eternal secret of human bondage—"das ewige Geheimnis der Verkettung alles Irdischen."

We are back to the "mystery of things" which the prisoner

---

4. Victor Hugo, *La Legende des siècles* (Paris: Garnier, 1962), poem XLVII, p. 629.

as God's spy will take upon himself; we have come full back
to the theme of the happy prison. It would appear that this
theme of the happy prison is only an apparent contradiction,
that there is here a dialectical logic. It is this kind of logic
that determines Benvenuto Cellini in his *Vita*—an autobiography much prized by the Romantics—to write a chapter
entitled "In Lode di detta prigione" and to insist—he the
fiery adventurer-artist!—on a spiritual initiation in prison.

> Chi vuol saper quant'è il valor de dio,
> e quant'un uomo a quel ben si assomiglia,
> convien che stie'n prigione, al parer mio.

Very similar effusions seem to inspire the famous *Le Mie
Prigioni* by Silvio Pellico, the Milanese liberal who experienced years of *carcere duro* in Metternich's political prison,
the Spielberg. Friends of Pellico later reproached him his
Christian lyricism, discovered in jail, as a weakness. But the
unusual success of the book (in France alone there were five
translations during the first year after publication, in 1833)
suggests that its tone had immense appeal. Beyond the clichés
of prison literature (the good jailer, the beautiful panorama,
the view of the sky, the familiarity and friendship with
spiders, the contrasts between the ugliness and horror of the
inside and the splendor of the surrounding landscape), Pellico
insists on the rediscovered light; he copies with deep emotion
the edifying graffiti on the walls (*"Benedico la prigione"*):
he glorifies suffering.

What does all this mean if not that the real and the metaphoric prison assume the value of holy place? "A prison is
a sacred asylum," affirms one of the characters in Petrus
Borel's *Madame Putiphar*. And Byron, whose *Prisoner of
Chillon* explains in the last stanza that "These heavy walls
to [him] have grown / A hermitage," writes even more ex-
plicity in the *Sonnet on Chillon* (referring to "the eternal
spirit of the chainless mind"):

> Chillon! thy prison is a holy place,
> And thy sad floor an altar . . .

Poets seem to entertain a particular affection for the world of walls, bars, and locks. Leopardi, in his imaginary dialogue between Tasso and his "genio familiare" exalts sequestration because it rejuvenates the soul ("ringiovanisce l'animo") and galvanizes the imagination—the "virtu di favellare": the locked-in individual in his solipsistic "recreation" learns how to enter into dialogue with the self, learns how to "conversare seco medesima." Gérard de Nerval imagines the jailer as eternally jealous of the prisoner's dreams. Tristan Corbière, in his poem entitled *Libertà—A la cellule IV bis (prison royale de Gênes)*, proclaims the joy of imprisonment:

> jamais [je] n'ai chanté
> Que pour toi, dans ta cage,
> Cage de la gaîté!

The joyous cage is here explicitly associated with the creative act. And this indeed is the most important feature of this "cage de la gaîté": it involves the very function of the poet.

> Prison sûre conquête
> Où le poète est roi.

The notion of a conquest relates no doubt to the unavoidable and fecund tension between vision and order, between the freedom of imagination and the discipline of form.

> Dans un cauchemar de verrous
> L'Ordre est né

writes a more recent poet.[5]

One could no doubt pause here to open several large parentheses. Aesthetically speaking, the Romantic mind, attracted to the picturesque, the historical detail, the ominous setting, exploits the dramatic and melodramatic potential of any situation of sequestration and exile. But this poetic pres-

5. Pierre Seghers, *Piranese* (Neuchâtel: Ides et Calendes, 1960), p. 33.

tige is not separable from an ethical valorization. What is involved is the significance of *any* condemnation, which also means the significance of any destiny and of any rebellion against it—even and perhaps especially if that destiny is self-chosen. If on one level the act of writing implies a tension and ideal reconciliation between "inspiration" and constraining will, this aesthetic dilemma is a figuration of an abstract struggle between forces of freedom and forces of constraint. It is revealing that Baudelaire, who lived this aesthetic and ethical conflict more acutely perhaps than any other Romantic writer, should have admired Edgar Allan Poe for his prisoner-destiny (all of the United States, according to Baudelaire, was for Poe a "vaste prison"), and at the same time also for his lesson of aesthetic control. What Baudelaire says of the sonnet, of the relationship between any constricting form ("formes contraignantes") and a perspective on infinity, is crucial to an understanding of his poetry.[6]

Balzac views the rapport of the writer to confinement in a different light; he is certainly not concerned with form as constriction (not he, Balzac!), but with the very locus of creative suffering in which the artistic creator, *any* creator, is himself locked up or chooses to be locked up. Hence the recurring image, in Balzac's work, of the writer's prison garret, the place of austerity and abnegation and self-discipline, from which, however, the roofs of the capital as well as the sky can be seen, much as an opening unto the world beyond. This garret, prison and watchtower, sordid enclosure of the loftiest vocation, is defined in the Balzacian metaphor as a *sépulcre aérien*, an almost supra-terrestrial tomb in which the artist dies to life (that is, to all the temptations of Paris beyond that window) in order to live the life of the

6. Charles Baudelaire, *Correspondance générale*, III (Paris: L. Conard, 1947–48), 39–40.

spirit, and by so doing, consents, not without regret and bitterness, to make a true monastic sacrifice in view of an ultimate salvation.

The Romantic quality of such an image becomes even more apparent if one recalls that Rousseau, in much the same spirit, conceives of the Bastille as the ideal place to write on the subject of liberty. In one of the key texts of Romanticism—the fifth "Promenade" in the *Rêveries* (where the Bastille image again occurs in association with the very notion of revery)—Rousseau describes his happy stay on the island of Saint Pierre, and expresses the desire to see the island-refuge become for him a "prison perpétuelle." The telling words in this text ("circonscrite," "enfermé," "asile," "confiné") all suggest an interiorization of the prison image which corresponds to the sense of almost divine self-sufficiency (this state in which "on se suffit à soi-même comme Dieu"), and all correspond in fact to the central metaphor of Rousseauistic solipsism: "ce séjour isolé où je m'étais enlacé de moi-même . . ." ("where I did *entwine* with myself").

Perhaps the most remarkable in this respect is the dialectical link—very strong throughout the Western tradition—between a visible loss and an invisible, secret victory. This paradox underlies the theme of the happy prison; it is of course not unrelated to the Christian notion of a lost paradise and a *felix culpa*. Robinson Crusoe, a hero very much in favor with the Romantics, declares that he has never been happier than in his "forsaken solitary condition," and gives thanks to God for having there opened his eyes, for providing cause "to praise Him for dungeons and prisons." [7]

We are touching here on one of the fundamental aspects of Romanticism: the value conferred on solitude. The title of Stendhal's novel, *The Charterhouse of Parma*, has puzzled

7. Daniel Defoe, *Robinson Crusoe* (New York: Signet-New American Library, 1961), pp. 146–47.

some readers, not only because Parma has no charterhouse, but because in the novel itself the charterhouse does not appear except as a withdrawal from Parma in the very last pages. But it is evident that the real charterhouse in the novel is the Farnese Tower which indeed does occupy the center of the landscape: in other words, the prison. The title of the novel thus proposes the central metaphor, as well as the parable of a fear translated into a blessing. Similarly, Julien Sorel, in *The Red and the Black,* discovers that the only discomfort in prison has to do with his not being able to lock the door from the inside, and thus shut out the world. He rediscovers the truth proclaimed by Saint Bernard: "O solitudo, sola beatitudo . . ."—a poetry of silence and serenity in which the gloomiest dungeon is metamorphosed into a felicitous space. Even the fearful incarceration in the *Prisoner of Chillon* is converted into a precious solitude, a second home. "Even I," he concludes, "regained my freedom with a sigh."

If even the most atrocious jail can be transformed into a mediating space where consciousness learns to love despair and takes full possession of itself, it is no doubt because—as Gaston Bachelard puts it—man is a "great dreamer of locks." [8] Even man's consolatory prison activities, as repeatedly viewed in Romantic literature, betray the urge to exploit creatively, as it were, the physical and abstract realities of concentration and expansion. On the one hand, mental prowess and experimentation (geometric progressions formulated without help of paper, imaginary chess games, sadistic or masochistic choreographies); on the other hand, an outward reach: love at a distance, conversation with the beloved (in fairy tales this often turns out to be the beloved changed into a bird!), an obsession with writing, secret alphabets, tappings on the walls, underground communications.

8. Gaston Bachelard, *La Poétique de l'espace* (Paris: Presses Universitaires de France, 1957), p. 79.

Two opposing and simultaneous movements can here be followed: the one toward an inner center (a search for identity, knowledge, discovery of self); the other toward a transcending outside which corresponds to the *ecstasy* of spirtual escape. Intimacy with the elusive self is the aim of the first movement, the quest within. Essentially unheroic (for heroism, or the heroic stance, requires an audience), the movement toward the internal cell of meditation corresponds to the quest for authenticity which, at its extreme point, tolerates no histrionics, leaves no room for any pose. Novalis speaks of the mysterious road that leads toward this interior region. The most diverse texts, in our literary tradition, confirm this association of the prisoner's descent into the self with the quest for a truth, even the quest for an identity. Robinson Crusoe, once again an exemplary figure, is quick to create on his prison-island further limits within limits: he builds a fortification, he surrounds himself with walls, not only to ward off danger but to *surround himself,* to confine himself—and thus to *define* himself. He makes a puritan inventory of his own being.

Yet, as Albert Béguin remarked—and precisely in talking about Novalis—the inward movement implies a glance toward external reality, an ascent, an expansion. Here again the most diverse texts confirm the crucial notion that the narrowest of cells does not, even metaphorically, represent an obstacle to the dynamics of escape. Nothing is more constant than the notion of freedom associated with the cell—freedom, as it were, from the imperatives of time and space. Poets repeatedly sing of this *utopia* and of this *atemporality*.

> There were no stars, no earth, no time,

writes Byron—a line on which Tristan Corbière seems to play his own variation:

> Plus de jours, plus de nuits.

What is involved, primarily, is the cult of liberty conceived in individualistic terms. "Die Freiheitsliebe ist eine Kerkerblume," explains Heinrich Heine. And in Schiller's *Die Raüber,* not exactly the setting of a happy imprisonment, it is nonetheless in the darkness of the dungeon that the dream of freedom penetrates "wie ein Blitz in der Nacht."

It is of course perfectly logical that the dynamics of escape —and this involves not just escape, but Romantic escapism— should affirm themselves within the context of captivity. Balzac evokes the *art* of these convicts who know how to conceive and execute masterful schemes. It is a proud sport, a challenge to the human potential of ingeniousness and perseverance. Nineteenth-century readers must have been particularly sensitive to Benvenuto Cellini's advice to his jailers to lock him up well ("guardatemi bene") because he promised them that he would do all in his power to escape. Romanticism has of course its own virtuoso jail-breakers in the works of Stendhal, Dumas, and above all Victor Hugo, who describes with poetic relish the "muscle science" of convicts eternally envious of all that which flies ("Ces éternels envieux des mouches et des oiseaux"), and the "incredible art" of rising perpendicularly. Hugo indeed sees in the most mediocre man obsessed by the frightful thirst for liberty an inspired dreamer tending toward the sublime.[9]

A wide range of mediating and stereotyped images links the dream-prisoner to a transcending reality: walls as a symbolic boundary, windows, hills, clouds, birds—even water. The bird seems favored—perhaps because the image of the bird lends itself to a fundamental ambiguity. For the bird flies freely, but in its flight it also recalls the cage from which it flew away, the cage that awaits it, perhaps the cage it regrets. The exploitation of the image confirms the double

9. Cellini, *Vita* (Milano: Rizzoli, 1954), Bk. I, par. 108, p. 207. Hugo, *Les Misérables* (Paris: Garnier, 1957), I, 117, 548, 959; I, 178.

movement inherent in the prison theme. If indeed the quest
of spiritual freedom and the redemptive thrust carry toward
an elsewhere, a reverse impulse tends toward the still center,
toward another form of release, a deliverance from the causal
world of phenomena. It is at this still center, this still point
of the turning world, that is to be found the hidden secret,
the ineffable treasure, the perception of the *numen*. It is, I believe, in this spirit that one must view Axel's castle in Villiers
de L'Isle-Adam's weird play: the isolated castle in the midst
of the dark forest, the dungeon atmosphere, and the funereal
vaults—all are the warrants of a perfect fulfillment. For Sara
and Axel, the protagonists of this spiritual drama, this fulfillment is intimately bound up with their ability to extract
themselves from the "geôle du monde," the worldly jail—that
is, from the world of Becoming.

One could almost trace how, within the context of the
prison theme, the dynamics of Romanticism can lead to the
stasis of Decadentism. "Vivre?" says one of the characters in
Axel, "les serviteurs feront cela pour nous" (to live—our
servants will do that for us!). It is revealing that Huysmans,
the author of *A Rebours,* that breviary of Decadentism, also
invokes the penitentiary of worldly existence to justify his
retirement into an inner exile. Nothing is in fact more characteristic of the mixture of decadentist and spiritualistic-
ally nostalgic literature than this inner exile, this contempt
for action, this taste for an enclosed, nocturnal, artificial
existence where rooms are furnished with ascetic elegance
and hermetically sealed, where it is possible to surround oneself with silence, and to surrender to the selfish enjoyment of
art as well as to a passive, vaguely onanistic eroticism sea-
soned by reveries of orgies and impotence. *A Rebours* proposes the comfortably heated cell—the "cellule tiède," the
"thébaïde raffinée," a sophisticated hermit retreat, a privileged and self-chosen encagement in which the aesthete lives

in fruitless comfort, surrounded by mirrors that reflect the image of his own haughty sterility. At the extreme point of this type of sensibility, the solipsistic prison ceases to have any tragic or lyric potential: it becomes the enervating enclosure for the self-centered hypochrondiac dilettante suffering from moral as well as physical dyspepsia. Very appropriately, when in his later work Huysmans begins to flirt with religion and toys with the idea of retiring to a monastery—but it must be a comfortable monastery!—he utilizes the expression "mettre son âme dans une pension."

Of course, in a tragically and poetically endowed temperament, such as Proust's (who owes a great deal to Huysmans), the combination of decadentist sophistication and aesthetic hedonism can, as though in an ultimate metamorphosis, transform the inner space, the sound- and light-proof room, into the symbolic area of poetic experimentation and poetic insight. A study of such inner spaces in the work of Marcel Proust would surely yield rich results. The novel begins in bed, in the most intimate space of the most intimate room; it is written by a recluse in his bed, and that bed stands in a cork-lined room that shuts out all the voices of this world. If one recalls moreover the importance, in Proust's work, of the very notion of imprisoned *essences* that have to be liberated in order to overcome death—essences saved by the almost divine grace of memory providing the individual with his identity—it does become clear that what is involved is an intensely private kind of salvation. Proust has spoken beautifully of his early, intimate experiences, when reading in his darkened room as a boy, he uncovered from the inside of this darkness the "spectacle total de l'été," and—even more dramatically—in a passage describing his childhood experience of sickness and reclusion: "I understood then that Noah was never able to see the world so clearly as from inside the ark, though it was locked and though there was darkness on the earth." [10]

It would of course be tempting to conclude on this note of happy confinement, glorifying redemptive artistic creation. The image of the ark seems like a promise of survival. Yet one cannot deny that artistic redemption is viewed here essentially as a form of private salvation. All suffering is justified to the extent that it can be assimilated to private needs. It is probably not a coincidence that the poetic prestige of the prison image corresponds culturally to a period when the writer becomes increasingly his own favorite subject—indeed almost his unique subject: art becomes the subject of art, and thought the subject of thought, as the nineteenth-century writer indulges in a mirror disease at the cost of delicious self-torture. Baudelaire, poet of artificial paradises, speaks of that inner theater, of that limpid tête-à-tête with the self, of the ironic and self-destructive inventory of one's impotence, while enjoying this private tragedy in which the self (already viewed posthumously) appears as an inviolable actor. His dream is one of dandyish, aristocratic self-sufficiency: "Le vrai héros s'amuse tout seul." [11]

"Solitude gives birth to the original in us, to beauty unfamiliar and perilous—to poetry," writes Thomas Mann. "But also, it gives birth to the opposite: to the perverse, the illicit, the absurd." [12] I have already alluded to the decadent aberrations. What remains to be stressed is the fundamental gloom that hides behind the conquest of intimacy and

10. Marcel Proust, *Du Côté de chez Swann* (Paris: Gallimard, 1939), I, 123; *Les Plaisirs et les jours* (Paris: Gallimard, 1924), p. 13.

11. Charles Baudelaire, *Oeuvres complètes,* ed. Claude Pichois (Paris: Gallimard [Pléiade], 1961), p. 1276.

12. Thomas Mann, *Death in Venice,* trans. H. T. Lowe-Porter (New York: Vintage-Knopf, 1958), p. 24.

images of self-possession. Behind the impregnable solitude and compulsive self-centeredness lurks the secret awareness that no relation can exist between man and man. There are no echoes to the cries of Sade's secret torture rooms—the cries cannot even be heard. And walls remain mute.

Of course, another story can be told; it also has deep roots in Romanticism, though it is our own period, alas, that was destined to experience it in the flesh. It is the story of *collective* imprisonment, whose historical and symbolic manifestations are the penal colony, the penitentiary. One recognizes, of course, the old tradition of the *Dies Irae,* of the purgatorial horrors, or worse, of a hopeless condemnation: "Lasciate ogni speranze voi ch'entrate." Victor Hugo in *Le Dernier Jour d'un condamné,* describes a grimacing prison-humanity in a purgatorial atmosphere. As for Dostoevsky's *House of the Dead,* Turgenev was quite right in saying that the famous passage of the bath provides a truly Dantesque image. The fact is that both Dostoevsky and Hugo are convinced that private salvation is not possible; both glorify the criminal-convict for being *other,* that is for being a meditator; both view the convict with "sacred awe" as a kind of demonic and collective Redeemer. For both are deeply convinced that man as individual cannot save himself, that he is implicated in a collective drama.

This sense of a collective drama has been confirmed most bitterly by our own era of totalitarianism and concentration camps. The catastrophic nature of the twentieth century seems to have cancelled out the possibility of dreaming within the context of a poetic privacy. The nostalgia for this privacy remains strong no doubt, but it is also steadily denied. If Camus still writes about what he himself calls the "cellular lyricism" in *The Stranger* and *The Fall,* he also recognizes the oppression of History, and in *The Plague* proclaims that there can be no individual destiny, that there can only be a *collective destiny.* The original title of *The Plague* was *Les Prisonniers*—and it is characteristic that the modern prison turns out to be the entire city. Much could be said on this notion of the collective habitat, metropolis or megalopolis, as the modern figuration of a dehumanizing penitentiary. Nightmarish or futuristically utopian texts—many of them Russian—deal with this prophetic subject: Briussov, Zamiatin, Biely in the geometrically oneiric Saint Petersburg . . . I recall in particular Briussov's story, *The Republic of Southern Cross,* in which the chief city, Star City, with its windowless buildings, is covered by an "impenetrable and opaque roof," a city that finally appears as an immense, black, polluted *coffer.* Whether in Briussov's, Zamiatin's, Orwell's, Walter Jens's, or Solzhenitsin's nightmare, the predominant feeling is that humanism and bourgeois culture, and even the concept of man, are doomed.

Finally, when the prison image has become so pervasive that the very notion of a prison-hermitage seems inconceivable, or at best an anachronistic revery, this seems to be evidence that individualism has become an impossible luxury. Stendhal, in the face of the increasing pressures and oppression of History, Ideologies, and anonymous, collective tyranny, could still believe that one can lock oneself out by locking oneself in—and thus protect a precious self-possession. Perhaps it is this that ultimately separates us most sharply from our Romantic heritage: the very dream of a happy prison has become hard to entertain in a world of penal colonies and extermination camps, in a world in which we may well fear that somehow even our suffering can no longer be our refuge.

II

INSTANCES

PAUL DE MAN

Theory of Metaphor in
Rousseau's Second Discourse

The place of the *Discourse on the Origins and the Foundations of Inequality among Men* (1754) in the canon of Rousseau's works remains uncertain. The apparent duality of
Rousseau's complete writings, a whole that consists in part
of political theory, in part of literature (fiction and autobiography), has inevitably led to a division of labor among the
interpreters, thus bringing to light latent incompatibilities
between political scientists, cultural historians, and literary
critics. This specialization has often prevented the correct
understanding of the relations between the literary and the
political aspects of Rousseau's thought. As the overtly political piece of writing that it undoubtedly is, the *Second Discourse* has primarily interested historians and social scientists.[1] It does not confront them with the same difficulties as
Julie, a book in which it is not easy to overlook the literary
dimensions entirely and where it takes some degree of bad
faith to reduce the text to "an intellectual experiment in the

1. The bibliography of studies wholly or in part devoted to the *Second
Discourse* is immense and one would welcome an updated *état de re-
cherches* on the text. In his notes to the edition of the *Second Discourse*
in the Pléiade Edition Jean Starobinski gives several useful indications
(see pp. 1297, 1299, 1305, 1315, 1317, 1319, 1334, 1339, 1359, 1370, 1372,
1377). Since then (1964) there have been numerous additions.

techniques and consequences of human engineering." [2] Despite the presence of at least one explicit passage on language in the *Discourse* the linguistic mediations can easily be ignored. The section on the origin of language [3] is clearly a polemical digression without organic links to the main argument and the *Discourse* can be considered as a literal model for a theory of history and of society, that is, a model that could be transposed *tel quel* from the text to the political or social situation that it represents or prefigures. Once this is assumed, the *Second Discourse* becomes highly vulnerable to a list of recurrent objections that reappear with remarkable persistance in all Rousseau studies and that any reader of the text will feel compelled to make himself.

It is by no means my intention to suggest that these objections are unfounded or that they are inspired by a deliberate malice that should be met with defensive counter-malice. The Rousseau interpreter should avoid the danger of repeating the paranoid gesture of his subject. The first task is to diagnose what, if anything, is being systematically overlooked by other readers, prior to asking why this particular area of Rousseau's thought possesses the curious privilege of rendering itself invisible, as if it were wearing the ring of Gyges referred to in the sixth *Promenade*. The literal reading that fails to take into account the figural dimensions of the language (despite the fact that this particular text explicitly draws attention to these dimensions) is not to be rejected as simply erroneous or malevolent, all the more since, in the *Second Discourse,* the political terminology and the political

2. Lester Crocker, *J. J. Rousseau* (New York: Macmillan, 1968), p. 20.
3. *Discourse,* pp. 146–151. All page references are to the French edition of the *Discourse, Discours sur l'origine et les fondements de l'inégalité,* texte établi et annoté par Jean Starobinski in J. J. Rousseau, *Oeuvres complètes,* III (*Ecrits politiques*), ed. Bernard Gagnebin and Marcel Raymond (Paris: Gallimard [Pléiade], 1964). All translations are my own.

themes postulate the existence of an extra-textual referent and raise the question of the text's relationship to this referent. Nor can we assume that this relationship is one of literal correspondence.

Consider, for instance, the status of what seems to be the inescapable *a priori* of the text itself, what Rousseau calls the "state of nature." Very few informed readers today would still maintain that Rousseau's state of nature is an empirical reality, present, past or future.[4] Most commentators would agree that, at least up to a point, the state of nature is a state "that no longer exists, that has perhaps never existed and that probably will never come into being" (*Discourse*, p. 123). It is a fiction; but in stating this, the problem has merely been displaced, for what then is the significance of this fiction with regard to the empirical world? Granted that the authority of the state of nature, the hold it has over our present thought, is no longer that of something that existed elsewhere or at other times and towards which our relation can therefore be described in terms of nostalgia and quest; granted that the mode of being of the state of nature and the mode of being of the present, alienated state of man are perhaps radically incompatible, with no road connecting the one to the other —the question remains why this radical fiction ("We must begin by discarding all facts"—*Discourse*, p. 132) remains indispensable for any understanding of the present, as if its shadow controlled once and forever the degree of light alotted to us. It is a state that we must "know well" and of which "it is necessary to have a correct understanding [des Notions justes] in order to evaluate our present condition" (*Discourse*,

4. For a recent statement to this effect, among many others, see Henri Gouhier, *Les méditations métaphysiques de J. J. Rousseau* (Paris: Vrin, 1970), p. 23. For a clear formulation of the fictional character of the state of nature, see Herbert Dieckmann's edition of Diderot, *Supplément au voyage de Bougainville* (Geneva: Droz, 1955), pp. lxxxiii–xciv.

p. 123). What kind of epistemology can hope to "know well" a radical state of Fiction? The *Second Discourse* hardly seems to provide a reliable answer. As a genetic narrative in which the state of nature functions at the very least as a point of departure or as a point of reference [5] (if no longer necessarily as a point of arrival), the *Second Discourse* seems to contradict the radical rejection of reality on which it bases its claim to free itself from the constraints of facts. Rousseau seems to want to have it both ways, giving himself the freedom of the fabulator but, at the same time, the authority of the responsible historian. A certain impatience on the part of the historians is certainly justified towards a man who, by his own admission, escapes in speculative fantasies but who, on the other hand, claims that in so doing, "one sweeps away the dust and the sands that cover the edifice [of human institutions], one reveals the solid foundations on which it is built and learns to consider them with respect" (*Discourse,* p. 127). How can a pure fiction and a narrative involving such concrete political realities as property, contractual law, and modes of government coalesce into a genetic history that pretends to lay bare the foundations of human society?

It seems difficult to avoid a prognosis of inconsistency, leading to the separation between the theoretical, literary and the practical, political aspects of Rousseau's thought. The literary faculty which, in the *Second Discourse,* invents the fiction of a natural state of man becomes an ideology growing out of the repression of the political faculty. A clear and concise statement of this recurrent critical interpretation of Rousseau —which goes back at least as far as Schiller—can be found in a recent study of the *Social Contract* by the French social philosopher Louis Althusser. He analyzes recurrent shifts

5. On this point, see Starobinski's preface, *Discourse,* p. LVII. He refers primarily to an article by Eric Weil, "J. J. Rousseau et sa politique," *Critique,* (January, 1952).

(décalages) in the key-terms of Rousseau's vocabulary and concludes that these shifts, or displacements, are

> to be explicitly understood, once and forever, as the very Displacement that separates the consequences of theory from reality, a displacement between two equally impossible *praxes* [*décalage entre deux pratiques également impossibles*]. Since we now have [in the text of the *Social Contract*] reached the stage of reality and since we can only keep going around in a circle (ideology—economy—ideology, etc.) no flight remains possible into the actual, real world [*dans la réalité même*]. End of the displacement.
>
> If no other displacement is available to us . . . only one single, different road remains open: a *transference* [*transfert*] of the impossible theoretical solution into the opposite of theory [*l'autre de la théorie*], namely literature. The fictional triumph of an admirable, unprecedented literary work.[6]

If the political side of Rousseau's work is indeed a reductive ideology that results from a repression carried out by means of literary language, then the theoretical interest of a text like the *Second Discourse* is primarily psychological. Conversely, the political writings can then themselves become a reliable way of access to the problematics of the self in Rousseau. And here the *Second Discourse* would be particularly useful, not only because, unlike the *Social Contract,* it explicitly involves the moment of transference into literary fiction, but precisely because, unlike the autobiographical writings, it hides its self-obsessions behind a language of conceptual generality. Rousseau's ambivalence with regard to such key notions as property, civil authority, and even technology [7] could then serve as a model for an understand-

---

6. Louis Althusser, "Sur le Contrat Social (Les décalages)" in *Cahiers pour l'Analyse,* 8 *L'impensé de J. J. Rousseau,* (Paris: Editions du Seuil, 1970), pp. 5–42.

7. The ambivalence of Rousseau's attitude toward property is one example: on the one hand, he makes it sound as if property were theft; on the other hand, law is at times glorified, in almost extravagant terms,

ing of his psychological self-mystifications. In strictly textual terms, the problem comes down to the inconsistency between the first and the second part of the text. Between the pure fiction of the first part, dealing with theoretical problems of man, nature, and methodology and the predominantly historical and institutional language used in the second part, there would exist a gap, an unbridgeable "décalage" that Rousseau, caught in a false claim of authentic self-knowledge, would be least of all able to perceive. The reading that follows puts this scheme into question.

In the *Second Discourse,* the state of nature, though fictional, is not static. Possibilities of change are built into its description as a synchronic *state* of being. The potentially dynamic properties of natural man are pity, "a principle anterior to reason [that] inspires a natural reluctance to see any sensitive being, and especially our fellow-man, suffer or perish" (*Discourse,* p. 126), and freedom: "Nature alone does everything in the actions of animals whereas man partakes in his own actions in his quality as free agent" (*Discourse,* p. 141). The concept of pity has been definitively treated by Jacques Derrida.[8] We can therefore begin with the concept of freedom.

The ambivalent nature of the concept of freedom in Rousseau has been noticed by several interpreters. To be free, for

as the defense of property (see, for example, *Discours sur l'économie politique,* in *Oeuvres,* III, 248–249). One is tempted to interpret the inconsistency psychologically by referring to Rousseau's lowly birth as a social misfit who both glorifies property as something he desires but cannot possess, and poverty as a self-redeeming moral virtue. On civil authority, see the discrepancy between, on the one hand, the glorification of the magistrates of Geneva and of his own father in the Dédicace of the *Second Discourse* (pp. 117–118) and the caricature of the harassed magistrate in the text of the *Discourse* proper (pp. 192–193).

8. Jacques Derrida, *De la Grammatologie* (Paris: Editions de Minuit, 1967), pp. 259–272.

Rousseau, is by no means a tranquil and harmonious repose within the ordained boundaries of the human specificity, the reward for a Kantian, rational sense of limitations. From the start, freedom appears as an act of the will ("the will still speaks when Nature is silent"—*Discourse,* p. 141) pitted against the ever-present obstacle of a limitation which it tries to transgress.[9] It is a consequence, or another version, of the statement at the beginning of the *Second Discourse,* that the specificity of man forever escapes our grasp since "the more we study man . . . the less we are in a position to know him" (*Discourse,* p. 123). Any confinement within the boundaries of an anthropological self-definition is therefore felt to be a restriction beyond which man, as a being devoid of natural specificity, will have to transgress. This will to transgress, in a pre-Nietzschian passage, is held by Rousseau to be the very definition of the Spirit: "the power to will or, rather, the power to choose, as well as the feeling of this power is a purely spiritual act" (*Discourse,* p. 142). Very little distinguishes power to will, or willpower (puissance de vouloir) from "will to power," since the power to choose is precisely the power to transgress whatever in nature would entail the end of human power.

The direct correlative of freedom thus conceived is mentioned in the paragraph that follows immediately upon the definition, although the transitional link is not explicitly stated: freedom is man's will to change or what Rousseau somewhat misleadingly calls "perfectibility." [10] The potential

9. As summarized in the admirable title of Starobinski's *Jean-Jacques Rousseau: La transparence et l'obstacle* (Paris: Plon, 1957). Rouseau's statement to the Polish nation is well known: "Le repos et la liberté sont incompatibles: il faut opter" (in *Considérations sur le Gouvernement de Pologne, Oeuvres,* III, 955). This aspect of Rousseau's thought is now generally recognized in contemporary studies.

10. Misleadingly, since "perfectibility" is just as regressive as it is progressive. Starobinski, in a lengthy footnote (p. 1317) asserts that per-

transgression that occurs whenever the concepts of nature and of man are associated—in the *Essay on the Origin of Language* all examples destined to illustrate the "natural" languages of man are acts of violence [11]—transforms all human attributes from definite, self-enclosed and self-totalizing actions into open structures: perception becomes imagination, natural needs (besoins) become unfulfillable passions, sensations become an endless quest for knowledge which deprives man forever of a central identity ("the more one meditates . . . the greater the distance becomes between our pure sensations and the simplest forms of knowledge" *Discourse,* p. 144). In the same consistent pattern, the discovery of temporality coincides with the acts of transgressive freedom: time relates to space in the same way that imagination relates to perception, need to passion, etc. The very conception of a future is linked with the possibility of a free imagination; the soul of the still-enslaved primitive man is "without any awareness of the future, however close it may be. His projects are as narrow as are his views: they hardly extend until the end of the day" (*Discourse,* p. 144). Consciousness of mortality is similarly linked to the freedom that distinguishes man from the animal: "the knowledge and the fear of death is one of the first things acquired by man as he moves away from the animal condition" (*Discourse,* p. 143).

This existential notion of freedom is impressive enough in

fectibility is a "néologisme savant"; the concept if not the word appears in Fontenelle's *Digression sur les anciens et les modernes* which dates from 1688. Fontenelle speaks of "le progrès des choses."

11. See *Essai sur l'origine des Langues,* text reproduit d'après l'édition A. Belin de 1817 (Paris, le Graphe, supplément au No. 8 des *Cahiers pour l'Analyse*), henceforth referred to as *Essay,* p. 502. Rousseau mentions the threatening gifts sent by the king of the Scythians to King Darius and especially the Old Testament story (*Judges*) of the Levite from Ephraim who sent the body of his murdered wife, cut in twelve pieces, to the Tribes of Israel to spur them on to revenge. The same theme is taken up in the later story *Le lévite d'Ephraim* (1762).

itself. It does not suffice, however, to make the connection with the political parts of the *Second Discourse*. It accounts for the ambivalent valorization of all historical change, since any change will always have to put into question the value-system that made it possible: any positive valorization as progress always also implies a regress, and Rousseau's text scrupulously maintains this balance.[12] The impossibility of reaching a rationally enlightened anthropology also accounts for the necessary leap into fiction, since no past or present human action can coincide with or be underway toward the nature of man. The question remains why the *Second Discourse,* in its second part, somehow manages to return to the concrete realities of political life in a vocabulary that reintroduces normative evaluations—why, in other words, the methodological paradox of the beginning (that the very attempt to know man makes this knowledge impossible) does not prevent the text from finally getting started, after many hesitations: a preface preceding a first part which is itself a methodological introduction and which, in its turn, is again introduced by another preface. What characteristic structures of freedom and perfectibility, in Part I, lead us to understand the political structures of Part II? And where are we to find a structural description of perfectibility in what seems to be a self-enclosed genetic text in which perfectibility simply functions as the organizing theme?

The section on language (*Discourse,* pp. 146–151) appears as a digression destined to illustrate the impossibility of passing from nature to culture by natural means. It runs parallel to a similar development that deals with the growth of technology. As such, it serves indeed a secondary function that belongs with the polemical and not with the systematic aspects of the *Second Discourse.* Starobinski rightly empha-

12. See *Discourse,* pp. 142, 162, 187, 193, especially note 9, pp. 207–208, and *passim*.

sizes that the passage is written "less in order to formulate a
coherent theory on the origin of language than to demonstrate the difficulties the question raises" (*Discourse,* p. 1322).
In fact, the entire passage has the tone of a mock-argument
directed against those who explain the origin of language
by means of causal categories that are themselves dependent
on the genetic power of the origin for which they are supposed to account.[13] The constant warning against the mysti-
fication of adopting a privileged viewpoint that is unable to
understand its own genealogy, a methodological theme that
runs throughout the *Second Discourse,* also applies to the
theory of language. But not selectively so. The science of language is one of the areas in which this type of fetishism (reducing history to nature) occurs, but it is not the only one.
The same error prevails with regard to ethical judgment
(Hobbes) or with regard to technology. From this point of
view, the section on language seems to have a primarily critical function and it could not serve to illuminate the central
problem of the text—that of the epistemological authority of
the normative second part.

The passage, however, contains its own theory on the structure of language, albeit in a highly fragmentary and oblique
form. More important still, Rousseau explicitly links language to the notion of perfectibility, itself derived from the
primal categories of freedom and will. "Moreover," he writes,
"general ideas can only enter the mind by means of words
and our understanding can seize upon them only by means
of propositions. This is one of the reasons why animals could
never acquire such ideas, nor the perfectibility that depends

13. "Dire que la Mère dicte à l'Enfant les mots . . . cela montre bien
comment on enseigne des Langues déjà formées, mais cela n'apprend
point comment elles se forment" (p. 147); "si les hommes ont besoin de
la parole pour apprendre à penser, ils ont eu bien plus besoin encore
de savoir penser pour trouver l'art de la parole" (p. 142). The conclusions are reached by substituting effect for cause (metalepsis).

on it" (C'est une des raisons pourquoi les animaux ne sauraient se former de telles idées, ni jamais acquérir la perfectibilité qui en dépend—*Discourse,* p. 149). Perfectibility evolves as language evolves, moving from particular denomination to general ideas: an explicit link is established between two distinct conceptual areas in the text, the first pertaining to perfectibility, freedom and a series of general concepts that are connected narratively and thematically but never described in terms of their internal structures, the second pertaining to the structural and epistemological properties of language. Besides, freedom and perfectibility are relay-stations on the itinerary by way of which the *Second Discourse* can move from the methodological language of the first to the political language of the second part. The sentence can therefore be interpreted to mean that the system of concepts at work in the political parts of the *Second Discourse* are structured like the linguistic model described in the digression on language. This makes the passage a key to an understanding of the entire text. For nowhere else do we find as detailed a structural analysis of the concepts involved in the subsequent narrative.

Yet the passage is avoided rather than stressed in most readings of the *Second Discourse*. In his notes to the Pléiade Edition, Jean Starobinski seems to be clearly aware of some of its implications, but he at once limits its impact by means of an argument that goes to the center of the problem involved in the interpretation of this text. Commenting on Rousseau's sentence—"C'est une des raisons pourquoi les animaux ne sauraient se former des idées générales, ni jamais acquérir la perfectibilité qui en dépend"—he writes: "The relative clause [qui en dépend] has here a determinative and not an explicative function. Rousseau refers here to one particular kind of perfectibility that depends on language. As for Perfectibility in general, which Rousseau has told us to be an essential and primitive property of man, it is not the result of language but much rather its cause" (*Discourse,* p. 1327). Since the French language does not distinguish between "which" and "that," it is impossible to decide by grammatical means alone whether the sentence should read: "animals could never acquire perfectibility since it is dependent on language" or, as Starobinski would have it, "animals could never acquire the kind of perfectibility that depends on language." The correct understanding of the passage depends on whether one accepts on the face of it that the principle of genetic causality introduced by Starobinski, in which chronological, logical, and ontological priority coincide,[14] is indeed the system at work in Rousseau's text. Can it be said of perfectibility that it is an "essential and primitive property of man," Starobinski's phrasing rather than Rousseau's, who said only that it was "une qualité très spécifique qui distingue [l'homme]" (*Discourse,* p. 142). Each of the terms is problematic and their combination, as if they could be freely interchanged, is the most problematic of all. Starobinski's phrasing not only assumes that the (temporally) primitive must also be the (ontological) essence, but that a property of what is presumably a substance (man) can be an essence. Since moreover the substance "man" is in this text a highly volatile concept that behaves logically much more like a property than like a substance, the essence perfectibility would then be the property of a property. Rousseau's main methodological point, his constant warning against the danger of substituting cause for effect [15] reveals at least a certain distrust of genetic continuities, for the substitution becomes aberrant only if such a continuity is in doubt. This should

14. See *Oeuvres,* III, 1285. Starobinski writes: "Rousseau has rigorously followed [Aristotle's] method, by giving to the word origin [*arche*] a meaning in which the logical antecedent necessarily entails a *historical* antecedent."

15. See preceding note.

make us wary of accepting uncritically the common sense and admirable prudence displayed in Starobinski's reading.

The statement—even if read to mean that perfectibility, in the general sense it is used in when we first encounter it in the *Second Discourse* (p. 142), is linked to language—does not at first sight seem to be so far-reaching as to justify its repression. Why then is it being overlooked or avoided? How curious that, when a text offers us an opportunity to link a non-linguistic historical concept—such as perfectibility— to language, we should refuse to follow the hint. Especially curious in the case of a text whose intelligibility hinges on the existence or non-existence of such a link between a "literary," language-oriented method of investigation and the practical results to which the method is assumed to lead. Yet a critic of Starobinski's intelligence and subtlety goes out of his way in order to avoid the signs that Rousseau has put up and prefers the bland to the suggestive reading, although it requires an interpretative effort to do so. For there is no trace to be found in Rousseau's works of a particular, linguistic perfectibility that would be distinct from historical perfectibility in general. In the *Essay on the Origin of Language,* the perfectibility of language, which is in fact a degradation, evolves exactly as the perfectibility of society evolves in the *Second Discourse.* There must be an unsuspected threat hidden in a sentence that one is so anxious to defuse.

Animals have no history because they are unable to perform the specifically linguistic act of conceptualization. But how does conceptualization work, according to Rousseau? The text yields information on this point, though not in a simple and straightforward way. It describes conceptualization as substituting one verbal utterance (at the simplest level, a common noun) for another on the basis of a resemblance that hides differences which permitted the existence of entities in the first place. The natural world is a world of

pure contiguity: "All individual entities appear in isolation
to the mind [of primitive man],[16] as they are in the picture of
nature. If one oak tree was called A, another was called B
. . . " (*Discourse*, p. 149). Within this contiguity certain
resemblances appear. By substituting for A and B the word
"tree" on the basis of certain properties that A and B have
in common, we invent an abstraction under which the irre-
ducible differences that separate A from B are subsumed.
The perception of these resemblances is not, in itself, a conceptualization: in the case of animals, it leads to acts that
satisfy needs but that remain confined to the limits of the
particular action. "When a monkey goes without hesitation
from one nut to another, do we think that he has in mind a
general idea of this type of fruit and that he compares his
archetype to these two individual entities? Certainly not
. . . " (p. 149). Conceptualization does not proceed on the
basis of mere perception: perception and imagination (in
the guise of memory) [17] intervene in recognizing the existence
of certain similarities—an act of which animals are said to
be as capable as men—but the actual process of conceptualization is verbal: "It is necessary to state propositions and to
speak in order to have general ideas; for as soon as the
imagination stops, the mind can only proceed by means of
discourse" (p. 150).

The description seems to remain within a binary system
in which animal and man, nature and culture, acts (or things)
and words, particularity (or difference) and generality, concreteness and abstraction stand in polar opposition to each
other. Antitheses of this kind allow for dialectical valoriza-
tions and although this particular passage of the *Second Dis-*

16. Rousseau says "des premiers Instituteurs," which may sound
cryptic in translation. The meaning refers to "primitive" men as the
"first" inventors who instituted language.

17. "La vue d'une de ces noix rappelle à [l]'a mémoire [du singe] les
sensations qu'il a reçues de l'autre" (*Discourse*, p. 150).

course (pp. 149–150) is relatively free of value judgments (nothing is said about an innate superiority of nature over artifice or of practical behavior over speculative abstraction), it nevertheless invites value judgments on the part of the interpreter. The most incisive evaluations of this and of similar passages are those which locate the tension within language itself by stressing that the implied polarity exists within the structure of the linguistic sign, in the distinction established by Rousseau between the denominative and the conceptual function of language. The text indeed distinguishes the act of naming (tree A and tree B) which leads to the literal denomination of the proper noun, from the act of conceptualization. And conceptualization, conceived as an exchange or substitution of properties on the basis of resemblance, corresponds exactly to the classical definition of metaphor as it appears in theories of rhetoric from Aristotle to Roman Jakobson.[18] The text would then, in a sense, distinguish between, on the one hand, figurative, connotative and metaphorical language and, on the other, denominative, referential and literal language, and it would oppose the two modes antithetically to each other. This allows for a valorization that privileges one mode over the other. Since Rousseau asserts the temporal priority of the proper noun over the concept ("Each object received *first* a particular name"—p. 149; "the *first* nouns could only have been proper nouns"—p. 150) it would indeed follow, within the genetic logic of the narrative, that he separates the literal from the metaphorical forms of language and privileges the former over the latter. This interpretation, nearly unanimously accepted in Rousseau studies, is well summarized, with a helpful reference to

18. The definition from the *Poetics* (1457 b) is well known: "Metaphor is the transfer (epiphora) to a thing of a name that designates another thing, a transfer from the genus to the species or from the species to the genus or according to the principle of analogy." Jakobson defines metaphor as substitution on the basis of resemblance.

Michel Foucault, by a recent commentator: [19] "The entire
history of Rousseau's work, the passage from 'theory to literature,' is the transference of the need to name the world to
the prior need of naming oneself. To name the world is to
make the representation of the world coincide with the world
itself; to name myself is to make the representation that I
have of the world coincide with the representation that I
convey to others." [20] Rousseau's increasingly subjective and
autobiographical discourse would then merely be the extension, within the realm of the self, of the referential linguistic
model that governs his thought. The failure of this attempt
to "name" the subject, the discovery that, in Grosrichard's
words, "le sujet est l'innomable" [21] undercuts the authority
of Rousseau's own language. It also relegates him, with
Condillac and, generally speaking, with all followers of
Locke, to what Foucault subversively calls "le discours clas-
sique." As far as the *Second Discourse* is concerned, such an
interpretation would have to conclude that the text is truly
incoherent, since it does not control the opposition between
the conceptual metaphor "State of nature" and the literal
reality of civil society, an opposition asserted in the *Discourse*
itself. Moreover, by starting out from the metaphor, the text

19. Alain Grosrichard, "Gravité de Rousseau" in *Cahiers pour
l'Analyse,* 8. Even the most rhetorically aware study of Rousseau available today, Jacques Derrida's "Linguistique de Rousseau," (*Revue internationale de Philosophie,* 82, [1967], 443–462) and his *De la Grammatologie,* cited above, remains within this scheme, though certainly
not without complications.

20. Grosrichard, "Gravité de Rousseau," p. 64. I give a free translation that attempts to explain the more elegant but more elliptical
French version: "Toute l'historie de l'oeuvre de Rousseau, la passage
de la théorie à la littérature, c'est le passage d'une exigence qui est de
faire se recouvrir la représentation du monde et le monde même, bref
de le *nommer,* à l'exigence préalable de faire coincider la représentation
que j'en donne à la représentation que j'en ai, bref de *me nommer.*"

21. "Gravité de Rousseau," p. 64.

reverses the priority of denomination over connotation that it advocates. In texts explicitly centered on the self, such as the *Confessions* or the *Dialogues,* this incoherence would at least be brought into the open, whereas it is merely repressed in the pseudo-conceptual language of the *Second Discourse.*

Before yielding to this very persuasive scheme, we must return to the particular passage in the *Discourse* and to the corresponding section in the *Essay on the Origin of Language.*[22] Does Rousseau indeed separate figural from literal language and does he privilege one type of discourse over the other? There is no simple answer to this question, for whereas, in the *Discourse,* it is said that "the first nouns could only have been proper nouns," the *Essay* states with equal assurance that "man's first language had to be figurative" and that "figural language predates literal meaning" (p. 506). And when we try to understand denomination in Rousseau as, in Foucault's words, "going through language until we reach the point where words and things are tied together

22. On the complex debate involving the chronological and thematic relationship between the *Discourse* and the *Essay,* see J. Derrida, *De la Grammatologie,* pp. 235–278. One can consider the *Essay* as an expanded footnote to the *Discourse.* As far as this particular point is concerned (animals lacking perfectibility because they lack conceptual language), the phrasing in the *Essay* runs entirely parallel to the phrasing in the *Discourse.* The parallel is close enough to allow for an extension of the *Discourse* to include the *Essay,* at least on this particular point. "Les animaux qui parlent [les langues naturelles] les ont en naissant: ils les ont tous, et partout la même; ils n'en changent point, ils n'y font pas le moindre progrès. La langue de convention n'appartient qu'à l'homme. Voilà pourquoi l'homme fait des progrès, soit en bien soit en mal, et pourquoi les animaux n'en font pas" (*Essay,* p. 504). That "langue de convention" has the same meaning as conceptual language is part of our argument. Starobinski is certainly right to say that "there is no contradiction between [this text] and the passage from the *Essai*" (p. 1327). On the combined reading of the *Essay* with the *Discourse* see also, for a divergent view, Michèle Duchet and Michel Launay, "Synchronie et diachronie; *l'Essai sur l'origine des Langues et le Second Discours*" in *Revue internationale de Philosophie,* 82 (1967).

in their common essence," [23] then we find that, in the *Second Discourse,* denomination is associated with difference rather than with identity. A note in the 1782 edition adds to the description of denomination ("If one oak were called A, another would be called B") the following remark: "for the first idea we derive from two things is that they are not the same; it often takes a great deal of time to observe what they have in common." We would then have to assume that an observer, so keenly aware of difference that he fails to notice the resemblance between one oak tree and another would be unable to distinguish the difference between the *word* A and the *tree* A, to the point of considering them as united in some "common essence." Another difficulty: following the traditional reading of Rousseau as it is here represented by Alain Grosrichard, we would want to seize upon the act of denomination in all the transparency of its non-conceptual literalness. We find instead that "the first inventors [of words] were able to give names only to the ideas they already possessed" (*Discourse,* p. 150), a sentence in which the word "idea," despite all pre-Kantian empiricist concreteness, denotes the presence of some degree of conceptuality (or metaphor) from the start, within the very act of naming. We know, moreover, from the previous quotation, what this "idée première" must be: it is the idea of difference ("the first idea we derive from two things"). But if all entities are the same, namely entities, to the extent that they differ from each other, then the substitution of sameness for difference that characterizes, for Rousseau, all conceptual language is built into the very act of naming, the "invention" of the proper noun. It is impossible to say whether denomination is literal or figural: from the moment there is denomination, the conconceptual metaphor of entity as difference is implied, and whenever there is metaphor, the literal denomination of a

23. Michel Foucault, *Les Mots et les choses* (Paris: Gallimard, 1966). The passage is quoted in Grosrichard, p. 64.

particular entity is inevitable: "try to trace for yourself the image of a tree in general, you will never succeed. In spite of yourself, you will have to see it as small or large, bare or leafy, light or dark" or "As soon as you imagine [a triangle] in your mind, it will be one specific triangle and no other, and it would be impossible not to make its contour visible and its surface colored" (*Discourse*, p. 150). Are we forced to conclude that Rousseau's paradoxes are genuine contradictions, that he did not know, in the *Discourse*, what he stated in the *Essay*, and vice-versa? Perhaps we should heed his admonition: "in order not to find me in contradiction with myself, I should be allowed enough time to explain myself" (*Essay*, p. 521).

In the third section of the *Essay on the Origin of Language*, Rousseau offers us an "example" in the form of a narrative parable, a brief allegory. It tells us how the proper name *man*, which figures so prominently at the beginning of the *Second Discourse*,[24] came into being:

A primitive man [un homme sauvage], on meeting other men, will first have experienced fright. His fear will make him see these men as larger and stronger than himself; he will give them the name *giants*. After many experiences, he will discover that the supposed giants are neither larger nor stronger than himself, and that their stature did not correspond to the idea he had originally linked to the word giant. He will then invent another name that he has in common with them, such as, for example, the word *man*, and will retain the word giant for the false object that impressed him while he was being deluded.   (*Essay*, p. 506)

This is a general and purely linguistic version of what Grosrichard calls "se nommer," in which the origin of *inequality*, in the most literal sense of the term, is being described. The

24. "La plus utile et la moins avancée de toutes les connaissances humaines me parait être celle de l'homme" (*Discourse*, p. 122). On the question of "man" in Rousseau, see especially Martin Rang, *J. J. Rousseaus Lehre vom Menschen* (Göttingen: Vandenhoeck & Ruprecht, 1959).

passage was possibly inspired, as has been pointed out,[25] by Condillac, except for the fact that Rousseau refers to full-grown men and not to children. The difference is important, for the entire passage plays a complex game with qualitative and quantitative notions of similarity, equality and difference.

In this encounter with other men, the first reaction of the primitive is said to be fear. The reaction is not obvious; it is certainly not based on objective data, for Rousseau makes it clear that the men are supposed to be of equal size and strength. Neither is it the fear of a single individual confronted with a multitude, since primitive men are entirely devoid of the sense of numbers or of groups. The similarity in size and in the observable attributes of strength should, at first sight, act reassuringly and make the reaction less anxious than if the man had encountered a bear, or a lion. Yet Rousseau stresses fright, and Derrida is certainly right in stating that the act of denomination that follows—calling the other man a giant, a process that Rousseau describes as a figural use of language—displaces the referential meaning from an outward, visible property to an "inward" feeling.[26] The coinage of the word "giant" simply means "I am afraid." But what is the reason for fear, if it is not due to observable data? It can only result from a fundamental feeling of distrust, the suspicion that, although the creature does not look like a lion or a bear, it nevertheless might act like one, outward appearances to the contrary. The reassuringly familiar and similar outside might be a trap. Fear is the result of a possible discrepancy between the outer and the inner properties of entities. It can be shown that, for Rousseau, all passions—whether they be love, pity, anger or even a borderline case between passion and need such as fear—are characterized by

25. Among others by Starobinski, *Oeuvres*, III, 1323, note 3.
26. Jacques Derrida, *De la Grammatologie*, p. 393.

such a discrepancy; they are based not on the knowledge that such a difference exists, but on the hypothesis that it might exist, a possibility that can never be proven or disproven by empirical or by analytical means.[27] A statement of distrust is neither true nor false: it is rather in the nature of a permanent hypothesis.

The fact Rousseau chose fear as an example to demonstrate the priority of metaphor over denomination complicates and enriches the pattern to a considerable degree, for metaphor is precisely the figure that depends on a certain degree of correspondence between "inside" and "outside" properties. The word "giant," invented by the frightened primitive to designate his fellow-man, is indeed a metaphor in that it is based on a correspondence between inner feelings of fear and outward properties of size. It may be objectively false (the other man is not in fact any taller) but it is subjectively candid (he seems taller to the frightened subject). The statement may be in error, but it is not a lie. It "expresses" the inner experience correctly. The metaphor is blind, not because it distorts objective data, but because it presents as certain what is, in fact, a mere possibility. The fear of falling is "true," for the potentially destructive power of gravity is a verifiable fact, but the fear of another man is hypothetical; no one can trust a precipice, but it remains an open question, for whoever is neither a paranoiac nor a fool, whether one can trust one's fellow man. By calling him a "giant," one freezes hypothesis, or fiction, into fact and makes fear, itself a figural state of sus-

27. The assertion has to be proven by a general interpretation of "passions" in the work of Rousseau. To indicate the direction of the argument, the following quotation from *Julie* is characteristic; recapitulating the history of her passion for Saint-Preux, Julie is said to write: "Je crus voir sur votre visage les traits de l'âme qu'il fallait à la mienne. Il me sembla que mes sens ne servaient que d'organe à des sentiments plus nobles; et j'aimai dans vous, moins ce que j'y voyais que ce que je croyais sentir en moi-même . . ." (*Oeuvres*, II, 340).

pended meaning, into a definite proper meaning devoid of
alternatives. The metaphor "giant," used to connote man,
has indeed a proper meaning (fear), but this meaning is not
really proper: it refers to a condition of permanent suspense
between a literal world in which appearance and nature coincide and a figural world in which this correspondence is no
longer *a priori* posited. Metaphor is error because it believes
or feigns to believe in its own referential meaning. This
belief is legitimate only within the limits of a given text: the
metaphor that connotes Achilles' courage by calling him a
lion is correct within the textual tradition of the *Iliad* because it refers to a character in a fiction whose function it is
to live up to the referential implication of the metaphor.
As soon as one leaves the text it becomes aberrant—if, for
example, one calls one's son Achilles in the hope that this
will make him into a hero. Rousseau's example of a man
encountering another man is textually ambiguous, as all sit-
uations involving categorical relationships between man and
language have to be. What happens in such an encounter is
complex: the empirical situation, which is open and hypothetical, is given a consistency that can only exist in a text.
This is done by means of a metaphor (calling the other man a
giant), a substitutive figure of speech ("*he* is a giant" substituting for "*I* am afraid") that changes a referential situation suspended between fiction and fact (the hypothesis of
fear) into a literal fact. Paradoxically, the figure literalizes
its referent and deprives it of its parafigural status. The figure
dis-figures, i.e. it makes fear, itself a para-figural fiction, into a
reality that is as inescapable as the reality of the original encounter between the two men. Metaphor overlooks the fictional, textual element in the nature of the entity it connotes. It assumes a world in which intra and extra-textual
events, literal and figural forms of language, can be distinguished, a world in which the literal and the figural are prop-

erties that can be isolated and, consequently, exchanged and substituted for each other. This is an error, although it can be said that no language would be possible without this error.

The intricacy of the situation is obviously tied to the choice of the example. The interplay of difference and similarity implied in the encounter between two men is more complex than if the encounter had been between two potentially antithetical entities such as man and woman, as is the case in *Julie* or parts of *Emile,* or man and things as is the case in the example of the *Second Discourse* in which a man is naming a tree instead of naming another man. It seems perverse on Rousseau's part to choose an example based on a more complex situation that that of the paradigm with which he is dealing. Should we infer, with the traditional interpreters of Rousseau, that the intersubjective, reflective situation of self-encounter, as in the specular self-fascination of Narcissus, is indeed for Rousseau the paradigmatic experience from which all other experiences are derived? We must remind ourselves that the element of reflective similarity mirrored in the example of man's encounter with man is not the representation of a paradigmatic empirical situation (as is the case in Descartes' *cogito* or in any phenomenological reduction) but the metaphorical illustration of a linguistic fact. The example does not have to do with the genetic process of the "birth" of language (told later in the text) but with the linguistic process of conceptualization. The narrative mode of the passage is itself a metaphor that should not mislead us into transposing a synchronic, linguistic structure into a diachronic, historical event. And conceptualization, as the passage of the *Second Discourse* on the naming of trees makes clear, is an intra-linguistic process, the invention of a figural meta-language that shapes and articulates the infinitely fragmented and amorphous language of pure denomination. To the extent that all language is conceptual, it always already speaks about language and not about things. The sheer metonymic enumeration of things that Rousseau describes in the *Discourse* ("if one oak was called A, another was called B") is an entirely negative moment that does not describe language as it is or used to be at its inception, but that dialectically infers literal denomination as the negation of language. Denomination could never exist by itself although it is a constitutive part of all linguistic events. All language is language about denomination, i.e. a conceptual, figural, metaphorical metalanguage. As such, it partakes of the blindness of metaphor when metaphor literalizes its referential indetermination into a specific unit of meaning. This statement about the metalinguistic (or conceptual) nature of language is the equivalent of the earlier statement, directly derived from Rousseau, according to which denomination has to postulate the concept (or idea) of difference in order to come into being.

If all language is about language, then the paradigmatic linguistic model is that of an entity that confronts itself.[28] It follows that the exemplary situation described in the *Essay* (man confronting man) is the correct linguistic paradigm, whereas the situation of the *Second Discourse* (man confronting a tree) is a dialectical derivation from this paradigm that moves away from the linguistic model toward problems of perception, consciousness, reflection and the like. In a text that associates the specificity of man with language and, within language, with the power of conceptualization, the

28. The implication is that the self-reflective moment of the *cogito,* the self-reflection of what Rilke calls "le Narcisse exhaucé," is not an original event but itself an allegorical (or metaphorical) version of an intralinguistic structure, with all the negative epistemological consequences this entails. Similarly, Rousseau's use of "fear" as the paradigmatic passion (or need) that leads to figural language is not to be accounted for in psychological but in linguistic terms. "Fear" is exemplary because it corresponds structurally to the rhetorical model of the metaphor.

priority belongs to the example from the *Essay*. The statement of the *Discourse* that "the first nouns could only have been proper nouns" is therefore a statement derived from the logically prior statement "that the first language had to be figural." There is no contradiction if one understands that Rousseau conceives of denomination as a hidden, blinded figure.

This is not yet the end of the parable. Actual language does not use the imaginary word "giant" [29] but has invented the conceptual term "man" in its stead. Conceptualization is a double process: it is this complexity that allows for the successive narrative pattern of the allegory. It consists first of all of a wild, spontaneous metaphor which is, to some degree, aberrant. This first level of aberration is however not intentional, because it does not involve the interests of the subject in any way. Rousseau's man stands nothing to gain from inventing the word "giant." The distortion introduced by the term results exclusively from a formal, rhetorical potential of the language. The same is not true at the second stage. The word "man" is created, says Rousseau, "after many experiences [when primitive man] will have discovered that the supposed giants are neither larger nor stronger than himself" (*Essay*, p. 506). The word "man" is the result of a quantitative process of comparison based on measurement, and making deliberate use of the category of number in order to reach a reassuring conclusion: if the other man's height is numerically equal to my own, then he is no longer dangerous. The conclusion is wishful and, of course, potentially in error—as

29. The actual word "giant," as we know it from everyday usage, presupposes the word "man" and is not the metaphorical figure that Rousseau, for lack of an existing word, has to call "giant." Rousseau's "giant" would be more like some mythological monster; one could think of Goliath, or of Polyphemos (leaving aside the temptation to develop the implications of Odysseus's strategy in giving his name to Polyphemos as no-man [οὖτις]).

Goliath and Polyphemos, among others, were soon enough
to discover. The second level of aberration stems from the use
of number as if it were a literal property of things that truly
belongs to them, when it is, in fact, just one more conceptual
metaphor devoid of objective validity and subject to the
distortions that constitute all metaphors. For Rousseau, as for
Nietzsche, number is par excellence the concept that hides
ontic difference under an illusion of identity. The idea of
number is just as derivative and suspect as the idea of man:

A primitive could consider his right and his left leg separately,
or consider them together as one indivisible pair, without ever
thinking of them as *two* [legs]. For the representational idea of
an object is one thing, but the numerical idea that determines
it is another. Still less was he able to count up to five. Although
he could have noticed, in pressing his hands together, that the
fingers exactly corresponded, he did not in the least conceive of
their numerical equality.   [*Second Discourse,* note 14, p. 219]

The concept of man is thus doubly metaphorical: it first
consists of the blind moment of passionate error that leads
to the word "giant," then of the moment of deliberate error
that uses number in order to tame the original wild metaphor into harmlessness (it being well understood that this
numerical terminology of "first," "doubly," "original," etc.,
is itself metaphorical and is used only for the clarity of
exposition). Man invents the concept man by means of
another concept that is itself illusionary. The "second"
metaphor, which Rousseau equates with the literary, deliberate and rhetorical use of the spontaneous figure [30] is
no longer innocent: the invention of the word man makes
it possible for "men" to exist by establishing the equality

30. "L'image illusoire offerte par la passion se montrant la première,
le langage qui lui répondait fut aussi le premier inventé; il devint en-
suite métaphorique, quand l'esprit éclairé, reconnaissant sa première
erreur, n'en employa les expressions que dans les mêmes passions qui
l'avaient produite" (*Essay,* p. 506).

within inequality, the sameness within difference of civil society, in which the suspended, potential truth of the original fear is domesticated by the illusion of identity. The concept interprets the metaphor of numerical sameness as if it were a statement of literal fact. Without this literalization, there could be no society. The reader of Rousseau must remember that this literalism is the deceitful misrepresentation of an original blindness. Conceptual language, the foundation of civil society, is also, it appears, a lie superimposed upon an error. We can therefore hardly expect the epistemology of the sciences of man to be straightforward.

The transition from the structure of conceptual language to society is implicit in the example from the *Essay* describing the genealogy of the word "man." It becomes explicit when, at the beginning of the second part of the *Discourse,* the origin of society is described in exactly parallel terms, this time no longer as a marginal example but as the central statement of the *Second Discourse,* forging the axis of the text in the coherent movement that extends from freedom to perfectibility, from perfectibility to language, from language to man and from man to political society. Neither the discovery of fire and technology, nor the contiguity of man's proximity to man on earth, accounts for the origin of society. Society originates with the quantitative comparison of conceptual relationships:

The repeated contacts between man and various entities, and between the entities themselves, must necessarily engender in the mind of man the perception of relationships. These relationships, which we express by words such as large, small, strong, weak, fast, slow, fearful, bold and other similar ideas, when compared to man's needs, produced, almost without his being aware of it, some kind of reflection, or rather some form of mechanical prudence that taught him to take the precautions most needed for his safety. . . . The resemblances that time allowed him to observe [between his fellow men], the human female and himself, made him infer [juger de] those which he could not perceive. Noticing that all of them behaved in the same way that he would himself have behaved in similar circumstances, he concluded that their way of thinking and feeling was entirely in conformity with his own.   [*Discourse,* p. 166] [31]

The passage describes precisely the same interplay between passion (fear), measurement and metaphor (inferring invisible properties by analogy with visible ones) as the parable from the *Essay on the Origins of Language.* In the lines that follow, the principle of conformity on which the concept of man and the possibility of government is founded is called "cette importante Vérité" (p. 166). We should now realize that what Rousseau calls "truth" designates, neither the adequation of language to reality, nor the essence of things shining through the opacity of words, but rather the suspicion that human specificity may be rooted in linguistic deceit.

The consequences of this negative insight for Rousseau's political theory are far-reaching. What the *Discourse on Inequality* tells us, and what the classical interpretation of Rousseau has stubbornly refused to hear, is that the political destiny of man is structured like and derived from a linguistic model that exists independently of nature and independently of the subject: it coincides with the blind metaphorization called "passion," and this metaphorization is not an intentional act. Contrary to what one might think, this enforces the inevitably "political" nature or, more correctly, the "politicality" (since one could hardly speak of "nature" in this case) of all forms of human language, and especially of rhetorically self-conscious or literary language—though certainly

31. The translation considerably simplifies the opening lines, quite obscure in the French text: [L]'application réitérrée des êtres divers à lui-même, et les uns aux autres, dut naturellement engendrer." The immediately preceding paragraph in the text makes clear that Rousseau refers to the interplay between several physical entities in technological inventions (such as the invention of the bow and arrow) or between man and nature, as in the discovery and conservation of fire.

not in the representational, psychological or ethical sense in which the relationship between literature and politics is generally understood. If society and government derive from a tension between man and his language, then they are not natural (depending on a relationship between man and things), nor ethical (depending on a relationship among men), nor theological, since language is not conceived as a transcendental principle but as the possibility of contingent error. The political thus becomes a burden for man rather than an opportunity and this realization, which can be started in an infinity of sardonic and pathetic modes, may well account for the recurrent reluctance to accept, or even to notice, the link between language and society in the works of Rousseau. Far from being a repression of the political, as Althusser would have it, literature is condemned to being the truly political mode of discourse. The relationship of this discourse to political praxis cannot be described in psychological or in psycholinguistic terms, but rather in terms of the relationship, within the rhetorical model, between the referential and the figural semantic fields.

To develop the implications of this conclusion would lead to a detailed reading of the second part of the *Discourse on Inequality* in conjunction with the *Social Contract, Julie* and Rousseau's other political writings. I have tried to emphasize the importance and the complexity of the transition that leads up to such a reading. Only if we are aware of the considerable ambivalence that burdens a theoretical discourse dealing with man's relation to man—"un homme [qui parle] à des hommes . . . de l'homme," as the *Second Discourse* puts it (p. 131)—can we begin to see how Rousseau's theory of literature and his theory of government could get translated into practical terms. The introductory analysis allows for the schematic formulation of some directives.

First of all, the passage from a language of fiction to a

language oriented toward political *praxis* implies a transition
from qualitative concepts such as needs, passions, man, power,
etc. to quantitative concepts involving numbers such as rich,
poor, etc.[32] The inequality referred to in the title of the
Discourse, and which must first be understood as difference
in the most general way possible, becomes in the second part
the inequality in the quantitative distribution of property.
The basis of political thought, in Rousseau, is economic rather
than ethical, as is clear from the lapidary statement that
opens the second part of the *Discourse:* "The first man who,
after having fenced in a plot of land went on to say '*this
belongs to me*' and found other men naive enough to believe
him [assez simples pour le croire], was the true founder of
civil society" (*Discourse,* p. 164). The passage from literal
greed to the institutional, conceptual law protecting the right
to property runs parallel to the transition from the spontaneous to the conceptual metaphor.[33] But the economic foundation of political theory in Rousseau is not rooted in a theory
of needs, appetites and interests that could lead to ethical
principles of right and wrong; it is the correlative of linguistic conceptualization and is therefore neither materialistic,
nor idealistic, nor merely dialectical, since language is deprived of representational as well as of transcendental authority.[34] The complex relationship between Rousseau's and

32. "Que les mots de *fort* et de *faible* sont équivoques (dans le cas
où l'on explique l'origine de la société par l'union des faibles entre eux);
que . . . le sens de ces termes est mieux rendu par ceux de *pauvre* et de
riche, parce qu'en effet un homme n'avait point, avant les lois, d'autre
moyen d'assujettir ses égaux qu'en attaquant leur bien, ou leur faisant
quelque part du sien" (*Discourse,* p. 179).

33. Thus confirming the semantic validity of the word-play, in
French, "sens *propre*" and "*propriété.*"

34. This, of course, does not mean that questions of virtue, of self
and of God are not being considered by Rousseau; they obviously are.
What is at stake is not the existence of an ethical, psychological or
theological discourse but their authority in terms of truth or falsehood.

Marx's economic determinism could and should only be approached from this point of view.[35]

Second, one sees why civil order and government are, in Rousseau, such fragile and threatened constructions, since they are built on the very sands of error.[36] "The vices that make social institutions necessary also make the abuse of these institutions inevitable" (*Discourse,* p. 187). This circular, self-destructive pattern of all civil institutions mirrors the self-destructive epistemology of conceptual language when it demonstrates its inability to keep literal reference and figural connotation apart. The literalism that makes language possible also makes the abuse of language inevitable. Hence the fundamental ambivalence in the valorization of literal reference throughout the *Second Discourse.* The "pure" fiction of the State of Nature precedes, in principle, all valorization, yet nothing can be more destructive than the inevitable transposition of this fictional model to the present, empirical world in which "the subjects have to be kept apart" (*Essay,* p. 542) and by which one reaches "the last stage of inequality and the extreme point that closes the circle and touches again upon our point of departure (namely the state of nature): this is where all individuals again become equal because they are nothing" (*Discourse,* p. 191).

35. Hints in this direction are present in the work of Lucien Sebag, *Marxisme et structuralisme* (Paris: Payot, 1964), whereas Althusser remains short of Engels's treatment of Rousseau in the *Anti-Dühring* (especially chapter 13 of Part I, "Dialectics. Negation of the negation"). I am not informed on the state of Rousseau studies outside Western Europe and the United States.

36. ". . . rien n'est permanent que la misère qui résulte de toutes ces vicissitudes; quand [l]es sentiments et [l]es idées [de l'homme] pourraient s'élever jusqu'à l'amour de l'ordre et aux notions sublimes de la vertu, il lui serait impossible de faire jamais une application sure de ses principes dans un état de choses qui ne lui laisserait discerner ni le bien ni le mal, ni l'honnête homme ni le méchant" (*Du Contrat social,* 1ère version, *Oeuvres,* III, 282).

Finally, the *contractual* pattern of civil government can only be understood against the background of this permanent threat. The social contract is by no means the expression of a transcendental Law: it is a complex and purely defensive verbal strategy by means of which the literal world is given some of the consistency of fiction, an intricate set of feints and ruses [37] by means of which the moment is temporarily delayed when fictional seductions will no longer be able to resist transformation into literal acts. The conceptual language of the social contract resembles the subtle interplay between figural and referential discourse in a novel. It has often been said that Rousseau's novel *Julie* is also his best treatise of political science; it should be added that *The Social Contract* is also his best novel. But both depend on their common methodological preamble in the theory of rhetoric that is the foundation of the *Discourse on the Origin and the Foundation of Inequality among Men*.

37. The furthest-reaching of these ruses being perhaps that of the legislator having to pretend that he speaks with the voice of God in order to be heard. "Voilà ce qui força de tout temps les pères des nations de recourir à l'intervention du ciel et d'honorer les dieux de leur propre sagesse, afin que les peuples soumis aux lois de l'Etat comme à celles de la nature, et reconnaissant le même pouvoir dans la formation de l'homme et dans celle de la cité, obéissent avec liberté et portassent docilement le joug de la félicité publique." The example of the true legislator is Moses and the passage concludes with a footnote reference to Machiavelli.

FREDERICK A. POTTLE

Wordsworth in
the Present Day

My own title for this paper originally was "The Secondary
Causes of the Respect Paid to Wordsworth in the Present
Day," but I was persuaded by some of my friends to adopt
one that was shorter and which seemed a little less allusive
and cute. I yielded when I remembered that Gibbon did not
put the irony of his notorious Chapter XV into its title: he
gave that chapter the bland heading "The Progress of the
Christian Religion," and revealed his subversive strategy
only in his third paragraph. I should like, however, to men-
tion my suppressed title, not just to be cute, but in order to
indicate the humble nature of my approach. Gibbon wrote
with solemn sneer, but if he had been a Christian instead of
a rather malicious ironist, it is hard to see how he could have
written at much greater length of his primary cause than he
actually did: "it was owing to the convincing evidence of the
doctrine itself, and to the ruling providence of its great Author." The workings of Divine Providence are not subject to
historical dissection. So, too, if I should try to develop the
dogmatic assumption that respect has been paid to Wordsworth in the last fifty years because he is at all times absolutely and irresistibly a great poet, I should very quickly run
out of words. All the evidence accessible to me seems his-

torical, seems like Gibbon's secondary causes. I can discern
several reasons why Wordsworth is not wholly uncongenial
to post-*Wasteland* sensibility, and I propose to write about
those. I must warn the reader that what I have to say will to a
considerable extent be an exercise in historical construction,
for I was born in the nineteenth century, and my own sensibility was already beginning to harden when *The Wasteland*
came along. Furthermore, my notions of what obtains at the
present day may be quaint. It may very well be that my assess-
ment would have been more appropriate for the Centenary
of Wordsworth's death in 1950 than for the Bicentenary of
his birth in 1970.

Significant modern criticism of Wordsworth has not been
ecstatic, but it has generally been respectful. We have had
acute and satisfying critical essays on Wordsworth from
Ransom, from Leavis, and from Brooks. Empson is irrever-
ent but even Empson shows admiration. One would hardly
have expected this, by which I mean that it is much easier for
one born in the nineteenth century to think of reasons why
modern critics should be hostile or cold to Wordsworth than
of reasons why they should respect him and perhaps enjoy
him. Let me specify.

The modern approval of Wordsworth cannot be due to
fondness for him as a person. Perhaps it is unfair even to
suggest that the moderns can be guilty of biographical involvement, for it was they who first established the doctrine
that biography and criticism are immiscible modes, and that
when you are engaged in biography, you cannot be criticizing
a poem. Undoubtedly the moderns have been clearer-headed
and more scrupulous on this score than any previous literary
generation, yet it would be strange if they had escaped all
contamination. Modern criticism of Keats and Shelley, I
fear, suffers from irrelevant personal affection for Keats and
irrelevant personal dislike of Shelley. Keats is indeed al-

most irresistibly attractive, but Wordsworth! Shelley called
him "a solemn and unsexual man." [1] We know a great deal
more about the facts of Wordsworth's life than Shelley did,
but for all his youthful revolutionary ardor and his French
daughter, Wordsworth remains an arrogant and rather un-
lovable personality. Perhaps, though it sounds like a paradox, that contributes to the moderns' esteem. A modern
critic is perhaps grateful when he comes on a poet whose
person he feels called upon neither to like nor to dislike,
a poet who does not distract him from his proper job. Milton
is perhaps a similar case.

But to turn to the poetry. Surely it is very hard to see how
Wordsworth's poetry meets New Critical specifications in
any obvious sense or in any large degree. Donne is still the
type poet of the New Criticism, and Wordsworth's poetry
was consciously opposed to the Metaphysical mode. Wit he
avoided on principle as being petty and cold-hearted.[2] Such
humor as he shows in his verse is of a waggish and earthy sort
that he called "drollery." One very seldom finds in his poetry
the large controlling figure beloved of the Metaphysicals; indeed, as Ransom was perhaps the first to point out, Wordsworth managed to write an astonishing number of respected
poems without employing any figurative language at all.
Though he is not wholly without irony and paradox, as
Brooks has demonstrated, his poetry at large (I quote Ransom again, this time directly) offers lean hunting in that
species of game.[3] He scorns all the density, the obliquity and
indirection treasured by the moderns: he not only tells you
straight out how you are to take his poems, he keeps on

1. *Peter Bell the Third,* VI. xix. 4.
2. "Upon Epitaphs (1)," in *Wordsworth's Literary Criticism,* ed.
Nowell C. Smith (London: Oxford Univ. Press, 1905 and later), p. 93.
3. "William Wordsworth: Notes toward an Understanding of Poetry,"
in *Wordsworth,* ed. Gilbert T. Dunklin (Princeton: Princeton Univ.
Press, 1951), pp. 99, 101.

telling you. Witness the relentless literal unfigurative iteration of the solitariness of the old Cumberland beggar, his
extreme old age and decrepitude: aged, aged, solitude, palsied, solitary, helpless, old, aged, aged, aged, old, solitary—all
in forty-four lines. Obscurity he certainly does offer, but
never of the compacted Metaphysical sort. When a poem of
Wordsworth's is obscure (*Simon Lee* is a good example), it is
not because you have any difficulty with the syntax or the
allusions. The sense is plain enough but not the point: you
feel as though the poem were so open that you have fallen
straight through it without touching it anywhere. Nearly all
of Wordsworth's poetry is vulnerable to ironic contemplation; he is probably the most parodied of English poets, evoking malicious attention from parodists as diverse as Bishop
Mant and Lewis Carroll. When D. B. Wyndham Lewis
wanted a title for an anthology of bad verse, he looked for
and found it in Wordsworth: *The Stuffed Owl.*[4] Wordsworth's verse is mild, grave, serene, noble—uncaptivating
qualities nowadays. And finally he obtrudes a great deal of
explicit doctrine of a kind not now in favor. He proclaimed
himself a Teacher; he preaches, indeed he preaches.

What then are the virtues that overbalance so formidable
an array of disqualifications? How *can* Wordsworth win respect from modern sensibility? My first reason, I am sure,
will come as a surprise. It is, I suggest, because he is so competent and scrupulous a craftsman. Modern criticism differs
from Romantic criticism in its determination to avoid general affective terms like "beauty" and to look for the cause of
poetic effect in specific verbal strategies. To a reader who
has trained himself to watch how a poet is doing his stuff, all,
literally all, of Wordsworth's poetry is rewarding. He published dull poems, flat poems, wrong-headed poems, but he
almost never published genuinely careless, genuinely uncrafts-

4. Sonnet: "While Anna's peers and early playmates tread," line 10.

manlike poems. I found this out through the extensive annual review I had to make while teaching the graduate course in the Age of Wordsworth at Yale. I came back to what I might call the silent majority of the poems of the other voluminous poets in that course with a sense of effort and duty, but I always moved into Wordsworth with pleased anticipation. I read on and on in his lesser-known verse, never finding anything I preferred to poems already in the anthologies, but with a constant sense of pleasure and a wish to continue. Next to Milton, Wordsworth is surely our most thoughtfully finished poet. He had a demon that drove him to rewrite. Too often he made changes, not because the poem was not finished as it stood, but because his ideas had changed, and that is a pity; but knowledgeable readers can always pick the best versions, and the others are the best commentary in the world.

Secondly, I think the moderns approve of and are attracted by Wordsworth's determination to look steadily at his subject.[5] This meant, among other things, that in serious poetry ("Poetry of the Imagination") he was determined to restrict himself to actually existing, concrete, everyday objects, the objects of "the very world, which is the world of all of us" (*Prelude* XI, 142–3). Serious poetry before Wordsworth made use of all kinds of consecrated superstition and traditional make-believe. The great Milton in *Paradise Lost* thought bees and elves equally eligible as matter for extended similes; Pope in his *Essay on Man* drew illustrations indiscriminately from observed nature and the medieval bestiaries.[6] Since Wordsworth it has not been so easy. Witness Coleridge, writing in 1796 before he had been much exposed to Wordsworth:

5. Preface of 1800, par. 9.
6. *Paradise Lost*, I, 768–75, 780–88; Frederick A. Pottle, "The Eye and the Object in the Poetry of Wordsworth," in Dunklin, pp. 34–36.

> Such a soft floating witchery of sound
> As twilight Elfins make, when they at eve
> Voyage on gentle gales from Fairy-Land,
> Where Melodies round honey-dropping flowers,
> Footless and wild, like birds of Paradise,
> Nor pause, nor perch, hovering on untam'd wing!
>
> (*Eolian Harp,* 20–25)

He tried too late to cut the footless birds of Paradise out of the poem in 1797 and eliminated the whole passage in 1803, pretty certainly, I should say, because of Wordsworth's example and doctrine.[7] He restored it in 1817, and it probably was too good to lose, but to modern sensibility do not the images look a little wilted? To a modern reader, how much more satisfying and effective are those of *Dejection,* written in 1802:

> This night, so tranquil now, will not go hence
> Unroused by winds, that ply a busier trade
> Than those which mould yon cloud in lazy flakes,
> Or the dull sobbing draft, that moans and rakes
> Upon the strings of this Æolian lute,
>   Which better far were mute.
> For lo! the New-moon winter-bright!
> And overspread with phantom light,
> (With swimming phantom light o'erspread
> But rimmed and circled with silver thread)
> I see the old Moon in her lap, foretelling
> The coming-on of rain and squally blast.

But I deviate into the diachronic mode. What I should be saying is that though one might find elves and footless birds of Paradise in Wordsworth's playful verse (he has a large section of poems called "Poems of the Fancy"), one does not have to cope with them in his serious verse:

> Long have I loved what I behold,
> The night that calms, the day that cheers;

7. *Collected Letters of S. T. Coleridge,* ed. Earl Leslie Griggs, I (Oxford: Clarendon Press, 1956), 330–31.

The common growth of mother-earth
Suffices me—her tears, her mirth,
Her humblest mirth and tears.

The dragon's wing, the magic ring,
I shall not covet for my dower,
If I along that lowly way
With sympathetic heart may stray,
And with a soul of power.

These given, what more need I desire
To stir, to soothe, or elevate?
What nobler marvels than the mind
May in life's daily prospect find,
May find or there create?

(*Peter Bell,* Prologue, 131–45)

Public approval by Robert Frost of anything in Wordsworth would always have been patronizing in tone. He would not have written that last stanza, and he would have worked some quizzical or ironical gestures into the other two. But I have no doubt that he would have pronounced all three stanzas good sense and good poetry.

Modern sensibility is notoriously wary of sentiment and recoils in strong distaste from sentiment that it considers excessive. Hoxie Fairchild, our great Inquisitor of Romantic heresy, is fain to admit that though Wordsworth is chockfull of sentiment, he almost never succumbs to sentimentalism in the pejorative sense of the term.[8] You may say, if you wish, that Wordsworth's sensibility was tough, mature, and well balanced, but it would be more useful to identify some of the techniques which he employs to keep himself within bounds. I consider Shelley's *Ode to the West Wind* a very great poem and can take in stride the now much-questioned line "I fall upon the thorns of life! I bleed!" but I grant that

8. *Religious Trends in English Poetry,* III (New York: Columbia Univ. Press, 1949), 187.

the strategy of that line is risky. (One of my undergraduate students of years ago—I wish I knew where he is now, for I did not appreciate him enough—once wrote in an examination, "Shelley is utterly without fear. He puts his hands right in the fire.") Shelley's poem at this point would undoubtedly have seemed more formidable to modern taste if he had followed more closely the method of the Hebrew poems that were in general the models for this ode. The Psalmist had never heard of the canon 'gainst self-pity: his songs often consist of prolonged and strident wail. But the imagery of his wail tends always to the harsh, the grotesque, the surrealistic:

I am poured out like water and all my bones are out of joint; my heart also in the midst of my body is even like melting wax. My strength is dried up like a potsherd, and my tongue cleaveth to my gums, and thou bringest me into the dust of death. For many dogs are come about me, and the council of the wicked layeth siege against me. They pierced my hands and my feet; I may tell all my bones; they stand staring and looking upon me. They part my garments among them and cast lots upon my vesture.   (Psalm 22: 14–18, Prayer Book version)

Wordsworth, too, curbs sentimentalism with grotesqueness, and the grotesque is never far to seek in the Wordsworthian sublime. Vision in Wordsworth is evoked by a dreary landscape and a solitary grotesque human figure:

> I fled,
> Faltering and faint, and ignorant of the road:
> Then, reascending the bare common, saw
> A naked pool that lay beneath the hills,
> The beacon on the summit, and, more near,
> A girl, who bore a pitcher on her head,
> And seemed with difficult steps to force her way
> Against the blowing wind. It was, in truth,
> An ordinary sight; but I should need
> Colours and words that are unknown to man,
> To paint the visionary dreariness

> Which, while I looked all round for my lost guide,
> Invested moorland waste, and naked pool,
> The beacon crowning the lone eminence,
> The woman and her garments vexed and tossed
> By the strong wind.
> > *(Prelude* XII, 246–61, "woman" in
> > line 260 from 1805 version)

Or that supremely grotesque old Man he suddenly came on upon the moors, again beside a naked pool, the oldest man that ever wore gray hairs, propping his bent body on a long shaved wooden staff:

> While he was talking thus, the lonely place,
> The old Man's shape, and speech—all troubled me;
> In my mind's eye I seemed to see him pace
> About the weary moors continually,
> Wandering about alone and silently.
> > *(Resolution and Independence,* 127–31)

Arnold, you will remember, picked as the best single line to represent Wordsworth that utterly literal, unheightened, straightforward line from *Michael:*

> And never lifted up a single stone.[9]

Any critic who asserts the attractive power of Wordsworth for modern readers must explain how that attraction can be reconciled with the strong modern distaste for direct statement in serious verse. I shall turn to R. P. Warren for an explanation, and shall cite as my fourth cause Wordsworth's remarkable power of *earning* direct statement. Warren, you remember, says that the impact of that line which Arnold seems to regard as the most infallible of all his touchstones, Dante's

> E la sua volontate è nostra pace,[10]

9. "Wordsworth," in *Essays in Criticism, Second Series.*
10. *Paradiso,* iii. 85.

does not come solely from that line but from that line in context. By packing a long stretch of earlier lines with vivid concretions, Dante *earns* his theology in verse.[11] I hope Warren does not mean that "E la sua volontate è nostra pace" is not in itself poetry. I read it detached in Arnold long before I read it in context in Dante and almost choked over it. In the same way I read "And never lifted up a single stone" in Arnold before I had read *Michael* or knew what *Michael* was about, and added it instantly to my store of personal treasures. It's hard for me now to say why, but I think it was because both lines, in the triumphant economy of their diction and meter, proclaimed themselves punch lines: I knew I could never in the world have imagined *them,* but I thought it would be easy to imagine contexts for them. Yet surely Warren is right in suggesting that a poem *all* in the style of "E la sua volontate è nostra pace" would in most cases be flat, and even when not flat, would be daringly austere. Here is Wordsworth asserting his right to be austere:

> I thought of Thee, my partner and my guide,
> As being past away.—Vain sympathies!
> For, backward, Duddon! as I cast my eyes,
> I see what was, and is, and will abide;
> Still glides the Stream, and shall for ever glide;
> The Form remains, the Function never dies;
> While we, the brave, the mighty, and the wise,
> We Men, who in our morn of youth defied
> The elements, must vanish;—be it so!
> Enough, if something from our hands have power
> To live, and act, and serve the future hour;
> And if, as toward the silent tomb we go,
> Through love, through hope, and faith's transcendent dower,
> We feel that we are greater than we know.
>   (*River Duddon* XXXIV, "After-Thought")

11. "Pure and Impure Poetry." Accessible in Robert W. Stallman, ed., *Critiques and Essays in Criticism, 1920–1948* (New York: Ronald Press, 1949), pp. 102–4.

One will never get Wordsworth right if one thinks of him as poetically timid. On the contrary, he was almost perversely daring: he saw poetic virtue in narrow misses; he loved to walk the tightrope over gulfs of declamation and bathos. It is most modern poets who are timid and shy away from risks. But one, perhaps the greatest of them all, was sometimes almost as fearless as Wordsworth. By two lines near the end of *An Irish Airman Foresees his Death* Yeats earns the perfectly simple prose directness of the other fourteen:

> I know that I shall meet my fate
> Somewhere among the clouds above;
> Those that I fight I do not hate,
> Those that I guard I do not love;
> My country is Kiltartan Cross,
> My countrymen Kiltartan's poor,
> No likely end could bring them loss
> Or leave them happier than before.
> Nor law nor duty bade me fight,
> Nor public men, nor cheering crowds,
> A lonely impulse of delight
> Drove to this tumult in the clouds;
> I balanced all, brought all to mind,
> The years to come seemed waste of breath,
> A waste of breath the years behind
> In balance with this life, this death.

But though *An Irish Airman* is in technique a very Wordsworthian poem, I ought to be illustrating from Wordsworth himself. Here is the way he earns that relentless iteration of denotative words I cited from *The Old Cumberland Beggar*, aged, aged, solitude, palsied, solitary, and the rest:

> I saw an aged Beggar in my walk;
> And he was seated, by the highway side,
> On a low structure of rude masonry
> Built at the foot of a huge hill, that they
> Who lead their horses down the steep rough road
> May thence remount at ease. The aged Man
> Had placed his staff across the broad smooth stone

That overlays the pile; and from a bag
All white with flour, the dole of village dames,
He drew his scraps and fragments, one by one;
And scanned them with a fixed and serious look
Of idle computation. In the sun
Upon the second step of that small pile,
Surrounded by those wild unpeopled hills,
He sat, and ate his food in solitude:
And ever, scattered from his palsied hand,
That, still attempting to prevent the waste,
Was baffled still, the crumbs in little showers
Fell on the ground; and the small mountain birds,
Not venturing yet to peck their destined meal,
Approached within the length of half his staff.
                    (*Old Cumberland Beggar,* 1–21)

I suspect that readers do not notice the denotative words, even when warned to be on the lookout for them. If a reader does notice them, he may perhaps consider the words superfluous. They tell him to get set for a response, but the response seems to come entirely from the poetic concretions: the serious mindless gaze of the old man, the showers of crumbs, the approaching birds. I feel sure that they are not superfluous, and that we need some kind of terminology that signals at once their non-poetic character and their poetic usefulness. I propose to call them catalysts: Ransom might call them looseners or clampers. A catalyst is a substance that accelerates a chemical reaction while remaining recoverable itself at the end of the reaction. For example, sulphur trioxide gas, an important chemical because from it one can make sulphuric acid merely by passing it into water, cannot be profitably manufactured simply by bringing sulphur dioxide and oxygen together. If, however, the mixed gases are passed at the proper temperature through platinum deposited on asbestos fibre, the reaction proceeds rapidly and none of the platinum is used up. When I studied chemistry more than fifty years ago, it was commonly assumed, I think, that the reaction proceeded in two steps: the platinum, that is, combined with one of the gases, and this intermediate compound then reacted with the other gas, the platinum being dropped out. Nowadays the favored explanation is stereo-chemical. In order for a reaction to proceed at optimum speed, it is now believed, the combining molecules must face each other in a certain way, and the bonds that unite the atoms must be loosened. The molecules of the catalyst, it is now assumed, clamp onto the molecules of one or both of the reacting substances and hold them in the required posture, at the same time loosening the bonds. A catalyst may in a real sense be inert and yet be the cause of a great deal of chemical activity. In the same way, I suggest, the output of poetic concretions may be greatly increased by judicious juxtaposition of language in itself merely denotative.

The reader must have anticipated my fifth reason from the start and must have been wondering why I didn't get to it sooner. Wordsworth is with the moderns in his passion for psychology and psychologizing. His great autobiographical poem, *The Prelude,* bears as its sub-title *Growth of a Poet's Mind.* In the Prospectus to *The Recluse,* that huge unfinished work of which *The Prelude* and *The Excursion* are only fragments, he matches himself proudly with Milton and announces that he has a greater subject than Jehovah with his thunder and the choir of shouting angels:

> Not Chaos, not
> The darkest pit of lowest Erebus,
> Nor aught of blinder vacancy, scooped out
> By help of dreams—can breed such fear and awe
> As fall upon us often when we look
> Into our Minds, into the Mind of Man—
> My haunt, and the main region of my song.

The Prelude does not merely look forward to authors like Proust, it can hold its own with any of them in the sharpness, vividness, and freshness of its recall of the past. No writing known to me has more compelling power than Wordsworth's accounts of what he happily calls "spots of time": recollected scenes of terror or intense uneasiness from his childhood which seemed to him in his later years paradoxically refreshing. I presented the latter part of one of these descriptions earlier in this paper. He tells how, when he was not yet six years old and hardly able to rein a horse, he had ridden out on the hills with an old servant of his father's, had lost his guide, dismounted through fear, led his horse stumbling down to the bottom, and there had come upon initials carved in the turf which he knew from previous report to mark the spot where a murderer had once been hung in chains. The part I read then followed:

> I fled,
> Faltering and faint, and ignorant of the road.

The Prelude is the first "stream of consciousness" poem in European literature. Its organization is more associational than logical: its organizing metaphor is not a building but a river.

Gibbon needed only five causes, but I should feel unsatisfied if I could not present one more. My sixth will need some explaining before I name it.

People are scared off from Wordsworth because they have been told—correctly—that he preaches a religion of nature variously called nature-mysticism, pantheism, panentheism. I was myself throughout my youth consciously wary of him for just this reason. I grew up on a farm in lake country (Cumberland County—Maine) not too unlike his; my boyhood experiences of the outdoors were remarkably like his; I had my spots of time just as he did. But though I experienced ecstasy or a sense of heightened awareness in confrontations with nature, I never recognized any element of religion in these encounters. I am not and never have been what I may call an experiencing pantheist or panentheist, and I felt that I would be disgusted or bored by a poet who preached such doctrine. Nobody told me that none of the better Wordsworthians—Coleridge, Arnold, Swinburne, Raleigh, Bradley, Whitehead, Sperry, Willey, Havens—was a practicing pantheist or panentheist either, but the fact is so, as I realized while I was writing this paper. I did not begin reading and rereading Wordsworth seriously till my mid-thirties, and I then began because I had begun teaching The Age of Wordsworth in a graduate course at Yale. And I found (it wouldn't be honest to say I soon found) that the preaching not only didn't bother me but that I had come to like most of it.

T. S. Eliot once remarked that meaning in poetry is the piece of meat that the burglar tosses to the watchdog to divert his attention while the burglar goes about his business.[12] R. P. Warren rebuked him rather sharply,[13] but there is truth that has to be faced under Eliot's cynicism. I get value out of Wordsworth, not by giving creedal assent to his doctrine, not by ignoring his doctrine, and certainly not in spite of his doctrine. I entertain the doctrine seriously but provisionally within the confines of a poem. A surprising amount of the doctrine is indeed stated provisionally ("Nor less, I trust . . ."; "If this be but a vain belief . . ."; "And so I dare to hope . . ."; "I would believe . . ."). Arnold said that we cannot do Wordsworth justice until we dismiss his formal philosophy; I would say that, save for the purposes of explicating his poetry or of fitting it into literary history, we ought not to abstract the philosophy, ought not to formalize it at all. We should take it within the poems exactly as we

12. *The Use of Poetry and the Use of Criticism* (Cambridge, Mass.: Harvard Univ. Press, 1933), p. 144.
13. "Pure and Impure Poetry," pp. 99–100.

take the literal iteration of *The Old Cumberland Beggar;* we
should take it, that is, because it serves as catalyst for invalu-
able concretions:

> For I have learned
> To look on nature, not as in the hour
> Of thoughtless youth; but hearing oftentimes
> The still, sad music of humanity,
> Nor harsh nor grating, though of ample power
> To chasten and subdue. And I have felt
> A presence that disturbs me with the joy
> Of elevated thoughts; a sense sublime
> Of something far more deeply interfused,
> Whose dwelling is the light of setting suns,
> And the round ocean and the living air,
> And the blue sky, and in the mind of man:
> A motion and a spirit, that impels
> All thinking things, all objects of all thought,
> And rolls through all things.
>   (*Lines composed . . . above Tintern Abbey,* 88–102)

But is my assent *all* provisional? Am I not perhaps letting a
real acceptance of part of his doctrine serve as sanction for
the rest? The Judaeo-Christian tradition has two great com-
mandments: Thou shalt love the Lord thy God with all thy
heart, and with all thy soul, and with all thy mind, and with
all thy strength; and Thou shalt love thy neighbor as thy-
self.[14] Theologians would say that it is the first commandment
that makes sense of the second. But do not many people for
whom the first commandment no longer has any reality continue to adhere to the tradition because of their warm assent
to the second? The first article of Wordsworth's poetical faith
is that God rolls through all things; the second is the connection and relation of things, the silence and the balm of mute
insensate things, the life of things. "The brooding, immediate presences of things are an obsession to Wordsworth," says

14. Mark 12. 30–31; Leviticus 19. 18.

Whitehead.[15] Wordsworth was the first poet to relate man to
his natural environment in a really modern way, the first to
insist passionately and endlessly on the folly and wickedness
of isolating him from his ground. He is sometimes very sharp
about this, too sharp indeed to be poetical:

> Sweet is the lore which Nature brings;
> Our meddling intellect
> Mis-shapes the beauteous forms of things;—
> We murder to dissect.
>
> *(The Tables Turned, 25–28)*

> Physician art thou?—one, all eyes,
> Philosopher!—a fingering slave,
> One that would peep and botanize
> Upon his mother's grave?
>
> *(A Poet's Epitaph, 17–20)*

You will see now what my sixth and last cause is. Wordsworth is the poet *par excellence* of the whole range of eco-
logical sentiment, and his sense of the interdependence of
man and his environment is expressed in an idiom which remains grateful to present-day sensibility. My demonstration
is one of his shorter poems which I shall print entire, because
I want even readers who are familiar with it to read it *now*
with this point in mind. It will, I hope, be more winning
than others I could have selected, because Wordsworth, who
tends to scold on this subject, here passes judgment on nobody but himself. As a fine example of Wordsworth's peculiar
power, I recommend the phrase "the intruding sky" in the
fourth line from the end.

> It seems a day
> (I speak of one from many singled out)
> One of those heavenly days that cannot die;
> When, in the eagerness of boyish hope,

15. *Science and the Modern World* (New York: Macmillan, 1925 and
later), p. 134.

I left our cottage-threshold, sallying forth
With a huge wallet o'er my shoulders slung,
A nutting-crook in hand; and turned my steps
Tow'rd some far-distant wood, a Figure quaint,
Tricked out in proud disguise of cast-off weeds
Which for that service had been husbanded,
By exhortation of my frugal Dame—
Motley accoutrement, of power to smile
At thorns, and brakes, and brambles,—and in truth
More ragged than need was! O'er pathless rocks,
Through beds of matted fern, and tangled thickets,
Forcing my way, I came to one dear nook
Unvisited, where not a broken bough
Drooped with its withered leaves, ungracious sign
Of devastation; but the hazels rose
Tall and erect, with tempting clusters hung,
A virgin scene!—A little while I stood,
Breathing with such suppression of the heart
As joy delights in; and with wise restraint
Voluptuous, fearless of a rival, eyed
The banquet;—or beneath the trees I sate
Among the flowers, and with the flowers I played;
A temper known to those who, after long
And weary expectation, have been blest
With sudden happiness beyond all hope.
Perhaps it was a bower beneath whose leaves
The violets of five seasons re-appear
And fade, unseen by any human eye;
Where fairy water-breaks do murmur on
For ever; and I saw the sparkling foam,
And—with my cheek on one of those green stones
That, fleeced with moss, under the shady trees,
Lay round me, scattered like a flock of sheep—
I heard the murmur and the murmuring sound,
In that sweet mood when pleasure loves to pay
Tribute to ease; and, of its joy secure,
The heart luxuriates with indifferent things,
Wasting its kindliness on stocks and stones,
And on the vacant air. Then up I rose,
And dragged to earth both branch and bough, with crash

And merciless ravage: and the shady nook
Of hazels, and the green and mossy bower,
Deformed and sullied, patiently gave up
Their quiet being: and unless I now
Confound my present feelings with the past,
Ere from the mutilated bower I turned
Exulting, rich beyond the wealth of kings,
I felt a sense of pain when I beheld
The silent trees, and saw the intruding sky.—
Then, dearest Maiden, move along these shades
In gentleness of heart; with gentle hand
Touch—for there is a spirit in the woods.

(*Nutting*)

Coleridge as a
Metaphysical Poet

The title of this essay may sound willfully perverse. For though Coleridge is often spoken of as a metaphysician, and Byron twitted him for "explaining metaphysics to the nation" in lieu of writing poetry, nobody, I believe, has ever claimed that Coleridge was a metaphysical poet. I shall not be so rash as to make that claim here. Nevertheless, it is evident that Coleridge took far more than a desultory interest in the metaphysical poets, particularly in John Donne, and what appealed to him in Donne's poetry was not the accidentals but the essence, its characteristic and animating principle. Witness the tribute that he pays to Donne's wit: he praises its "Wonder-exciting vigour" and speaks of the "intenseness and peculiarity of [Donne's] thought, using at will the almost boundless stores of a capacious memory, and exercised on subjects, where we have no right to expect it." [1] In scribbling down these comments, Coleridge has in fact given us a good description of his own vein of wit—at least as it displays itself in his earlier letters.

I choose the following example almost at random: it is a

1. From notes written in a copy of "Chalmer's Poets, belonging to Mr. Gillman." See Roberta F. Brinkley, *Coleridge on the Seventeenth Century* (Durham: Duke Univ. Press, 1955), pp. 526–527.

letter addressed to Francis Wrangham, dated December 19, 1800. He writes:

Rather than not answer your kind letter immediately, I have made up my mind to write but a half a dozen Lines, as a sort of promissory Note. Wordsworth received your letter, & meant to have answered it immediately. I'll write to him *to day,* quoth he. For you must understand, that *W.* has innovated very vilely the good old *Common-Law* of Procrastination—instead of To morrow, & To Morrow, & To Morrow, it is To Day, To Day, and To Day, which I the more disapprove of, as it appears to me a tame Plagiarism from the Lie of the Taverns & Coffee Houses— "Coming *this instant,* your *Honor!"* [2]

Perhaps Coleridge did have principally in mind contemporary tavern practice, but he has nevertheless given us in passing two Shakespearian echoes: Macbeth's melancholy series of *tomorrows* together with a hint of Prince Hal's bedevilment of poor Francis, the drawer who kept parroting, "Anon, anon." The pleasantest part of the joke, of course, is that Coleridge was himself the great procrastinator.

Toward the end of the letter, Coleridge describes the view from his window. He goes on to say:

In truth, my [looking] Glass being opposite to the Window, I seldom shave without cutting myself. Some Mountain or Peak is rising out of the Mist, or some slanting Column of misty Sunlight is sailing cross me / so that I offer up soap and blood daily, as an Eye-servant of the Goddess Nature.

I shall not quote further from the letter except for the postscript which includes a pleasant morsel of etymological lore:

> My house stands on the River Grieta, which is a
> literal Translation of the Word Cocytus—
>   Nam'd from lamentation loud

2. *Collected Letters of Samuel Taylor Coleridge,* ed. Earl Leslie Griggs (Oxford: Clarendon Press, 1956), pp. 657–658.

Heard on the rueful Stream.[3]
To griet is to lament aloud, and a is the masculine
termination of the substantive—

Would that correspondents in our days wrote so wittily and
with so much light-hearted learning.

Here is a further example excerpted from a letter written
four years later. It is addressed to Sara Hutchinson, Wordsworth's sister-in-law, the young woman with whom Coleridge
had fallen hopelessly in love in 1799. As someone has observed, it did not take Coleridge very long to discover that
Wordsworth was a far better poet than Bob Southey, nor
to discover that Sara Hutchinson who was Wordsworth's
sister-in-law would have made him a much better wife than
Sarah Fricker, who was Southey's sister-in-law, but to whom
Coleridge was unfortunately already married.

The letter to Sara [4] is written on the fly leaves of a folio
volume of *Pseudodoxia Epidemica* bound up with other
works by Sir Thomas Browne. Dr. Samuel Johnson, one remembers, found in Browne almost the same combination of
faults and virtues that he found in the metaphysical poets.
Browne's style, Johnson said, is "a mixture of heterogeneous
words, brought together from distant regions, with terms
originally appropriated to one art, and drawn by violence
into the service of another." [5] This echoes almost precisely
Johnson's reprehension of the metaphysical conceit as con-
sisting of "heterogeneous ideas yoked by violence together." [6]
Coleridge's comment on Browne is therefore very much to
our present purpose.

Coleridge writes to Sara that Browne has a

3. *Paradise Lost,* II, 579–580.   4. *Collected Letters,* pp. 1080–1083.
5. *The Works of Samuel Johnson, Ll.D.* (Oxford: Talboys and
Wheeler, 1825), VI, 500.
6. "Life of Cowley," *Lives of the Poets,* ed. George Birkbeck Hill
(Oxford: Clarendon Press, 1905), I, 20.

strong tinge of the Fantast, the Humourist constantly mingling with & flashing across the Philosopher. . . . In short, he has brains in his Head, which is all the more interesting for a *little Twist* in the Brains. . . .—So compleatly does he see everything in a light of his own, reading Nature neither by Sun, Moon, or Candle-Light, but by the Light of the faery Glory around his own Head, that you might say, that Nature had granted to him in perpetuity a Patent and Monopoly for all his Thoughts.

With special regard to Browne's "Urn Burial," Coleridge exclaims:

how *earthy,* how redolent of graves & Sepulchres is every Line!— You have now dark mould, now a thigh-bone, now a Skull, then a bit of mouldered Coffin / a fragment of an old tombstone with moss in it's Hic Jacet—a ghost, or a winding Sheet, or the echo of a funeral Psalm wafted on a November wind—& the gayest thing you shall meet with shall be a silver nail or gilt Anno Domini from a perished Coffin Top.

William Hazlitt was to come down very hard on this account of *Hydriotaphia.* He wrote:

There is not a word in the Hydriotaphia about "a thigh-bone, or a skull, or a bit of mouldered coffin, or a tomb-stone, or a ghost, or a winding-sheet, or an echo," nor is "a silver nail or a gilt *anno domini* the gayest thing you shall meet with." You do not meet with them at all in the text.[7]

Hazlitt—though in this instance I regret to have to point it out—is correct. No ghosts or winding sheets or relatively gay silver coffin nails are to be found in Browne's *Urn Burial.* It would seem that Coleridge had read *Urn Burial* not by sun or candle light but by the "faery-glory around *his own* head." There was evidently something in Coleridge which made him respond to Browne's subject matter and language, something not unrelated to his delight in Donne's mingling of

7. "Lectures on the Dramatic Literature of the Age of Elizabeth," *Works,* ed. A. R. Waller and Arnold Glover (London: Dent, 1902), V, 340–341.

the most diverse material—bracelets of bright hair about skeleton forearms, or the placing of sun dials within graves.

Ernest Hartley Coleridge notes that the letter just quoted "is the sole survivor of the correspondence between . . . [Coleridge and Sara Hutchinson.] Mrs Wordsworth, so her granddaughter Mrs Jane Kennedy told me, burnt all the rest of S. T. C.'s letters to Sara H. . . ." A modern editor, Earl Leslie Griggs, adds, however, that "Fortunately a few of Coleridge's letters to Sara Hutchinson escaped Mrs. Wordsworth's vigilance." [8] But the refugees are few and many of them fragments—perhaps a half dozen scraps rather than complete letters. There are good reasons for wishing that Mrs. Wordsworth had been less thorough in dealing with the missives that emanated from this passionate though quite platonic love affair, for it was the force that shaped much of Coleridge's life and gave rise to many of his poems.[9] Some of Coleridge's most nearly "metaphysical" poems are addressed to her or are inspired by her. One of these, "Recollections of Love," [10] seems to echo a theme congenial to Donne and to be found in several of his lyrics.

In "Recollections," Coleridge, walking on the Quantock Hills, is mindful of another walk there, eight years earlier, not long before he set out for the north where he and Sara Hutchinson were to have their "first . . . and fatal interview." On that earlier day, the very landscape had seemed to the poet filled with expectancy—there was, he says, a

8. *Collected Letters,* p. 1081, n.

9. See the impressive list of poems referring to, or inspired by, Sara Hutchinson in George Whalley's *Coleridge and Sara Hutchinson and the Asra Poems* (London: Routledge and Kegan Paul, 1955), pp. 151–80.

10. *The Complete Poetical Works of Samuel Taylor Coleridge,* ed. Ernest Hartley Coleridge (Oxford: Clarendon Press, 1912), I, 409–410. Subsequent quotations from Coleridge's poems are drawn from this edition.

"sense of promise everywhere." And so, when he actually met Sara for the first time, it was not like a meeting of strangers:

> I met, I loved you, maiden mild!
> As whom I long had loved before . . .
>
> You stood before me like a thought,
> A dream remembered in a dream.

In "Air and Angels" Donne expresses a like sentiment:

> Twice or thrice had I lov'd thee,
> Before I knew thy face or name;
> So in a voice, so in a shapeless flame,
> *Angells* affect us oft.[11]

Coleridge knew Donne's poem and admired it. In Lamb's copy of Donne, Coleridge set down some marginal comments: "The first stanza is noble," he writes, though he makes the frank admission that "The 2nd I do not understand." [12]

In Donne's "The Good Morrow," the speaker tells the loved one:

> If ever any beauty I did see,
> Which I desir'd, and got, 'twas but a dreame of thee.

And in his poem "The Dream," Donne pursues a similar thought:

11. *John Donne: The Elegies and the Songs and Sonnets,* ed. Helen Gardner (Oxford: Clarendon Press, 1965), p. 75. The next two quotations from Donne also follow Gardner.

12. The volume was the 1669 edition of Donne's poems. This copy is now in the Beinecke Library at Yale. Most of the marginal notes it contains were published soon after Coleridge's death and are now perhaps most readily available in Brinkley's *Coleridge on the Seventeenth Century.* In 1963 the rest of Coleridge's marginalia contained in the 1669 volume was published by Kay Davis in *Notes and Queries,* vol. 208, 187–189. For Coleridge's comments on "Air and Angels," see Davis p. 188.

> My Dreame thou brok'st not, but continued'st it,
> Thou art so true, that thoughts of thee suffice,
> To make dreames truth.

Coleridge knew "The Good Morrow" and in his marginalia expressed his admiration of it.[13] But the comments I
have quoted above were written down in 1811.[14] Did Coleridge know Donne's poems as early as 1807, the probable date
of the composition of "Recollections of Love"? George
Whalley writes: "One of the least expected things about
Coleridge's reading of Donne is how early he noticed Donne's
work with admiration: that was in 1796, at the age of 24, and
probably in the small type and corrupt text of Anderson's
British Poets, which he acquired at that time." [15]

Yet even if one concedes that Coleridge admired Donne
enough to borrow from him occasionally a theme or a dramatic situation, how reconcile such admiration with Coleridge's general reprehension of the artifical, the contrived,
the witty, and the fanciful when offered as serious poetry?
What, for example, are we to make of the squib of verse that
he scribbled in a copy of Chalmers' *British Poets?*

> With Donne, whose muse on dromedary trots,
> Wreathe iron pokers into true-love knoths;
> Rhyme's sturdy cripple, fancy's maze and clue,
> Wit's forge and fire-blast, meaning's press and screw.[16]

To call Donne a cripple of rhyme and to say that his muse
bounces along upon a trotting dromedary is essentially to
reiterate Ben Jonson's complaint that "for not keeping of
accent Donne deserved hanging." Coleridge's indictment
here is in fact rather good-natured, and some of his other

13. "Too good for mere wit." See Brinkley, p. 521.
14. See Davis, p. 187.
15. "The Harvest on the Ground: Coleridge's Marginalia," *University
of Toronto Quarterly,* 38 (1969), 263.
16. Brinkley, p. 526.

comments go far to soften the censure. For example, Coleridge again and again praises the versification of Donne's Satire III. He exclaims of it: "A fine instance of free, vehement, verse—disguising verse. Read it as it wants to be read, and no Ear will be offended." [17] In another comment Coleridge calls Donne a "Knotty, double-jointed Giant"—a decidedly more favorable epithet than "sturdy cripple"—and he says that Donne's apparent violations of meter—for Coleridge thinks that some were occasioned by corruptions of the text—are the result of what he calls Donne's "Cramp of Strength!"

Yet, we are hardly surprised that Coleridge did not imitate Donne's handling of meter. What Coleridge tends to stress is Donne's analogical power: as we would put it today, his ability to think through his images. Here the dromedary squib offers more than a grudging tribute. Donne's masculine strength and his fire—his ability to shape recalcitrant materials—come in for genuine praise. Another bit of marginalia in Lamb's edition of Donne makes clear just what Coleridge means by characterizing Donne as "meaning's press and screw." Coleridge is here annotating the following lines from Satire III:

> To will implyes delay, therefore now doe:
> Hard deeds, the bodies paines; hard knowledge too
> The mindes indeavours reach.

Coleridge writes: "i.e. The body's pains reach hard deeds; and likewise so do the mind's Endeavours reach hard knowledge. Here's Brama's Hydraulic Packing Engine! a scrouge of sense." Miss Davis, who in 1963 was the first to publish this last bit of marginalia, tells us that "In 1796, Joseph Bramah built a press to be used for packing or printing." It was a hydraulic press, capable of exerting enormous pressure, and made something of a sensation in its day. Coleridge's added

17. For Coleridge's marginalia on "Satire III," see Davis, p. 188.

phrase, "a scrouge of sense," enforces the point. The OED
defines *scrouge* as a crush or a squeeze, but gives as a second
meaning (which incidentally it characterizes as "U.S.," citing
College Words, 1851) "a very long lesson or any hard and
unpleasant task." It's amusing to notice that nineteenth-
century American college students developed a literal meaning for *scrouge* that answers almost exactly to that which
Coleridge applies to Donne: that is, Donne has so powerfully
packed his poems with meaning that the mind struggles as
with a hard lesson. (Perhaps the meaning that the OED lists
as U.S. is simply one more example of a locution that crossed
the Atlantic with the colonists and only surfaced into print
in the nineteenth century).

Donne's masculine power elicits Coleridge's genuine admiration. But what of Donne's choice of materials on which
he exercised his wit? Could Coleridge bring himself to believe that they were the legitimate ingredients of a serious
poetry?

In considering this question one is forced to take into account Coleridge's famous distinction between fancy and
imagination. Imagination, the superior power, "dissolves, dif-
fuses, dissipates, in order to recreate; or where this process
is rendered impossible, yet still at all events it struggles to
idealize and to unify. It is essentially *vital,* even as all objects
(as objects) are essentially fixed and dead." [18] Thus Coleridge
speaks in one of the most well-thumbed chapters of the *Biographia Literaria.* On the other hand, Fancy, the inferior
power, in the end leaves the objects with which it works as
thoroughly fixed and dead as they were in the beginning. For
Fancy simply shuffles and rearranges the "fixities and definites" with which it is condemned to deal. Fancy is powerless
to render them part of an organic whole that is vibrant with
its own individual life.

18. *Biographia Literaria,* ed. J. Shawcross (Oxford: Clarendon Press,
1907), I, 202.

Yet Donne's iron pokers would seem all too definite—quite inflexible fixities—and if they are to be woven into such arabesques as true-love knots, the weaver will indeed have to have recourse to the forge, pump the bellows hard, and raise a real fire-blast to render the recalcitrant metal workable. Does not Coleridge imply therefore that the triumph, even so, will be merely that of a *tour de force?*

There is more than a hint of this in Coleridge's praise of Donne's wit, for in the passage I have quoted earlier, Coleridge calls attention to the "peculiarity" of Donne's thought and to the fact that Donne exercises his wit "on subjects, where we have no right to expect it." [19] The term *wit* in itself is for Coleridge normally a term of disparagement. Abraham Cowley, who is for Coleridge much inferior to Donne, attempts to excite his reader by "compulsory juxtaposition[s]" and his work is therefore most often to be regarded as "a species of *wit,* a pure work of the *will."* [20]

Yet Donne's best witty poetry, Coleridge has to admit, is really "Too good for mere wit." [21] Moreover, in Coleridge's vocabulary, "metaphysical" as applied to poetry usually carries some note of disparagement. It requires apology or explanation if the poem in question is deemed to be really good. Thus, Coleridge writes of Donne's "Ecstasy": I should never find fault with metaphysical poems, were they all like this, or but half as excellent."

This last comment is, of course, splendidly generous, as are many of Coleridge's other comments on Donne's poems. Of "The Sun Rising," he exclaims: "Fine, vigorous exultation, both soul and body in full puissance." "The Canonization," he calls "One of my favourite poems. As late as ten years ago, I used to seek and find out grand lines and fine stanzas; but my delight has been far greater since it has con-

19. Brinkley, pp. 526–527.   20. *Biographia,* II, 68.
21. This and the next four of Coleridge's marginal notes on Donne may be found in Brinkley, pp. 521–524.

sisted more in tracing the leading thought thro'out the whole. The former [way of reading] is too much like coveting your neighbour's goods; in the latter you merge yourself in the author, you *become He*."

The last of the comments on Donne's poetry that Coleridge wrote in Lamb's copy concludes thus: "I am tired of expressing my admiration; else I could not have passed by *The Will, The Blossom,* and *The Primrose* with *The Relic.*"

This praise is so fervent and so obviously genuine that one is tempted to ask whether Coleridge did not radically modify his censure of wit and the fancy's "compulsory juxtaposition[s]" of recalcitrant materials. Did he finally satisfy himself that iron pokers may after all be suitable materials if worked by an ingenious smith using an intense fire-blast and a Bramah's hydraulic press? Surely, Coleridge's account of the imagination in Chapter XIV of the *Biographia* will provide a measure of support for such an interpretation. When Coleridge stresses the power of the imagination to bring into unity "opposite and discordant qualities," what else is he talking about other than the ability of a poet like Donne to fuse the apparently contradictory and to harmonize the discordant?

The temptation to answer yes here is almost overwhelming, and to the modern critic it is particularly inviting. Thus, Coleridge's concept of the imagination as a reconciling and unifying power has made its fortune in modern criticism. It has been invoked in a dozen critical contexts: to destroy the notion that there is any special "poetic" subject matter; to affirm the principle of tension within the structure of a literary work; to provide a charter for the difficult and, for some readers, the deliberately shocking kind of poetry written by the moderns; to suggest why the metaphysical poets of the seventeenth century are to be regarded not as bemused vagrants who took a bypath leading off into the wilderness of eccentricity, but as travelers along the king's highway of the

English poetic tradition. Some of Coleridge's very phrases—the imagination's power to achieve the "reconciliation of opposite or discordant qualities," or the imagination's blending of "the natural and the artificial"—might seem to be designed to take account of the special qualities of metaphysical poetry.

Yet, though I have myself made such use of this passage, and though I am willing to accept Coleridge's theory of poetry—at least as typified here—as providing the basis for a general theory of poetry, I must agree with Professor William K. Wimsatt's estimate of what Coleridge probably meant to say. Coleridge's theory, Wimsatt has written, has in fact to be regarded as "slanted very heavily toward a particular kind of poetry, one in which [he and Wordsworth] excelled." [22] Professor Wimsatt has made it plain that he himself is not opposed to extending Coleridge's account in the direction of a general theory, but that if we attempt to ascertain what Coleridge himself meant by it, we are forced to a rather different conclusion: that is, that Coleridge's theory of poetry is much more limited than the interpretation that the enthusiastic modernizing theorist would like to place upon it. Wimsatt points out that the primary quality that we discern in the metaphysical poets, "the element of tension in disparity," may not be prominent in Coleridge's conception of poetry. In Romantic poetry "the interest derives not from our being aware of disparity in stated likeness, but in the opposite activity of our discerning the design and the unity latent in a multiform sensuous picture. This is no doubt," Wimsatt observes, "a form of 'reconciliation.' At the same time there are [in Coleridge's account] certain clearly anti-'metaphysical' tendencies," including "the absence of overt definition" and the "reduction of disparity."

One might add that there seems to be in Coleridge's ac-

22. William K. Wimsatt, Jr., and Cleanth Brooks, *Literary Criticism: A Short History* (New York: Knopf, 1957), p. 398.

count even a preference for a special privileged subject matter, a subject matter usually drawn from the English landscape, the several details of which are not "fixities and definites" but entities almost infinitely plastic, constituting a subject matter which—I paraphrase Wimsatt again—at once yields reflections on the "one life within us and abroad," and similitudes by means of which these reflections may be symbolized.

In sum, we had best be cautious in attributing to Coleridge any serious attempt to make room for Donne and the metaphysicals in his theory of poetry, at least as he has stated it in the *Biographia* and his other published work. Yet what a pity that he did not make a serious attempt to reconcile with his general theoretical position the judgments he made on particular poems by Donne and George Herbert.

Because Coleridge's scattered comments on Donne, Herbert, and Crashaw as well, do reflect genuine evident admiration, I. A. Richards reproached Eliot for remarking that Coleridge did nothing to bring the poetry of the metaphysicals to bear on the poetry of his own time.[23] In his Charles Eliot Norton lectures Eliot had observed that the metaphysical poets were irrelevant to "the interest which [Wordsworth] and Coleridge had at heart." Eliot went on to ask: "did . . . Coleridge acclaim Donne?" And answered himself: "No, when it came to Donne . . . Wordsworth and Coleridge were led by the nose by Samuel Johnson: they were just as eighteenth century as anybody." [24]

Richards countered with the statement: "The right answer [to whether Coleridge acclaimed Donne] is, Yes, repeatedly and especially for his passion: see, for example, B.L., II, 56,

23. *Coleridge on Imagination* (New York: Harcourt Brace, 1935), p. 74.
24. *The Use of Poetry and the Use of Criticism* (Cambridge, Mass.: Harvard Univ. Press, 1933), p. 63.

65." In the first of these passages, Coleridge praises "the descriptions or declamations in DONNE or DRYDEN" for their "force and fervor" which he says is as often derived from the passion of the describer as from the forms or incidents that constitute his materials. In the second passage, Coleridge makes a related point in praising Donne's language for its "poetic fervor self-impassioned," language that Coleridge regards as excellent. He illustrates by quoting two stanzas from Donne's "Progress of the Soul." Yet Coleridge's praise of Donne's passionate language has to be weighed against his earlier complaint in the *Biographia* that "our faulty elder poets"—Donne is mentioned by name—"sacrificed the passion and passionate flow of poetry, to the subtleties of intellect, and to the starts of wit."

Indeed, lacking the evidence of the marginalia—and such highly private evidence does not in itself amount to a public proclaiming—could one really judge the warmth of Coleridge's appreciation of Donne? Coleridge's reaction seems mixed. It might even suggest that Coleridge was confused in his own mind—though perhaps what seems to be a muddle is due to the confused nature of the *Biographia* itself, that wonderful ragbag of a book.

Is there evidence in Coleridge's own poetry that he was strongly influenced by Herbert or Donne? On an earlier page I have suggested that one or two of Coleridge's poems seem to reflect themes and dramatic situation derived from Donne. Was Coleridge also influenced by the poetic methods and techniques of Donne?

Clearly Coleridge would have had nothing to do with Donne's metrics. Coleridge always seats his muse on an animal of more regular and conventional gait. No dromedaries for him! Just as obviously Coleridge eschews the special complexities of tone in Donne—even though he confessed to an amused admiration for such a poem as Donne's "The Flea."

Coleridge much admired the famous geometrical conceit that concludes "A Valediction: Forbidding Mourning." Of it, he wrote: "Nothing was ever more admirably made out than the figure of the Compass." [25] Scientific phenomena evidently fascinated Coleridge, and more than once he tried to use them as similitudes in serious poems. "Lines at Shurton Bars" concludes with this elaborated similitude:

'Tis said, in Summer's evening hour
Flashes the golden-colour'd flower
  A fair electric flame:
And so shall flash my love-charg'd eye
When all the heart's big ecstasy
  Shoots rapid through the frame!

To this stanza, Coleridge appends the following note.

Light from plants. In Sweden a very curious phenomenon has been observed on certain flowers, by M. Haggern, lecturer in natural history. One evening he perceived a faint flash of light repeatedly dart from a marigold. Surprised at such an uncommon appearance, he resolved to examine it with attention; and, to be assured it was no deception of the eye, he placed a man near him, with orders to make a signal at the moment when he observed the light. They both saw it constantly at the same moment.

The note goes on to relate in very circumstantial detail other aspects of Haggern's experiment such as the fact that the phenomenon occurred more often in the months of July and August and the varieties of flowers that were most active in sending out the flashes: the marigold, monkshood, the orange lily, and the Indian pink. Coleridge concludes that "it may be conjectured that there is something of electricity in this phenomenon."

Again, in Act II, Scene ii of his verse play *Remorse*, Coleridge tried another scientific or pseudo-scientific simile:

25. For Coleridge's notes on "The Flea" and "A Valediction," see Brinkley, pp. 521–525.

> In the future,
> As in the optician's glassy cylinder,
> The indistinguishable blots and colours
> Of the dim past collect and shape themselves,
> Upstarting in their own completed image
> To scare or to reward.

This simile is neither very successful nor very intricate. Its interest rests in the fact that it represents another of Coleridge's attempts to incorporate mathematical fixities and definites into elevated poetry. What is this "optician's glassy cylinder" that resolves into a "completed image" what would otherwise be mere "indistinguishable blots and colours"? It is almost certainly the kaleidoscope, which nowadays we think of as a child's toy, but which was invented by one of Britain's best known authorities on optics, Sir David Brewster, and which caused quite a stir in its own day. What is worth noting is that though Brewster did not patent his invention or, as far as I know, give it a name until 1817, Coleridge's *Remorse* was published four years earlier, in 1813. Our poet was here abreast of the times, anticipating Byron's allusion to the kaleidoscope by some six years.

One scientific phenomenon at least *did* provide Coleridge with the vehicle for a rich and powerful simile: it occurs, perhaps significantly, in a late poem, "Constancy to an Ideal Object." It is also significant that this successful use of an intricate and specialized analogy occurs in a poem about Sara Hutchinson. It would seem that in his poems on or about her —Coleridge's "confessional poems," to borrow a contemporary term—he did move toward the metaphysical poets. His earlier conversational poems had certainly taken him in another direction. One might add a further observation. As he grew older, Coleridge's liking for the metaphysical poets seems to have grown stronger: he had been used to reading Herbert's poetry to amuse himself "with its quaintness," he tells us, but in 1826 he wrote: "Every time I read Herbert anew, the more he grows in my liking." [26]

When Coleridge wrote "Constancy," his close friendship with Wordsworth had long since lapsed, and with it his special relation to Sara Hutchinson. He saw very little of Sara after 1810. But the *idea* of Sara was too important and too precious for him to abandon, though, when he wrote "Constancy," she had in truth become simply an ideal object, a "yearning Thought! that liv'st but in the brain." In the poem he addresses this "ideal object" directly, and in the second person:

> Yet still thou haunt'st me; and though well I see,
> She is not thou, and only thou art she,
> Still, still as though some dear embodied Good,
> Some living Love before my eyes there stood
> With answering look a ready ear to lend,
> I mourn to thee and say—"Ah! loveliest friend!"

This poem is what might be called a "private poem." Sara Hutchinson is nowhere in the poem mentioned directly. In fact, we must know a good deal about Coleridge's intimate life in order to see what the poem is talking about.

"She is not thou and only thou art she," the speaker exclaims. The statement is puzzling and may seem to involve a real contradiction: if X is not Y, then how can Y be X? And yet in the context, the meaning, though packed as by Bramah's press, gradually emerges. Coleridge's ideal woman is not the aging, rather dumpy little woman whom he no longer saw and to whom he no longer wrote letters. In fact, the woman who had affected his whole life and still matters intensely to him has become essentially an idea. Yet the poet cannot repress his desire that it should be clothed in flesh and blood. The idea of Sara stands before him "as though [she were] some dear *embodied* Good" (italics mine). In his yearn-

26. Brinkley, p. 540.

ing, he appeals to this idea as if it might make some womanly response—might give an "answering look." "Ah! loveliest friend!," he says,

> "That this the meed of all my toils might be,
> To have a home, an English home, and thee!"
> Vain repetition! Home and Thou are one.

Again, the language here has felt the force of meaning's press and screw. "Vain repetition" does not mean, or at least does not mean merely, that he is simply vainly repeating his yearning for a home with her. The essential vanity of the repetition is that the statement which couples "home" and "thee" is tautological. For Coleridge to name one is to name the other. Without her, even "the peacefull'st cot, the moon shall shine upon" would be no more than a "becalmed bark, / Whose Helmsman on an ocean waste and wide / Sits mute and pale his mouldering helm beside." Bereft of her, he lives a life-in-death like his own ancient mariner.

Then comes the great simile:

> And art thou nothing? Such thou art, as when
> The woodman winding westward up the glen
> At wintry dawn, where o'er the sheep-track's maze
> The viewless snow-mist weaves a glist'ning haze,
> Sees full before him, gliding without tread,
> An image with a glory round its head;
> The enamoured rustic worships its fair hues,
> Nor knows he makes the shadow, he pursues!

In a note appended to the word "image," Coleridge tells us that "the Author has himself experienced" this phenomenon and refers the reader to a description of it to be found "in one of the earlier volumes of the *Manchester Philosophical Transactions*." [27]

Miss Kathleen Coburn has reprinted this account as set down by Coleridge in his notebooks:

27. *Poetical Works,* I, 456, n. 2.

Vide Description of a Glory, by John Haygarth, Manchester Trans. Vol. 3 p. 463. On the thirteenth of February, 1780, as I was returning to Chester . . . in the road above me, I was struck with the peculiar appearance of a very white shining cloud, that lay remarkably close to the ground. The Sun was nearly setting but shone extremely bright. I walked up to the cloud, and my shadow was projected into it; the head of my shadow was surrounded at some distance by a circle of various colours whose centre appeared to be near the situation of the eye, and whose circumference extended to the Shoulders. The circle was complete except where the shadow of my body intercepted it—it exhibited the most vivid colors red being outermost—all the colors appeared in the same order & proportion that the rainbow presents to our view.[28]

In its fullness and richness, the simile beautifully answers to Coleridge's own plight. The vision with a glory round its head, nimbused like an angel, like a spirit "gliding without tread," is only a projection of himself.[29] The enamored rustic who sees it does not know this. Unfortunately, Coleridge does; yet since the vision still retains its beauty and attraction, he is still tormented by his yearning for it.

Earlier in this essay, I quoted, from his letter of 1804 to Sara Hutchinson, Coleridge's characterization of Sir Thomas Browne as one who read nature "neither by Sun, Moon, or Candle-Light, but by the Light of the faery Glory around his own Head." Now, sadly, it is Coleridge himself saying that he had viewed Sara by the light of the faery glory round his own head. Did Sara ever read the poem? It would be interesting

28. *The Notebooks of Samuel Taylor Coleridge* (New York: Pantheon, 1957), I, Item 258. Miss Coburn's own note tells us that Coleridge borrowed volume II of *The Memoirs of the Literary and Philosophical Society of Manchester* from the Bristol Library, 20 April–22 May 1798.

29. In his note on "Constancy" (see *Poetical Works*, I, 456, n. 2) Coleridge tells us that he had made a figurative use of this phenomenon in his *Aids to Reflection: viz.*, "The beholder either recognises it as a projected form of his own Being, that moves before him with a Glory round its head, or recoils from it as a Spectre."

to know. One *could* shade the figure to mean: in seeing you I saw a part of my own self but glorified. But Sara could hardly have missed the more somber meaning: I never saw *you* at all. You were merely a delusion—a projection of my own need for love.

"Constancy to an Ideal Object" contains another of Coleridge's most striking similes. But its merit will become apparent only if we take into account the lines that precede it.

> Since all that beat about in Nature's range,
> Or veer or vanish; why should'st thou remain
> The only constant in a world of change,
> O yearning Thought!

The notion expressed here is essentially Platonic. Things which embody ideas—clumsily and approximately—inhabit a world of change. Only the pure idea is unchanging: the ideal object exists not in nature at all but in a transcendent world. Yet this idea yearns—or is it the thinker who yearns?— to see itself embodied and existent here and now, in the world of nature.

> O yearning Thought! that liv'st but in the brain?
> Call to the Hours, that in the distance play,
> The faery people of the future day—
> Fond Thought! not one of all that shining swarm
> Will breathe on thee with life-enkindling breath,
> Till when, like strangers shelt'ring from a storm,
> Hope and Despair meet in the porch of Death!

The concluding figure has something of the paradoxical quality of metaphysical poetry and it comes to the reader with a fine rhetorical shock. But does it contribute to the enrichment of the poem? What, in short, does the simile add to the simple assertion that the fond thought will never be embodied in this life?

It adds a great deal. Strangers, even people of sharply different character and circumstance, do sometimes meet unexpectedly, taking shelter from a common peril. If the shelter is "the porch of Death," what is the peril from which they seek refuge? What is the storm? In this poem, the storm can only be life itself. When we write that the poem is saying that hope and despair flee from life as from a storm, the meaning of the simile comes with great poignance. Death ends hope's yearning for realization and just as certainly ends the despair occasioned by watching the days go by with hope unrealized. It is only in terms of a future reference that hope and despair have a meaning.

With death—but in death only, the poet suggests—hope and despair will at last recognize that they are really sister and brother—siblings, the offspring of the human heart caught in the human predicament. Then, but only then, the speaker of the poem will no longer be vexed by hope and despair, for it will no longer matter whether or not the yearning thought is embodied. It cannot matter to the mortal body, locked in the eternal sleep of death; nor could it matter to Coleridge as a Christian soul holding to the faith that with the death of the body the spirit enters into a transcendent realm. When that occurs, the mortal will have been put aside. Besides, in heaven there is no marrying or giving in marriage.

Though Coleridge's figure of Hope and Despair impinges on the reader with an appropriate shock, it is followed by aftershocks, reverberations of meaning, that expand and deepen the total import. It is a splendid simile. Donne, either as Dean of St. Paul's or as the poet who wrote "I long to talk with some old lover's ghost / Who died before the god of love was born" would surely have understood the meaning and approved the method by which it is expressed.

HAROLD BLOOM

Emerson: The Glory and Sorrows of American Romanticism

"Evil Tendencies Cancel" is the title of a tough little poem by Robert Frost, in which the blight fails to end the chestnut, which goes on growing, while waiting for another parasite, which "shall come to end the blight." I choose to read this as the governing fable of our American Romanticism, which means of Emersonianism, our true and glorious, if also disastrous, literary tradition. It keeps on sending up shoots, it keeps on catching the blight, and one blight keeps on slaying another, but the old chestnut lives. Emerson lives, because we are still alive, and all the exorcisers—Eliot, Winters, and their ilk—could not dissolve this brave ghostly father.

An American student of British Romanticism, when he turns to the study of the domestic variety, soon finds himself obsessed with, lost in, dazed by—Emerson. Otherwise, he can't hope to find himself at all. Emerson is appalling and peculiar—at first. Then he is—simply—ourselves, perhaps for worse. But—a certain way into him—he is what Matthew Arnold asserted him to be—the friend and the aider of anyone whatsoever who would live in the spirit.

"Whose spirit is this?" Stevens asked, listening to his singing girl at Key West, knowing that it was the spirit that he sought, but skeptical as to the spirit's sanction, its autonomy as against the world of wind and wave. Whose spirit is the spirit that Emerson perpetually invokes? What is the authority that he so beautifully and yet so arbitrarily assumes, nearly every day of his writing life? Aged twenty-seven, he writes this in his Journal as his first great declaration of self-reliance:

> Every man has his own voice, manner, eloquence, and, just as much, his own sort of love and grief and imagination and action. Let him scorn to imitate any being, let him scorn to be a secondary man, let him fully trust his own share of God's goodness, that, correctly used, it will lead him on to perfection which has no type yet in the universe, save only in the Divine Mind.

Very few among us are going to offer our neighbors that Emersonian admonition. I won't, even though I am haunted by Stevens' line in which he calls Narcissus "Prince of the secondary men." I get scared, sensibly so, when my students start fully trusting in their own share of God's goodness, and start acting as though that share will lead them on to a "perfection which has no type yet in the universe, save only in the Divine Mind." Why then should I be moved rather than skeptical when Emerson urges me to scorn being a secondary man, which means that I mustn't imitate any other being whatsoever? Am I then only another armchair Emersonian, like the voice in "The Man with the Blue Guitar" that cries out:

> Am I a man that is dead
>
> At a table on which the food is cold?
> Is my thought a memory, not alive?
>
> Is the spot on the floor, there, wine or blood
> And whichever it may be, is it mine?

The Emersonian way of answering such dreadful questions is to ask a much happier one, a rather more rhetorical one.

Here he is five years further on, writing in his Journal, aged thirty-two:

Far off, no doubt, is the perfectibility; so far off as to be ridiculous to all but a few. Yet wrote I once that, God keeping a private door to each soul, nothing transcends the bounds of reasonable expectation from a man. Now what imperfect tadpoles we are! an arm or a leg, an eye or an antenna, is unfolded,—all the rest is yet in the chrysalis. Who does not feel in him budding the powers of a Persuasion that by and by will be irresistible?

This, the vision proper of the earlier Emerson, sees in the universe primarily the possibility for an original relation to the universe on the part of everyone, again whomsoever. Whether this sees the universe at all, in whole or in part, is dubious; Emerson dwelt in possibility, a fairer house than prose. Through its more numerous windows, its superior number of doors, he saw, and he knew, and he became a kind of liberating god. But what did he see, what did he know, and what kind of man-godhood was this? What bread did he eat, what wine did he drink, to find in himself the real presence of a kind of giant of the imagination?

In his little book or manifesto, misentitled "Nature," Emerson writes: "Of that ineffable essence which we call Spirit, he that thinks most, will say least." Emerson fortunately did not stop there, at saying least, but ventured the following giant formula: "The ruin or the blank that we see when we look at nature, is in our own eye. The axis of vision is not coincident with the axis of things and so they appear not transparent but opaque."

That is the more-than-Coleridgean formula, beautiful and extreme, which made possible the Romantic poem in America, down to this present day. Not the Romantic poem of Bryant or of Poe or of Longfellow, but of Thoreau, Whitman, Dickinson, Melville, Robinson, Frost, Stevens, Williams, Hart Crane, Roethke, and all their followers. For, if our own eye contains the ruin or blank we see in nature, then it contains also the joy and color we see there. And, in that ecstasy when the axis of vision and the axis of things coincide, and we see into the life of things, we behold a transparency that is also ourselves. The Emersonian or American Sublime is a wildness or holistic freedom in which the spirit, transparent to itself, knows its own splendor, and by knowing that knows again all things. This is not a mystical reverie that I am describing, but a rather sober, even matter-of-fact state. Perhaps it is the most American of states-of-mind, since it is the most impatient. Mysticism, according to one famous definition, has not the patience to wait for God's revelation of Himself. Emersonianism has not the patience to wait for mysticism. Let us, without delay, examine the Emersonian impatience at its most sublime and most notorious, by chanting the great epiphany from his "Nature":

Crossing a bare common, in snow puddles, at twilight, under a clouded sky, without having in my thoughts any occurrence of special good fortune, I have enjoyed a perfect exhilaration. I am glad to the brink of fear. . . . Standing on the bare ground,— my head bathed by the blithe air and uplifted into infinite space, —all mean egotism vanishes. I become a transparent eyeball; I am nothing; I see all; the currents of the Universal Being circulate through me; I am part or parcel of God. The name of the nearest friend sounds then foreign and accidental: to be brothers, to be acquaintance, master or servant, is then a trifle and a disturbance. I am the lover of uncontained and immortal beauty.

To sandbag this rapture would be disgusting, if one sought the origins of such ecstasy only to reduce it. But the journal entry Emerson builds upon is so strikingly different, and so moving, that a contrast should help us to a vision of the Emersonian impatience. Listen for the plangency of loss in this, and you may hear a deeper sorrow than Emerson himself intended:

As I walked in the woods I felt what I often feel that nothing can befall me in life, no calamity, no disgrace (leaving me my eyes), to which Nature will not offer a sweet consolation. Standing on the bare ground with my head bathed by the blithe air, and uplifted into the infinite space, I become happy in my universal relations. The name of the nearest friend sounds then foreign and accidental. I am the heir of uncontained beauty and power. And if then I walk with a companion, he should speak from his Reason to my Reason; that is, both from God. To be brothers, to be acquaintances, master or servant, is then a trifle too insignificant for remembrance. O, keep this humour (which in your lifetime may not come to you twice), as the apple of your eye. Set a lamp before it in your memory which shall never be extinguished.

Though even this journal entry is in a mode of what I will describe as divination, I hear no impatience in it, whether impatience with natural continuities or with human limitations. Though Emerson centers on his eyes, he *sees* nothing, but inherits beauty and power. He is joyous because he is wholly taken up into what Wordsworth called "Reason in her most exalted mood." He speaks and hears as God, and in this humor possesses as he would be possessed. At the climax of his greatest poem Stevens proclaims: "I have not but I am, and as I am I am." Beauty is not in things seen, not even by seeing into the life of things, but is the recognition of self, and power is one with self. But this humor is very rare; the walker in the woods is thirty-two, the age at which his master Wordsworth wrote "Resolution and Independence" and the first four stanzas of the "Intimations" ode. The fear that this humor may never return creates the extraordinary image of the transparent eyeball, an image impatient with all possibility of loss, indeed less an image than a promise of perpetual repetition. As he rewrites the journal entry into the passage of "Nature," Emerson raises himself from the mere exercise of a Divine faculty to being a part or particle of God Himself. This raising is not at all akin to that muscular exertion by

which Whitman, according to the young Henry James, en-
deavoured to wrestle himself into poetry. The Emersonian
elevation authentically is shamanistic—it bears all the splendid and barbarous stigmata that E. R. Dodds, in his study of
the Greeks and the irrational, comprehensively located in the
Siberian shamans who had descended into Thrace, and whose
egregious raptures lurk in the dark abysses from which Western poetic tradition emerged. Emerson, as we ought never
to be suprised to realize, is at once our sweetest and most
civilized writer and our wildest and most primitivistic. The
spirit that speaks in and through him has the true Pytha-
gorean and Orphic stink. Compared to Emerson, poor Allen
Ginsberg is a pallid academic imposter, a gentle donkey mas-
querading as an enraged waterbuffalo. The ministerial Emerson, who lived to sit on the Harvard Board of Overseers and
to cast his vote there for compulsory chapel attendance, is full
brother to the Dionysiac adept who may have torn living
flesh with his inspired teeth.

The late Yvor Winters, who was not very fond of Emerson,
attempted to dismiss our dialectically shamanistic ancestor
by accusing him of what might be called rhetorical hypocrisy.
I quote from Winters at his most morally passionate best:

[Emerson] . . . was able to present the anarchic and anti-moral
doctrines of European Romanticism in a language which for two
hundred years had been capable of arousing the most intense and
the most obscure emotions of the American people. He could
speak of matter as if it were God; of the flesh as if it were spirit;
of emotion as if it were Divine Grace; of impulse as if it were conscience; and of automatism as if it were the mystical experience.
And he was addressing an audience which, like himself, had been
so conditioned by two hundred years of Calvinistic discipline,
that the doctrines confused nothing, at the outset, except the
mind: Emerson and his contemporaries, in surrendering to what
they took for impulse, were governed by New England habit; they
mistook second nature for nature. They were moral parasites

nign, knowing not what we do and these may be—as Wordsworth said—the best portions of a good man's life. But to act without knowing *how* we act—at its best this may be Yeats's celebratory kind of *sprezzatura* (as derived from Castiglione) but more usually we meet this in Swift's dreadful and dreaded "Mechanical operation of the spirit." I suppose that Emerson, always a more-than-Platonic-Idealist, really means here what earlier he had oddly called Self-Reliance, a principle whose closest twentieth-century equivalent formula is Freud's "Where It was, there I shall be," or the progressive displacement of the id by the maturing ego. Yet that cannot be wholly what Emerson means. Freud, like one strain in Pre-Socratic thought, is telling us that a person's character is his fate. Emerson, like quite another strain in the Pre-Socratics, a shamanistic one, is telling us as Yeats did that the daimon is our destiny. Our longing for the wider circumference is daimonic, and belongs to personality as against character, to use an Emersonian dialectic which Yeats inherited from that brilliant rhetorician, his own father. The daimon knows how we do it or why it is done; we are along for the glory, and the sorrows, of the ride.

I divide the remainder of this essay equally between the glory and the sorrows of the Emersonian daimonic. The glory I take to be Emerson's beautiful self-confidence as to his own spiritual authority; the sorrows I shall invoke all belong to the great Serpent *Ananke*, Necessity, upon whose altars Emerson was to sacrifice the joy of his authority. What is a poet's or sage's authority? Vico gives us the certain answer: authority is precisely property, the author's sole possession, his commerce as granted him by Hermes, god of ownership and of thievery. Authority was at first titanic, belonging to such giants of the imagination as Prometheus, but then became divine, by Jove's expropriation, in Vico's account. Authority or property is power of divination, not only

upon a Christian doctrine which they were endeavoring to destroy.

With so directly moral a critic as Winters (whose judiciousness resembled Dr. Johnson's about as closely as an avocado resembles a potato) I always like to cope by juxtaposition rather than direct attack, because it is not much fun just to say "You're another," in that you are a moral parasite upon a Romantic doctrine which you are endeavoring to destroy. Emerson did not allow himself much irony, ever, as he had far too many imprisoned truths that he rightly felt only he could set free. But against the Winters vision I set Emerson in an uncharacteristic but wholly apposite ferocity, anticipating and to my mind wholly thawing out the Winters vision. In the great essay "Circles," to which I shall circle back later, Emerson attains a height from which all moral virtue is seen to fall away, until at last he can declare:

There is no virtue which is final; all are initial. The virtues of society are vices of the saint. The terror of reform is the discovery that we must cast away our virtues, or what we have always esteemed such, into the same pit that has consumed our grosser vices.

Emerson's eloquence gives us that grand phrase, "the terror of reform" but hardly tells us how we are to interpret "reform" or distinguish it from mere unamiable antinomianism, whose true enemy is never "the virtues of society" but frequently approximates any principle of coherence whatsoever. Emerson—as Winters never saw—demands very close reading, for his prose is as evasive and vacillating as Pater's or Yeats's though instead of their elaborate, marmoreal hesitation he seems to offer us the rhapsode's impatient rushes, divine moments in which known truths take on overwhelming immediacy. This is his power over us—his rhetorical authority—but not a power he possesses over himself, as he is all too aware. For, in "Circles," he goes on to meditate upon the phenomenon of his afflatus, and its tendency to abolish remorse, in the manner of Blake and Shelley. Emerson reverses the process, as he reverses so many Romantic influxes. In him, the sweetness flows in, and the effect is the abolition of all remorse. "It is the highest power of divine moments" he writes, "that they abolish our contrition also. I accuse myself of sloth and unprofitableness day by day; but when these waves of God flow into me I no longer reckon lost time. I no longer poorly compute my possible achievement by what remains to me of the month or the year; for these moments confer a sort of omnipresence and omnipotence which asks nothing of duration, but sees that the energy of the mind is commensurate with the work to be done, without time."

We can begin by noting that the axis of vision suddenly has been made coincident with the axis of things, so that Emerson stands in his radiance of transparency, without time. But for this once the transparent eyeball darts out a balefully ironic light, as the American rhapsode responds to his version of that grand Blakean character, the Idiot Questioner, here the precursor of our recently departed sage of Stanford. Listen to the following, and wonder what any Emersonian could add to this uncharacteristic but wholly central outburst, this astonishing, formidable irony:

And thus, O circular philosopher, I hear some reader exclaim, you have arrived at a fine Pyrrhonism, at an equivalence and indifferency of all actions, and would fain teach us that *if we are true*, forsooth, our crimes may be lively stones out of which we shall construct the temple of the true God!

I am not careful to justify myself. I own I am gladdened by seeing the predominance of the saccharine principle throughout vegetable nature, and not less by beholding in morals that unrestrained inundation of the principle of good into every chink and hole that selfishness has left open, yea into selfishness and sin itself; so that no evil is pure, nor hell itself without its extreme satisfactions.

When I encounter this mode of irony in Blake or Nietzsche, or even muted in Pater or Yeats, I know how to read it, but not when it rises against me from the pages of Emerson. For he is not an apocalyptic, Rabelaisian satirist, like Blake, nor a heroic vitalist like his admirer Nietzsche, nor an uneasy naturalizer of the psychic flux like Pater, nor a pseudo-apolcalyptic charlatan and necromancer like the still indubitably great Yeats. "Circles," read close, as Emily Dickinson clearly read it, is a genuinely shocking and unsettling essay, but unlike "The Marriage of Heaven and Hell," "Beyond Good and Evil," or some of the "Imaginary Portraits" or the drama "Purgatory," it does not intend to startle us into reconceptualizations by its rhetorical dissociations. What then is our circular philosopher up to, why does he so blandly tell us that he unsettles all things and simply experiments, an endless seeker with no past at his back? He has, as he well knew, and as Perry Miller and others have shown, Jonathan Edwards at his back, which is a formidable enough past for any man, even an American. Why does Emerson disown perpetually what he takes such ferocious pride in owning, the influx of power, the election as theorist of the poem of the mind in the act of finding what will suffice, the exhilaration of becoming a liberating god?

At the close of "Circles," Emerson speaks for the perpetual quest of virtually every American artist or person of sensibility when he declares that: "The one thing which we seek with insatiable desire is to forget ourselves, to be surprised out of our propriety, to lose our sempiternal memory and to do something without knowing how or why; in short to draw a new circle." Let us read close: circumference can be widened only by self-forgetfulness, surprise, loss of memory and—most crucially—by doing something (does he mean anything, just anything?), something without knowing how we do it or why it is done. A motiveless act is one thing; we do much that is not malignant, much indeed positively be-

in the sense of augury but in the sense of gaining immortality, in becoming a god. The making that is poetry is god-making, and even the ephebe or starting-poet is already as much daimon as man or woman. Emerson quotes Empedocles in this context, as approvingly as Yeats does, but with a little more self-referential irony. Yet the whole quotation, which Emerson does not give, must have alarmed him, for the daimonic in the shamanistic Empedocles is much starker than in Emerson's favorite Neoplatonic visionary, Proclus, whose daimons are benign interpreters between gods and men. But the same Empedocles who proudly says "I go about among you an immortal god, no mortal now, honored . . . crowned with . . . flowery garlands" is also the tormented consciousness of the great fragment 115, which I shall quote entire, to show the large range of sorrow upon which Emerson had opened:

There is an oracle of Necessity, an ancient ordinance of the gods, eternal and sealed fast by broad oaths, that whenever one of the daemons, whose portion is length of days, has sinfully polluted his hands with blood, or followed strife and forsworn himself, he must wander thrice ten thousand seasons from the abodes of the blessed, being born throughout the time in all manners of mortal forms, changing one toilsome path of life for another. For the mighty Air drives him into the Sea, and the Sea spews him forth on the dry Earth; Earth tosses him into the beams of the blazing Sun, and he flings him back to the eddies of Air. One takes him from the other, and all reject him. One of these I now am, an exile and a wanderer from the gods, for that I put my *trust* in insensate strife.

The actual Empedocles is thus already an authentic High Romantic ruined quester, closer to Manfred than he is to Matthew Arnold's tiresome worrier, and closest of all to Byron and Shelley themselves, and to their greatest fictive descendant, Browning's Childe Roland. Emerson, though, is an Empedocles-in-dialectical-reversal, a happy pilgrim whose

daimonic drive irradiates every Dark Tower he astonishingly
bypasses, almost indeed a Buster Keaton in his amazing sur-
vivals that thread through what ought to be the destructive
labyrinths of the self. Yet, as quester, he is the Don rather
than Sancho, most Faustian where he is most amiable. Is it
then Emerson's outrageous accomplishment so to have purified Romanticism or internalized quest that it loses all its
Empedoclean and Byronic hazard and sorrow? Can one surrender the darkness of the daimonic ground and yet retain its
enchantment? We know that Hawthorne, Emerson's uneasy
neighbor and walking companion, rather resentfully thought
otherwise, and that *his* friend Melville satirized Emerson as
only another Confidence Man, or as the Plotinus Plinlimmon
whose abstractions drained life of its vitality as much as of its
suffering. Emerson—to them—for all his uncanny greatness
remained the sophist of the visionary lie, the poet of ideas
who blandly sought—in Dickinson's terms—to know the
transport without the pain. Any American—for we are still,
in our accursedness, Emerson's contemporaries and his involuntary disciples—needs to ask of this central American
sage: "How can you hope to teach us to purify our selves and
lives without teaching us some, any, mode of purgation? How
can you urge us to daimonic expansion, from the Soul to the
Oversoul, without our becoming what Stevens so bitterly calls
"The Rabbit as King of the Ghosts," a giant of consciousness
utterly devoid of any being whatsoever? What do you offer
us which we do not already possess in quantities rather too
large for our own exasperated good?"

I think that Emerson more than answers these questions,
by making us see what it is in us that persists in asking them,
and I will turn to the essay "Circles" again for demonstration, but first I ask the indulgence of a personal excursus.
Whatever Romanticism *is*—and I am convinced it *is* now
what it has been for at least the past two hundred years—I

am certain it is not a Napoleonic obsession with titanic forms, and not a subtle, charming shrug that says "This is not the place, this not the time and you—there confronting me—you are not the person for me, nor am I the person for you." The Titanic form and the diffident ironist are not even the diseases of Romanticism, but symptoms of that greater malady Romanticism came hoping to heal. Romanticism, even in its most remorseless protagonists, is centrally a humanism, which seeks our renewal as makers, which hopes to give us the immodest hope that we—even we—coming so late in time's injustices can still sing a song of ourselves. Despite all its studying of the nostalgias, the high song that is Romanticism persists in saying: "Nothing need be lost—nothing is lost—if we will learn to listen again, and with the ear of the mind too, to see into the life of things and to see with the eye of the mind, to touch without self-appropriation." We live, of course, amid a parody of this high song. We are now afflicted—more than we need be—by what masquerades as a new sensibility or consciousness but is only another exhausted sentimentality, a pseudo-shamanism, indeed what Blake prophesied accurately as a revival of what he sardonically called Druidism, a virulent natural religion exalting what Blake ironically termed "The selfish virtues of the natural heart." Our baffled younger questers who go apart peculiarly assert their discipleship to Blake, or to Emerson's one surly follower who was also a genius in his own stance and right, Thoreau, whose one consistent teaching was the Emersonian insistence upon continuous intellectual effort.

The last line of Emerson's verse-epigraph to "Circles" speaks of a new genesis that would be here, could we but know the full dimensions of our perceptions, our scanning of nature's sphere. Throughout, Emerson speaks for Blake's prolific half of the contraries, for outwardly pulsating energy which makes a new idea of reason with each fresh circumfer-

ence. "Every action admits of being outdone," he insists, and
again: "There is no outside, no inclosing wall, no circumference to us." This denial of Necessity, of the contrary that
Blake calls the Devourer, reaches the moral extreme of in-
sisting that "The only sin is limitation." And even natural
context must yield to influx, as it does in a fine sentence that
reverberates throughout Dickinson: "The natural world may
be conceived of as a system of concentric circles, and we now
and then detect in nature slight dislocations which apprise
us that this surface on which we now stand is not fixed, but
sliding." In Dickinson's terms, we have gone out upon Circumference, but Emerson betrays not the slightest sign of her
wariness of our risk. Why is it that no plank in precarious
fresh reason can give way for the Concord rhapsode; why does
he not fear that we may fall through, as so many of us certainly will—indeed as we certainly must—in fact as we certainly do? An extraordinarily cunning brief paragraph answers
us, and needs as much pondering as we can bring to it:

> Yet this incessant movement and progression which all things
> partake could never become sensible to us but by contrast to
> some principle of fixture or stability in the soul. Whilst the
> eternal generation of circles proceeds, the eternal generator
> abides. That central life is somewhat superior to creation,
> superior to knowledge and thought, and contains all its circles.
> Forever it labors to create a life and thought as large and excel-
> lent as itself, but in vain, for that which is made instructs how
> to make a better.

We could—after reading this—burst out as did the elder
Henry James, who loved Emerson yet who understandably
protested: "O you man without a handle!" But even a moder-
ately close reading gives us handle enough, and tells us
plainly the central truth within ourselves that the earlier or
primary Emerson insists we learn and acknowledge. The
soul stands sure, if it stands at all; there is a substance in us

that prevails, because it always was. No more was it ever made than God was made. How does it manifest itself to us? We know the flux and outward move of our boundaries because there is a place surely enough fixed within us that we can take firm stance. At the center of us is a divinity that hopes to look upon its makings and find them good, but that will be frustrated only because the mind in creation is not—as Shelley skeptically conceived—like a fading coal, but more like Isaiah's and Blake's expanding furnace, which teaches itself to go beyond itself. Isaiah would have recoiled from Emerson's paradox, but Blake expresses the same celebratory fury many times. The circles of creation emanate out from the Merkabah's or Divine Chariot's fire-bursts, but the vehicular form of divinity, as Blake oddly calls it, is not itself affected. At the center of Emerson's central mind is a point where no change can come, but this point is not in itself a final excellence or central truth. It will and must be bettered, not by what it makes, but by what comes after, that is, by what its own creation will teach to successors. This vision of Emerson's is not so much difficult as it is frustrating, for it leaves us asking: "What are *we* to do when *we* must choose? Do we abandon the fixed point, the soul's stability, and go with our own creation, to see what fresh excellence it will instruct into existence, or do we abide where our stance abides, secure and snug while our naked conceptions live and die in the world of what is becoming?" Just here, I am afraid, is where Emerson's answerings stop, and his Yankee caution inherits. He will not say, unlike Blake or Shelley, Nietzsche and Pater and Yeats, indeed unlike his disciples Thoreau and Whitman, all of whom in very different but parallel ways would send us out from our fixed souls and into a freedom they found terrible but necessary. Emerson is not a Trimmer, and he does not grow suddenly silent. Like Wordsworth, he has anchored upon a "possible sublimity," upon "something ever more about to be," upon a final step not quite taken. Why then are his answerings true answers? Nietzsche, who loved Emerson and scorned Carlyle, denied that Emerson gave answers at all. His best and funniest comment on Emerson can help us here. He wrote, in his "Twilight of The Idols":

Emerson has that gracious and clever cheerfulness which discourages all seriousness; he simply does not know how old he is already, and how young he is still going to be; he could say of himself, quoting Lope de Vega: "I am my own heir." His spirit always finds reasons for being satisfied and even grateful; and at times he touches on the cheerful transcendency of the worthy gentleman who returned from an amorous rendezvous, as if he had accomplished his mission. "Though the power is lacking," he said gratefully, "the lust is nevertheless praiseworthy."

Potency is indeed the point at issue, for I take "Power" to be Emerson's key term. Either he opens us to more power in ourselves, or he is a cheerful and charming self-deceiver, and hardly the dangerous deceiver of others that Winters, sincere apostle of moral virtue, found him to be. The answer, and his answer, I judge to be in the formula: "opening towards power." The power is in him all right, as it is in you; he tells you it is there, tells you how to open yourself to it, and then abandons you either to abandon it yourself, or somehow, anyhow, decide what to do with it, while he quests off to his later, darker broodings about Fate and Necessity. He finds you simmering, brings you to a boil, but does not stay to make the coffee. Freud also passes beyond the Pleasure Principle to the confrontation with Ananke, Necessity, the Reality Principle, but Freud is a much firmer moralist, and achieves some useful balancings in his comments on the Pleasure Principle. Emerson, like all true questers, cares about the journeying and not the goal. Childe Roland, after a lifetime spent training for the sight, cannot see the Dark

Tower until it is upon him. Emerson would not even see *then* that it *was* dark, and would bustle by cheerful and unharmed.

Yet his disciples, coming after him, have come to their griefs there one by one, from Whitman on to Hart Crane, Roethke, and our immediate contemporaries. Thoreau, whose Journals are not exactly heaped with praise of his fellow men, said there that his relation with Emerson was one long tragedy, but grudgingly added that: "There is no such general critic of men and things, no such trustworthy and faithful man. More of the divine realized in him than in any. A poetic critic, reserving the unqualified nouns for the gods."

What *is* this more of the realized divine that even the embittered Thoreau had to acknowledge? I return for a last time to "Circles." Emerson, stable at his own center, observes the farthest circumferences emanating out from him, rejoices that they will lead someone on out to a perfection greater than his own, and then hunkers down cheerfully in his center. This is an awfully canny godhood, but at least is *is* transparent to itself. And there I locate the final clue, in this transparency, this sense that all things have stopped revolving except in crystal, to adapt a highly Emersonian line of Stevens. I venture the generalization that Emersonian Transcendentalism is not a transcendence at all, but is the program of attaining this transparency, which is the peculiarly American mode of the Romantic epiphany or privileged moment. Immanence and transcendence are both spatial concepts; the Divine is either *in* the world or above and *over* the world, but the Emersonian transparency gives us the Divine as being found *through* the world, which is not a spatial category at all, but discontinuous in the extreme, and as much an ebbing out as a flowing in, as Whitman, Hart Crane, and their compeers discovered.

ᴜut I will not leave our father Emerson there, happily circulating like his own Uriel in his own bright and transparent cloud, while chuckling—in what became the mode of his disciple Frost—that "Evil will bless and ice will burn." His conscious glory was solipsistic and to some degree self-castrating; his greater glories came unconsciously and where they had to, even for him: in his sorrows, personal and intellectual. The later Emerson moves from the High Romanticism of *Nature*, "Self-Reliance," and "Circles" through the growing skepticism of "Experience" and *Representative Men* on to the extraordinary worship of the serpent Ananke in *The Conduct of Life*, particularly in its three great essays— "Illusions," "Power," and the devastating "Fate." This Emerson has abandoned the American Romanticism that he invented, and gives us instead a demonic parody of Romantic hopefulness. No new genesis is here, but only the most ancient of entropies, as Emerson—in spite of himself—at last becomes Browning's Childe Roland, who at the Dark Tower calls what comes to claim him by the dread name of Necessity. Only a decade after writing "Circles," he writes the essay "Fate," and we witness again what Shelley—brooding on Wordsworth and Coleridge while tracing the exemplary destiny of Rousseau—grimly called "The Triumph of Life." After the transparency, the spectral shadowing; after the celestial light, the colder light of common day. "Circles" had said: "Men cease to interest us when we find their limitations. The only sin is limitation." To which "Fate" replies as follows:

Let us build altars to the Beautiful Necessity, which secures that all is made of one piece; that plaintiff and defendant, friend and enemy, animal and planet, food and eater are of one kind. . . . Why should we fear to be crushed by savage elements, we who are made up of the same elements?

No—I want to reply, as Blake did to Wordsworth—you shall not bring me down to such fitting and being fitted, I

will not join you in building altars to the Beautiful Necessity, which you of all men should not be doing in any case.
If the daimon was your destiny, then you should have followed him out to the farthest rings of the circumferences he
drew for you, since you knew better than I that the transparency is most absolute out there, where no Necessity can
come. But I do not make this reply, because I am haunted by
a Journal entry that Emerson had made a few years before,
shortly after the death of his greatly loved five-year-old son,
Waldo. The true Emersonian dialectic of imaginative autonomy as against Necessity, of transparency as against enforced
opaqueness, is in this journal passage. I close this essay by
quoting it, without final comment, as the epitome of the
glory and sorrows of Emerson, and of our American Romanticism, wildest and freest at last, most a giant of the imagination where it most confronts its own dwarf of disintegration.
Emerson writes:

In short, there ought to be no such thing as Fate. As long as
we use this word, it is a sign of our impotence and that we are
not yet ourselves. There is now a sublime revelation in each of
us which makes us so strangely aware and certain of our riches
that although I have never since I was born for so much as one
moment expressed the truth, and although I have never heard
the expression of it from any other, I know that the whole is here,
—the wealth of the Universe is for me, everything is explicable
and practicable for me. And yet whilst I adore this ineffable
life which is at my heart, it will not condescend to gossip with
me, it will not announce to me any particulars of science, it will
not enter into the details of my biography, and say to me why
I have a son and daughters born to me, or why my son dies in his
sixth year of joy. Herein, then, I have this latent omniscience
coexistent with omni-ignorance. Moreover, whilst this Deity
glows at the heart, and by his unlimited presentiments gives me
all Power, I know that tomorrow will be as this day, I am a
dwarf, and I remain a dwarf. That is to say, I believe in Fate.
As long as I am weak, I shall talk of Fate; whenever the God
fills me with his fulness, I shall see the disappearance of Fate.

I am *Defeated* all the time; yet to Victory I am born.

III

CONTINUITIES

ROGER SHATTUCK

This Must Be the Place:
From Wordsworth to Proust

In the 1814 Preface to *The Excursion,* Wordsworth quotes from an unpublished section of the same poem. The lines make plain statement of his subject: himself. He will be his own case history.

> For I must tread on shadowy ground, must sink
> Deep—and, aloft ascending, breathe in worlds
> To which the heaven of heavens is but a veil.
> All strength—all terror, single or in bands,
> That ever was put forth in personal form—
> Jehovah—with his thunder, and the choir
> Of shouting Angels, and the empyreal thrones—
> I pass them unalarmed. Not Chaos, not
> The darkest pit of lowest Erebus,
> Nor aught of blinder vacancy, scooped out
> By help of dreams—can breed such fear and awe
> As fall upon us often when we look
> Into our Minds, into the Mind of Man—
> My haunt, and the main region of my song.

These are also the lines that afflicted another William, William Blake, so seriously we are told that they gave him a bowel complaint of which he nearly died.[1] Could there be

1. Helen Darbishire, *The Poet Wordsworth* (Oxford: Clarendon Press, 1958), p. 139.

any more blatant declaration of arrogance and pride before Jehovah? To explain the "unexampled opposition" that met Mr. Wordsworth's writings, Coleridge had to work out a footnoted psychological theory about "a state of mind, which is the direct *antithesis* of that, which takes place when we make a bull." In other words, Wordsworth threw into jeopardy certain "opinions of long continuance."[2] Our opposition to, or partial neglect of, Wordsworth today springs from our sense of his didactic purpose, our insensitivity to his diction and the novelty of it, and his pastoral tone. If we really did detect in him some of the defects Coleridge taxes him with later on in the *Biographia Literaria* (pp. 216–224), like "disharmony of style," "matter-of-factness," and "eddying of thought," we would probably rate him a great modern and a precursor of Eliot and Pound. Two hundred years after Wordsworth came into this world trailing the clouds of glory he noticed later, it is a special task to read him.

I propose to speak of a few elementary and elemental aspects of Wordsworth's verse, confining myself almost entirely to *The Prelude,* the *Ode on Intimations of Immortality* and the *Lines Composed above Tintern Abbey*. It is primarily the first, a posthumous book-length poem written between 1795 and 1805, revised intermittently until his death, that will permit me to compare Wordsworth to Marcel Proust.

The Prelude is a mammoth hybrid. It presents itself as a letter to a dear friend—Coleridge. It served as a kind of professional time-step to fill vacant intervals when other poets might have done translations or written prose. It offers a tapestry of detachable lyrics and odes. And it narrates in careful, deliberate discourse "the history of a Poet's mind." As a letter, it rings hollow. The time-step served its purpose admirably. The detachable parts are superb and are therefore

2. Samuel Coleridge, *Biographia Literaria* (London: Dent; New York: E. P. Dutton, 1906), pp. 36–37.

usually read without the connective tissue. The autobiographical story seems remote and inflated without the lyric break-
throughs, yet it displays a sturdier structure than one suspects
at first.

After an elaborate and self-conscious introduction, Book I
of *The Prelude* and two-thirds of Book II depict in vivid and
direct terms what Wordsworth calls "this infant sensibility"
(II. 270)—"scenes which were a witness of that joy," "did
become / Habitually dear," and "Were fastened to the affec-
tions" (I. 599–612). Then, through ten books and probably
twelve years, he traces a gradual falling off of the pristine
communion with Nature. First it is only "a trouble" in his
mind (II. 276); later, "imagination slept" (III. 257); then a
"deep vacation" (III. 509)—though always with assurances
that he has not lost his powers. Throughout the books about
the years in Cambridge and London and the two trips to
France, an intermittent light of reminiscence and passionate
inwardness keeps the spirit alive in this "loiterer" (III. 578)
whose "thoughts by slow gradations had been drawn / To
human-kind" (VIII. 677–678). However, as we learn in the
twelfth book, "the degradation . . . was transient . . . I
shook the habit off / Entirely and for ever, and again / In
Nature's presence stood, as . . . a *creative* soul" (193–207).
This affirmation is followed by a new burst of early memories,
the famous "spots of time" passage, and the truly majestic
strains of the two closing books.

The most fundamental thing to observe about this poem of
a poet's progress back to his infant sensibility is also the most
evident: the poet's decisive experiences arise from and direct
their power not toward people or works of art or historic
occasions, but toward a sense of place, or of "scene" as Wordsworth often preferred to say, much to Coleridge's disgust.[3]
The best of Wordsworth's poetry is always what Dr. Johnson

3. *Ibid.,* p. 203 n.

would have called "local poetry." Even the discursive sonnets and the later poems carry a sense of situation, like Socrates in the *Phaedrus* strolling along the banks of the Ilissus, or the Savoyard priest making his profession of faith to Emile against the carefully described Alpine backdrop of mountains, lake, forest, and light effects.

But Wordsworth's sense of place has its peculiar powers. The scenes he prefers are unpeopled, except perhaps by his own alter ego in the form of a lone stranger. There is little need to point to the poems in which the poet communes alone with the presence of Nature; this in the heart of Wordsworth. But he can also describe the gaiety and bustle of a rustic fair, and then, in a line, hold it off in a frame in order to establish the attitude of contemplation most natural to him. After fifty colorful lines about the fair, a period, a dash, and then this:

> Immense
> Is the recess, the circumambient world
> Magnificent, by which they are embraced.   (VIII. 55–57)

"Recess" is precisely the word to describe the area Wordsworth hollows out in space, and in time, and in the world of men.

His handling of place partakes of a further and probably subtler element that I cannot develop here, yet which forms one of the most alluring aspects of his work. We know that Wordsworth composed not at a desk but on foot, peripatetically, either pacing up and down a path or covering as much as thirty miles of countryside in a day. De Quincey estimates that in his lifetime Wordsworth "must have traversed a distance of 175,000 to 180,000 English miles—a mode of exertion which, to him, stood in stead of alcohol and all other stimulants whatsoever to the animal spirits; to which, indeed, he was indebted for a life of unclouded happiness, and we for

much of what is most excellent in his writings." [4] I suspect
that one could trace a connection between the diction of his
blank verse and the rhythm of walking, as is true also of
Rousseau's and Rimbaud's poetic prose. And the innner contour of his longer poems, particularly *The Prelude,* follows
that of the journey or *journée*—distance steadily covered, in-
terrupted by long pauses for the major sites and scenes of
landscape, inner and outer.

But Wordsworth's reaction to place is by no means uniform
or simple. It is remarkably easy to read right over his earliest
emotion, even though he takes pains to describe it. In his
walks and encounters as a child, particularly at night of
course, he feels fear. But it was not the dark alone he was
afraid of. "Many times," he says in a note, "while going to
school have I grasped at a wall or tree to recall myself from
this abyss of idealism to the reality. At that time I was afraid
of such processes" (note to *Ode on Intimations of Immortality*). *The Prelude* is equally explicit in the first book. "I grew
up / Fostered alike by beauty and by fear" (I. 301–302). The
first and third childhood incidents he relates turn on the sensation of something ominous coming after him. But with time,
fear yields to a more rewarding and elevating emotion; in
Tintern Abbey he describes what he has felt as:

> . . . a sense sublime
> Of something far more deeply interfused,
> Whose dwelling is the light of setting suns,
> And the round ocean and the living air,
> And the blue sky, and in the mind of man;
> A motion and a spirit, that impels
> All thinking things, all objects of all thought,
> And rolls through all things. (95–102)

These lines preesnt a condensed version of what he extends to
a hundred lines in the gorgeous description of the ascent of

4. Thomas De Quincey, *Recollections of the Lake Poets,* ed. Edward
Sackville-West (London: John Lehman, 1948), p. 118.

Mt. Snowden at the end of *The Prelude,* a scene which he
recreates as "the emblem of a mind / That feeds upon infinity" (XIV. 70–71). The closeness with which this passage repli-
cates Petrarch's account of his ascent of Mont Ventoux marks
them as belonging to one of the *topoi* of modern sensibility.

I find the key to these solitary experiences in two places: in
what we might call Wordsworth's two bad trips in *The Prelude,* and in his refrainlike use of certain lexical forms. The
opening of *The Prelude* describes Wordsworth's thoughts
during a walk from Bristol to Racedown to inspect the lodge
where he and Dorothy would soon move, for almost a year,
after six bleak months in London. The new freedom of the
country has given him "a renovated spirit" (I. 53). Yet when
in midafternoon he tries to find some communion with
Nature, he has to acknowledge defeat:

> It was a splendid evening, and my soul
> Once more made trial of her strength, nor lacked
> Æolian visitations; but the harp
> Was soon defrauded.   (I. 94–97)

The moment of insight does not come. The poem begins with
a gently accepted failure. Five books later he has a much
worse trip on Lake Como. He and his walking companion,
Robert Jones, apparently misunderstood the Swiss church
bells which ring up to twenty-four in that locality, got up
far too early, set out in pitch dark, and lost their way in the
woods. They waited hours for the sunrise, and wondered if
they had been "ensnared by witchcraft" (VI. 709):

> At last we stretched our weary limbs for sleep,
> But *could not* sleep, tormented by the stings
> Of insects, which, with noise like that of noon
> Filled all the woods.   (VI. 710–713)

It is the most human moment in Wordsworth, his tiny signa-
ture in a corner of the edifice. In both these scenes, the cur-

rent of imagination and communication is just not on, with or without bugs. What that current is I look for behind a cluster of verb forms that sprinkle the opening pages of *The Prelude*. Referring to the Soul that is "the eternity of thought," he writes:

> not in vain
> By day or star-light thus from my first dawn
> Of childhood didst thou intertwine for me
> The passions that build up our human soul.
>
> (I. 404–407)

Intertwine yields interfuse, yields intercourse (cf. I. 346: "Regrets, vexations, lassitudes interfused"): "In solitude, such intercourse was mine" (I. 422): "I held unconscious intercourse with beauty" (I. 562). The mingling of elements, whether during nighttime ice skating or daytime kite-flying, depends essentially on a particular identified and remembered *place* as the median between the poet's self and universal organic Nature, always capitalized. Again, the vocabulary makes its own acknowledgment: bond, relation linked (III. 130). The sense of communion with the world never comes upon him alone in his study; the visible properties must be spread before him, even if furled in suggestive mist. When they are in place, they can "almost make remotest infancy / A visible scene . . . " (I. 634–635). The vividness of these scenes reaches so great a degree of intensity that he claims them as his own creation:

> I had a world about me—'twas my own;
> I made it, for it only lived to me,
> And to the God who sees into the heart.   (III. 141–143)

Here is the ultimate statement. The complete act of beholding corresponds to independent creation.

Why then, since we spend our lives moving among "objects that endure" and through scenes that might give us this ex-

perience, why does it so seldom happen? Why don't we live in
constant ecstasy just by dint of being alive and in the world?
Because we could not stand it, and because other things forever distract us from our "infant sensibility." Here I find the
explanation of what Wordsworth means when he opens *The
Prelude* talking about a "gift."

> Dear Liberty! Yet what would it avail
> But for a gift that consecrates the joy?   (I. 31–32)

When he comes back to it, several books later, each poet has
"heaven's gift,"

> a sense that fits him to perceive
> Objects unseen before . . .   (XIII. 304–305)

Because the exposition and explanation of that gift cover so
many pages, we may tend to think that Wordsworth is speaking of a very complex, almost ineffable quality. But thanks to
the faithful De Quincey we have another down-to-earth
account of it. One dark night Wordsworth put his ear to the
ground several times to listen for the mail coach he and
De Quincey were waiting for. Just as he got up and relaxed
his attention, a "bright star . . . fell suddenly upon my eye,
and penetrated my capacity of apprehension with a pathos
and a sense of infinite, that would not have arrested me under
other circumstances." [5] Across the years, I would surmise,
Wordsworth had developed, even practiced, a knack, a quirk
of mind. There is a kind of noticing so forceful that the object noticed appears to move. In this case, the star "fell."
De Quincey had the insight to link this vivid nocturnal ap-
perception with the celebrated section of the fifth book of
The Prelude, "There Was a Boy." It is too tight and delicate
a passage to quote just a fragment of it. The boy, while mim-
icking owls and listening for their response, suddenly perceives the scene before him and receives it into his heart as

5. *Recollections of the Lake Poets,* p. 144.

it is received "into the bosom of the steady lake." To notice is not a passive but rather an excitingly active and reciprocal process. It entails motion and surprise, even shock.

The "gift" of which Wordsworth often speaks is more precise than a general poetic bent. As I read the texts, he meant a kind of psychological or metaphysical squint, an attentiveness formed of physical energy and of dreaminess. To notice was for him an act of imagination: forming an image so strong and integral it transformed the world and left his companions thinking of him as rather mad (III. 146).

The consequence of Wordsworth's powerful sense of place, and of his psychic alertness, was the feeling of rugged self-sufficiency conveyed by his poetry, especially by the works in blank verse. This peasant of the imagination, during his long marches back and forth across England and France, has retrieved his childhood and gained some measure of self-understanding. Except when he speaks briefly of Chaucer (III. 276), comedy does not furnish a dimension for this work of steady affirmation. His sense of belonging to his own sensibility is so strong and steady that we begin to accept his definition of poetry as "the spontaneous overflow of powerful feelings." Over this sturdy dam spilled in a steady stream the words that portray his mind seated directly in front of Nature.

One of the most remarkable intellectual results of that interchange, that intercourse, is his refusal to separate the faculties of mind. In the fifth book of *The Prelude* Wordsworth refers to

> all the meditations of mankind,
> Yea, all the adamantine holds of truth
> By reason built, or passion, which itself
> Is highest reason in a soul sublime. (V. 38–41)

Later he will speak of imagination as "Reason in her most exalted mood" (XIV. 192). In the final coda-invocation addressed to Man and anticipating the closing lines of *The Prelude* which exalt the mind of Man as approaching the divine, Wordsworth afirms an undissociated sensibility or consciousness: "feeling intellect" he calls it. At the opening of the *Confessions,* Rousseau makes the simple yet presumptuous claim, "Je sens mon âme." "I feel my soul." In the low-keyed, slow-pulsing lines of *The Prelude,* Wordsworth makes the same claim with a more massive calmness than the Frenchman could summon.

Climbing Snowden at the end of *The Prelude,* the poet again describes his psychic squint. It happens just as he emerges from the clouds and catches the outspread world and himself in one lingering glance. Notice the first verb:

> For instantly a light upon the turf
> Fell like a flash, and lo! as I looked up
> The Moon hung naked in a firmament.   (XIV. 38–40)

The sense of self-and-site-together that always *falls* upon him in these moments is the feeling I have tried to describe with the trite and even jocular words of my title: "This must be the place."

The distance between Wordsworth and Proust seems very great, more than a matter of chronology. Wordsworth is all directness and nakedness. Proust reaches reality, and himself, only through an elaborate feint. Things do not interfuse; they interfere. What is starkly absent in Wordsworth fills Proust's universe. The bulk of his novel develops around three un-Wordsworthian themes: the idolatries of love, of social success or prestige, and of art. Yet there are considerations which provide the basis for a fruitful comparison and which may help to display the vitality of Romanticism. When Wordsworth writes, "There are in our existence spots of time" (XII. 208), he has provided the precise translation for Proust's term *pan.* Until resuscitated by the *madeleine,* Combray, Marcel's landscape of childhood, was reduced to a *pan lumineux.* He uses the *pan* as a heightened synonym for *impression,* the element out of which we construct consciousness by a kind of inner optics. Wordsworth's phrasing is simpler and briefer: "Nature spake to me / Rememberable things" (I. 587–588). Both Wordsworth and Proust faced toward their childhood as they moved backward toward the future.

But the principal parallel that could be drawn between them is the way in which they trace through a lengthy work of alternating incident and reflection, the development of a single sensibility, their own. In each case, what holds the massive work together is a tripartite structure: the sonata form, *ABC(A).* *A* is the world lying about them "apparelled in celestial light" in childhood: in *Remembrance of Things Past,* the place and the mood of Combray; in *The Prelude,* "those hallowed and pure motions of the sense" (I. 551) which compose the first two books. *B* is the long middle section of the sensibility gone astray—Marcel pursuing Gilberte's elusive person, or the equally elusive, and fictive, secret to the Guermantes noble name; Wordsworth stumbling from Cambridge to the continent to London and knowing that within him were dwindling gradually the "Dear native Regions" (VIII. 468) that alone could nurture his gift. Then *C* (in both cases resurrecting *A*): time recaptured, the world beheld afresh from on high—Wordsworth's Snowden, Proust's stilts of time. This large-scale tidal movement of the action, as well as their length, gives the books a similar narrative feeling.

But the terms in which I have tried to approach Wordsworth will also serve to make certain revelations about the author of *A la recherche du temps perdu.* Let us take a look at Proust's sense of place. Proust never to my knowledge either read Wordsworth or mentioned him. But the literary

links can be established if need be. He went out of his way
to praise George Eliot, and the two pages in the *Mill on the
Floss* that he said could make him cry [6] must be those at the
end of the first book dealing with the experiences of childhood—possibly the elderberry bush. Recently we have
learned of a Proust text about a profoundly Romantic author
whose reactions to landscape are very close to Wordsworth's:
Senancour. In 1919, when most of his novel had been written,
Proust began some notes for an article by exclaiming: "Senancour, c'est moi. Rêverie morale inspirée par la nature."—
"Senancour is myself. 'Moral' daydreams inspired by nature." [7] But the outburst, coming so late in Proust's career, is
deceptive. In *Remembrance of Things Past,* the meditations
in a natural setting decrease markedly after Marcel's visit to
Balbec; Paris apartments and *salons* replace landscape and
countryside. The last two-thirds of the novel presents scenes
which are as significant as Wordsworth's, but they differ in
two ways. They are interiors, and they display not the dur-
able objects of Nature but the metamorphoses of men. The
last exterior in Proust comes only a few pages before the
ultimate *matinée chez la princesse de Guermantes* which will
transform everything. Marcel's train stops in the countryside
next to a line of obliquely lit trees, and he reports his thought
in direct quotations: " 'Trees,' I thought, 'there's nothing
more you can say to me, my chilly heart can no longer hear
you. Yet here I am in the very lap of nature. Well, I feel only
indifference and boredom when my eyes follow the line that
separates your illuminated forehead from your shadowy trunk.
If I could never before fully *believe* myself a poet, I now

6. Christopher Salvesen, *The Landscape of Memory* (London: Edward Arnold, 1965), p. 22; see also André Maurois, *A la recherche de
Marcel Proust* (Paris: Hachette, 1949), p. 29.

7. Marcel Proust, *Textes retrouvés* (Urbana: Univ. of Illinois Press,
1968), p. 51.

know that I am *not* one.' " [8] Landscape no longer serves. In this long meandering of the novel, the collection of vivid scenes originally kept by Marcel to slip more or less at will into his interior stereoscope has been subordinated to the characters of the action and absorbed by them. Albertine, the unknowable mixture of innocence and vice, stands in front of Balbec and contains it. Unlike the sense of permanence that accompanies Wordsworth's natural scenes, Proust's richly colored landscapes in Combray and Balbec fade into the background as the cast of characters moves forward. The most clearly etched scene of response to the sensuous mode of feeling occurs when Marcel, strolling near Combray, passes a little pond whose surface reflects the light effects on the tile roof of a shed. A chicken is perched there in a strong wind. The scene is both more fragile and more convincing than any description in Wordsworth. Marcel doesn't know what to do about the enthusiasm this glimpse of reality inspiries in him, except to brandish his umbrella and cry aloud, "Gosh, gosh, gosh" (in French, "Zut"; *RTP:* I, 155). Proust's comic effect is fully intended. But those "impressions" (he calls them precisely that and attaches great weight to the word) occur along a falling curve. In the last volume, when Marcel catches sight of the steeple of the Combray church, its strong emotive charge is contained and rechanneled by the fact that he sees it framed in the window of the room where he is a guest in Gilberte's house. People have interfered so much with landscape as to render it nearly invisible. Outward nature is little more than a memory.

The decline of landscape in Proust contrasts with the steadiness of that experience in *The Prelude*. The contrast may be explained in great part by the fact that the quirk of mind,

8. Marcel Proust, *A la recherche du temps perdu* (Paris: Gallimard [Pléiade], 1954), III, 855. Future references will be to this edition; translations are my own.

the metaphysical tic with which Proust had to live was markedly different from Wordsworth's trick of noticing things.

I am not referring to involuntary memory. That spasmodic doubling of consciousness in time gave Marcel a clue to the workings of his mind, but not the key to the moral content of his life. For that we must look elsewhere, in a theme that works its way increasingly into the texture of the action. In its earliest guise, it seems only a kind of poutiness or perverseness in a spoiled boy. In Combray, at an unspecified age less than ten, Marcel goes to Machiavellian extremes to lure his mother up to his bedroom to say good night to him when she should be down attending to her guests. The scene is justly celebrated, for it sets the novel in motion and provides the taproot of its later growth. Yet the close of the incident brings the most revealing moment. When finally his mother does come and is permitted by his father to compromise herself and her principles by spending the entire night in Marcel's room and reading him to sleep, then Marcel reverses himself. He cannot cope with so great success. "If I had dared to now, I would have said to maman: 'No, I don't really want you to, don't sleep here with me' " (*RTP:* I, 38). From this seed will grow a new tree of forbidden knowledge. In a letter to Princess Bibesco, he generalizes the same thought: "A sensation, no matter how disinterested it may be, a perfume, or an insight, if they are present, are still too much in my power to make me happy." [9] The novel develops this theme, or this mental setting, steadily and disturbingly. Toward the end of the almost tediously described evening when he has dined for the first time with the Duke and Duchess of Guermantes, Marcel has to take stock of his disappointment. This entry into the most elegant and inaccessible layers of society has not lived up to expectation. But he finds the explanation not

9. *Correspondance générale de Marcel Proust,* V (Paris: Plon, 1935), 142.

in those people but in himself: "Several times already I had wanted to leave, and more than for any other reason, because of the insignificance which my presence imposed on the party. . . . At least my departure would allow the guests, once rid of the interloper, to form a closed group. They would be able to begin the celebration of the mysteries" (*RTP:* II, 543). Because this is still a young debutant among the dowagers, we can laugh off such a moment as something like a failure in social depth perception. It should straighten out as Marcel makes his way and picks up experience. But by the last volume, he is looking to art itself to provide him with "other eyes" with which to behold the universe, for that would be the true fountain of youth (*RTP:* III, 258), or with other worlds, for our own is always so inconsequential (*RTP:* III, 896).

One further quotation will illuminate this particular twist. Marcel has just read and been deeply impressed by a (parodied) passage from the Goncourt brothers' journal describing many of the people he knows well, their houses, and their lives. And in the Goncourt version they all seem bathed in a prestigious light of historic and literary importance. In consequence, everything tumbles down again about his ears. How could he have gone so far astray as to consider the Verdurins a couple of mediocre bourgeois social climbers if they could inspire such artistic prose? "It amounted to wondering if all these people whom one regrets not having known (because Balzac described them in his books or dedicated his works to them in admiring homage, about whom Sainte-Beuve or Baudelaire wrote their loveliest verses), or even more if all the Recamiers and the Pompadours would not have struck me as insignificant characters, either because of some infirmity in my nature . . . or because they owed their prestige to an illusory magic belonging to literature" (*RTP:* III, 722–723). Once again, in context, the effect is in large part comic. Marcel paces about wondering just how far off base he has been. Either he has misjudged all the apparently tiresome and fraudulent people of fashion he has met, or else all those great historic figures may participate in this same inflation of the ordinary by literary processing. But just what does he mean when he refers to an "infirmité dans ma nature"? This, I believe, puts into our hands the end of the thread that will lead us to Marcel's and to Proust's quirky moral posture. But in order to follow it, I must make a digression.

Throughout the seventeenth and eighteenth centuries, in England and on the continent, the psychological investigations of men's motives concentrated on the theme of pride— the search for fame, for what was in French called *gloire*. La Rochefoucauld and La Bruyère keep *gloire* very much in the foreground. In a book called *Reflections on Human Nature,* Arthur Lovejoy plots the differing estimates of what he calls "approbativeness" or the quest for esteem in others' eyes. When Milton, in *Lycidas,* tells us that "Fame is the spur," and implies that the desire for fame is a socially beneficial infirmity, he is only echoing scores of his contemporaries, including Voltaire and Rousseau, Hume and Kant. This powerful heritage, which accepts human vanity or pride as the necessary motor of culture, the source of the fair edifices of civilization, still ran strong through the nineteenth century in the novels of Stendhal and Balzac, in the myth of the young man out to make his mark in the world, and even in the figure of the revolutionary.

Against this background of *gloire,* Proust's "infirmity in my nature" looks almost grotesque. Marcel cannot win, not so much because he lacks talent or looks, *but simply because he is Marcel*—his very presence discredits in his own eyes whatever he does. He has a real case. We laugh, and rightly so; after the most elaborate efforts he succeeds in winning what turns out to be valueless precisely because he has won it. The triumph is always empty. When, years after he first wanted to kiss Albertine, he is invited by her to do so, her complex and long desired image disintegrates, as his face approaches hers, into ten different Albertines, none of which belongs to her and none of which he desires. By a fatality that lodges in his bones or his name or his look, Marcel casts a pall wherever he goes. His situation is much like that of Pierre Bezukov in *War and Peace,* who carries with him everywhere a sense of uncertainty. When Pierre goes out to get a taste of action at the battle of Borodino, he keeps looking for the center of the battle, riding forward toward mysterious maneuvers. And Tolstoy finally gives the signal after Pierre, more or less at random, climbs up to Raevsky's Redoubt: "In line with the knoll on both sides stood other guns which also fired incessantly. A little behind the guns stood infantry. When ascending that knoll Pierre had no notion that this spot, on which small trenches had been dug and from which a few guns were firing, was the most important point of the battle. On the contrary, just because he happened to be there, he thought it one of the least significant parts of the field." [10] Pierre, in fact, even after the full heat of combat and after he has had to confront an enemy soldier face to face, never fully grasps that he has stood and fought in the very eye of the battle, in the decisive juncture not just for his own sense of reality but also for the whole historic engagement of Borodino. In this respect Tolstoy's scene is even more dramatic and ironic than Stendhal's picture of Fabrice wandering through the confusion of Waterloo.

It is not really surprising that the liveliest, coolest reckoning with this habit of self-deprecation should turn up, not in one of the so-called "moralists," but in the great, gnarled, live

10. Leo Tolstoy, *War and Peace,* trans. Louise and Aylmer Maude (London: Oxford Univ. Press, 1922–1923), III, 509.

oak of a writer we call Montaigne. In the first version of the essay "On Presumption," he speaks of the outward signs of vainglory and pride. And suddenly—it feels sudden when you read it—he inserts this chunk ten years later. He is close to sixty. Just listen, it is the true clinamen:

I feel oppressed by an *erreur d'âme* [error of soul or mind] which offends me both as unjust as even more as annoying. I try to correct it, but I cannot root it out. It is that I attach too little value to things I possess, just because I possess them; and over-value anything strange, absent, and not mine. This frame of mind extends very far. As the prerogative of authority leads men to regard their wives with monstrous disdain, and sometimes their children, so too am I afflicted. Whatever I am responsible for can never, as I see things, meet the competition. To an even greater degree, any desire for advancement and improvement clouds my judgment and closes off the path to satisfaction, just as mastery in itself breeds scorn of whatever one holds in one's power. Exotic societies, customs, and languages attract me, and I realize that the dignity of Latin impresses me more than it should, just as it does children and common folk. My neighbor's house, the way he runs his affairs, his horse, though no better than my own, are all worth more than mine precisely because they are not mine.[11]

In these words Montaigne is right on pitch, perfectly in tune with himself and with that human condition we all share with him. Here is the subtlest fault of all, and the most far-reaching; for it strikes at our very sense of reality. *Erreur d'âme* is his exact phrase. Florio and Cohen translate it as "error of the mind." Frame says an "error of my soul." But Montaigne does not use the genetive, *erreur de l'âme*. The French syntax implies substance, essential composition, as in the forms *état d'esprit,* or *chemin de fer.* The up-to-date English or American version would have to be *soul error:* the incapacity to give full status to one's own life and ex-

11. Montaigne, *Essais* (Paris: Gallimard [Pléiade], 1962), pp. 616–617; my own translation.

perience. It forms a kind of running metaphysical fiasco which Montaigne recognizes in order to oppose. This quiet southern gentleman who retired to a tower and devoted his life to writing about himself would seem to be the least self-deprecating of men. Yet it is still he who tells us: "It would be difficult for any man to have a poorer opinion of himself." [12]

Proust, our modern Montaigne, never shrank from the irony and the perverseness of soul error. It lurked in the air he breathed. Possession kills the mystery we desire to penetrate (*RTP:* I, 717). In self-defense, we seek an impossible perfection (*RTP:* II, 46), or the inaccessible (*RTP:* III, 385). When Marcel finally makes the journey to see the statue of the Virgin in the church of Balbec, at least half of his experience consists in disappointment. Everything we know is subject to what he calls "the tyranny of the Particular" (*RTP:* I, 660). The Particular, squarely encountered, casts itself loose from the image and the ideal with which we approached it. Often, that is more than we can take. And since we are, if we dare face ourselves, our own principal particular, we find ourselves very hard to take. If you follow what I am saying, if you can see through the eyes of Montaigne and Pierre Bezukov and Marcel, you will know why, wherever and whenever you are, this cannot be the place.

This grasp of soul error was Proust's mental quirk, the response to weakness which became his strength. And he had the astuteness to observe that there are variations in the condition, best dealt with by dividing the world into two parts: "She [the Princesse des Laumes, later the Duchesse de Guermantes] belonged to that half of humanity in whom the other half's curiosity about beings it does not know is replaced by interest in the beings it does know" (*RTP:* I, 335).

Now, in all this pursuit of soul error, am I talking about

12. *Ibid.,* p. 618.

anything more profound than a few proverbs about where
the grass always looks greener? Perhaps not. But proverbs
are surely not to be dismissed when they come forward at
the end of the journey offering the wisdom we have been toil-
ing toward all along. Raymond Radiguet talked about literature as a means to "déniaiser les lieux communs"—giving
meaning to common places, initiating them to the facts of
life, making a man out of a proverb. In the present context a
venerable saying takes on new life: Familiarity breeds contempt. In college stores a poster is on sale which carries these
words: "If nearness kills love, what hope is there for humanity (Sudborough)."

I think we are approaching two complementary definitions
of the old rascal, Romanticism. Proust's Romanticism arises
from metaphysical envy. A desire for anything truly other,
anything with beauty, with prestige, or with mystery, engaged his huge hunger to know. Anywhere out of the world.
His Don Juanism gave him a powerful sense of the mixture
of qualities that makes up the bulk of mankind.

The cumulative effect of Wordsworth, on the other hand,
and in particular of *The Prelude,* is the portrait of a consciousness resolved to assimilate its surroundings as a fully
sufficient expression of the universe, as the locus of a whole
life. Those surroundings are primarily pastoral, and in them
he retrieves the child's immediacy of response to Nature—
fear and wonder. In the "review of his own mind" as he calls
The Prelude, he states early on that he seeks to "fix the
wavering balance of my mind" (I. 622). Though it probably
infected Wordsworth's moods many times, the worm of self-
contempt is ultimately driven out. The inner sturdiness of
Wordsworth's mind, which accompanied his physical sturdiness, rested on this genuine sense of his own existence where
he was. He was a waterfall. He made his own stationary blast.

After Wordsworth, after Proust, *after our own experience*

without which Proust and Wordsworth would be lost monuments in the forest of culture, there are two statements we can make about where we are and about how we are. Just because we are here, and for no further reason, this cannot be the place. For the very same reason and no more, this must be the place.

PETER BROOKS

The Melodramatic Imagination:
The Example of Balzac and James

There is at the start of Balzac's novel *La Peau de chagrin* a passage which suggests how we should read Balzac, how he locates and creates his drama, and, more generally, what the melodramatic imagination is up to. When Raphaël de Valentin enters a gambling house to play roulette with his last franc, a shadowy figure crouched behind a counter rises up to ask for the young man's hat. The gesture of surrendering one's hat forthwith elicits a series of questions from the narrator:

Is this some scriptural and providential parable? Isn't it rather a way of concluding a diabolical contract by exacting from you a sort of security? Or may it be to oblige you to maintain a respectful demeanour toward those who are about to win your money? Is it the police, lurking in the sewers of society, trying to find out your hatter's name, or your own, and if you've inscribed it on the headband? Or is it, finally, to measure your skull in order to compile an instructive statistic on the cranial capacity of gamblers? [1]

The gestures of life call forth a series of interrogations aimed at discovering the meanings implicit in them. The narrative

1. Honoré de Balzac, *La Peau de chagrin*, in *La Comédie Humaine*, ed. Marcel Bouteron (Paris: Gallimard [Pléiade], 1955–56), I, 11–12. Subsequent references are to this edition, and will be given in the text. Translations are my own.

voice is not content to describe and record gesture, to see it simply as a figure in the interplay of people one with another. Rather, the narrator applies pressure to the gesture, pressure through interrogation, through the evocation of more and more fantastic possibilities, to make it yield meaning, to make it give up to consciousness its full potentialities as "parable."

Throughout these first pages of *La Peau de chagrin*, we can observe the narrator pressuring the surface of reality in order to make it yield the full, true terms of his story. In the face of the old man who takes the hat, says the narrator, we can read "the wretchedness of hospital wards, aimless wanderings of ruined men, inquests on countless suicides, life sentences at hard labor, exiles to penal colonies." The gambling house itself elicits a contrast between the "vulgar poetry" of its evening denizens and the "quivering passion" of daytime gamblers. The crowd of spectators is like the populace awaiting an execution at the Place de Grève. Finally we reach this comment: "Each of the spectators looked for a *drama* in the fate of this single gold piece, perhaps the final scene of a noble life."

Use of the word "drama" is authorized here by the kind of pressure which the narrator has exerted upon surface reality. We have in fact witnessed the creation of drama—of an excessive, hyperbolic, parabolic story—from the banal stuff of reality. States of being beyond the immediate context of the narrative, and in excess of it, have been brought to bear on it, to charge it with intenser significances. The narrative voice, with its grandiose questions and hypotheses, leads us in a movement through and beyond the surface of things to what lies behind, to the spiritual reality which is the true scene of the highly colored drama to be played out in the novel. We have entered into the drama of Raphaël's last gold piece; that coin has become the token of a super-drama involving life and death, perdition and redemption, heaven and hell, the force of desire caught in a death struggle with the life force. The novel is constantly tensed to catch this essential drama, to go beyond the surface of the real to the truer, hidden reality, to open up the world of spirit.

One could adduce a multitude of other examples. There is always a moment in Balzac's descriptions of the world where the eye's photographic registration of objects yields to the mind's effort to pierce surfaces, to interrogate appearances. In *Père Goriot,* after a few initial lines of description of Mlle. Michonneau, the narrator shifts into the interrogatory: "What acid had stripped this creature of her female forms? She must once have been pretty and well-built: was it vice, sorrow, greed? Had she loved too much, been a go-between or simply a courtesan? Was she expiating the triumphs of an insolent youth?" (II, 855). Reality is both the scene of drama for Balzac, and mask of the true drama, which lies behind, is mysterious, and can only be alluded to, questioned, then gradually elucidated. His drama is of the true, wrested from the real; the streets and walls of Paris under pressure of the narrator's insistence become the elements of a Dantesque vision, leading the reader into infernal circles: "as step by step daylight fades and the song of the guide goes hollow when the visitor descends into the Catacombs."

The same process may be observed in Balzac's dramatizations of human encounters: they tend toward intense, excessive representations of life which strip the façade of manners to reveal the essential conflicts at work, moments of symbolic confrontation which fully articulate the terms of the drama. In *Gobseck,* for instance, the sinning Comtesse de Restaud, struggling to preserve her fortune for her two illegitimate children, is caught in the act of trying to wrest her husband's secrets from the oldest son (the legitimate one) when the Count rises from his deathbed:

"Ah!" cried the Count, who had opened the door and appeared suddenly, almost naked, already as dried and shrivelled as a skeleton . . . "You watered my life with sorrows, and now you would trouble my death, pervert the mind of my son, turn him into a vicious person," he cried in a rasping voice.

The Countess threw herself at the feet of this dying man whom the last emotions of life made almost hideous and poured out her tears. "Pardon, pardon!" she cried.

"Had you any pity for me?" he asked. "I let you devour your fortune, now you want to devour mine, and ruin my son."

"All right, yes, no pity for me, be inflexible," she said. "But the children! Condemn your wife to live in a convent, I will obey; to expiate my faults toward you I will do all you command; but let the children live happily! Oh, the children, the children!"

"I have only one child," answered the Count stretching in a gesture of despair his shrivelled arm toward his son.   (II, 665)

I have deliberately chosen an extreme example here, and in quoting it out of its context, I run the risk of confirming the view, popularized by Martin Turnell and others, that Balzac is a popular melodramatist whose versions of life are cheap, overwrought and hollow. Balzac's use of hyperbolic figures, of lurid and grandiose events, masked relationships and disguised identities, abductions, slow-acting poisons, secret societies, mysterious parentage and other elements from the melodramatic repertory; and even more, his forcing of narrative voice to the breathless pitch of melodrama, his insistence that life be always seen through highly-colored lenses, have of course always been the object of critical attack. "His melodrama," Turnell comments, "reminds us not so much of Simenon or even Mrs. Christie as of the daily serial in the BBC's Light Programme." In his most waspish *Scrutiny* manner, Turnell adds: "it must be confessed that our experience in reading Balzac is not always very elevated and that his interests are by no means always those of the adult." [2]

2. Martin Turnell, *The Novel in France* (New York: Vintage, 1958), p. 220.

To the extent that the "interests of the adult" imply repression, sacrifice of the pleasure principle, and a refusal to
live beyond the quotidian, Turnell is right, but his rightness
misses the point of Balzac's drive to push *through* manners
to deeper sources of being. Such representations as the scene
I quoted from *Gobseck* are necessary culminations to the
kind of drama Balzac is trying to evoke. The progress of the
narrative elicits and authorizes such terminal articulations.
The scene represents a victory over repression, a climactic
moment at which the characters are able to confront one
another with full expressivity, to fix in large gestures the
meaning of their existences. As in the interrogations of *La
Peau de chagrin* we saw a desire to push through surfaces to a
"drama" in the realm of emotional and spiritual reality, so
in the scene from *Gobseck* we find a desire to make articulate
all that this family tragedy has come to be about.

This desire to express all seems a primary characteristic of
the melodramatic mode. Nothing is spared because nothing is
left unsaid; the characters stand on stage and utter the unspeakable, give voice to their deepest feelings, dramatize
through their heightened and polarized words and gestures
the whole lesson of their relationship. Life tends, in this fiction, toward ever more concentrated and totally expressive
gestures and statements. Raphaël de Valentin is given a lesson by the old antiques dealer, "Desire sets us afire and power
destroys us"—terms which reveal the true locus and the
stakes of his drama. Eugène de Rastignac, in *Père Goriot,* is
summoned to choose between Obedience, represented by the
family, and Revolt, represented by the outlaw Vautrin. The
metaphoric texture of the prose itself suggests polarization
into moral absolutes: Rastignac's "last tear of youth," shed
over Goriot's grave, from the earth where it falls "rebounds
up to heaven." The world is subsumed by an underlying
manichaeism, and the narrative creates the excitement of its

drama by putting us in touch with the conflict of good and evil played out under the surface of things—just as description of the surfaces of the modern metropolis pierces through to a mythological realm where the imagination can find a habitat for its play with large moral entities. If we consider the prevalence of hidden relationships and masked personages and occult powers in Balzac, we find that they derive from a sense that the novelist's true subject is hidden and masked—because the center of his interest and the scene of his drama is in fact what we might call the "moral occult," the domain of operative spiritual values which is both indicated within and masked by the surface of reality. The moral occult is not a metaphysical system; it is closer to unconscious mind: a sphere of being where our most basic desires and interdictions lie, a realm which in quotidian existence may appear closed off from us, but which we can get in touch with, must get in touch with since it is the realm of meaning and value. The melodramatic mode exists to locate and to articulate the moral occult.

I shall come back to these formulations. I want first to try to extend our understanding of the melodrama of manners, and the kinds of representations of social life that it gives. And I want to extend the argument beyond Balzac by calling upon his greatest admirer among subsequent novelists, Henry James. The melodramatic tenor of James's imagination was beautifully caught by his secretary, Theodora Bosanquet, when she wrote:

When he walked out of the refuge of his study into the world and looked about him, he saw a place of torment, where creatures of prey perpetually thrust their claws into the quivering flesh of the doomed, defenceless children of light.[3]

3. Theodora Bosanquet, *Henry James at Work* (London: Hogarth Press, 1924), p. 32. This passage is also cited by Leo B. Levy in *Versions of Melodrama: A Study of the Fiction and Drama of Henry James, 1865–1897* (Berkeley and Los Angeles: Univ. of California Press, 1957).

James's moral manichaeism is the basis of a vision in which the social world is made the scene of dramatic choice between heightened moral alternatives, where every gesture, no matter how frivolous or insignificant it may seem, is charged with the conflict between light and darkness, salvation and damnation—where people's destinies and choices of life seem finally to have little to do with practical realities of a situation, and much more to do with an intense drama in which consciousness must purge itself and assume the burden of moral sainthood. The theme of renunciation which sounds through James's novels—Isabel Archer's return to Gilbert Osmond, Strether's return to Woollett, Densher's rejection of Kate Croy—is incomprehensible and unjustifiable except as a victory within the realm of a moral occult which may be so inward and personal that it appears restricted to the individual consciousness, predicated on the individual's "sacrifice to the deal."

As Jacques Barzun has emphasized, James always creates a high degree of excitement from his dramatized moral dilemmas, partly because of his preoccupation with evil as a positive force ever menacing violent conflict and outburst.[4] Balzac did an apprenticeship in the *roman noir*, nourished himself from gothic novel and frenetic adventure story, and invented cops-and-robbers fiction. These are modes which insist that reality can be exciting, can be equal to the demands of the imagination, its play with large moral conflicts. With James, the same insistence has been further transposed into the drama of moral consciousness, so that excitement derives from characters' own dramatized apprehension of clashing moral forces. A famous sentence from the Preface to *Portrait of a Lady* suggests James's intent. He is describing Isabel's vigil of discovery, the night she sits up and makes

4. See Jacques Barzun, "Henry James Melodramatist," in *The Question of Henry James,* ed. F. W. Dupee (New York: Holt, 1945).

her mind move from discovery to discovery about Gilbert Osmond. "It is," says James, "a representation simply of her motionless *seeing,* and an attempt withal to make the mere still lucidity of her act as 'interesting' as the surprise of a caravan or the identification of a pirate." [5] The terms of reference in the adventure story are mocked; yet they remain the terms of reference: moral consciousness must be an adventure, its recognitions must be the stuff of a heightened drama.

The excitement and violence of the melodrama of consciousness are obviously and derivatively Balzacian in *The American.* Newman's initiation into the epistemology of good and evil is represented as a dark ancestral crime hidden beneath—and suggested by—the gilded surface of Faubourg Saint-Germain society: depths open beneath the well-guarded social image of the Bellegarde family; crisis is revelation of sin, and Newman's consciousness must expand to receive the lurid, flashing lights of melodrama. But even in James's latest and most subtle fiction—probably most of all in this fiction —the excitement of plot is generated exclusively from conflict within the realm of the moral occult. There is a pressure similar to Balzac's on the surface of things, to make reality yield the terms of the drama of this moral occult. To take deliberately a fairly low-keyed example, from *The Ambassadors:* following the revelation of Mme de Vionnet's relationship with Chad, Strether goes to pay her a final visit. He stands for the last time in her apartment:

From beyond this, and as from a great distance—beyond the court, beyond the *corps de logis* forming the front—came, as if excited and exciting, the vague voice of Paris. Strether had all along been subject to sudden gusts of fancy in connexion with such matters as these—odd starts of the historic sense, suppositions and divinations with no warrant but their intensity. Thus

5. *The Portrait of a Lady* (New York: Scribner's, 1922), I, xxi.

and so, on the eve of the great recorded dates, the days and nights of revolution, the sounds had come in, the omens, the beginnings broken out. They were the smell of revolution, the smell of the public temper—or perhaps simply the smell of blood.[6]

That this vision is ascribed to Strether's "gusts of fancy" does not really hedge the bet. James makes the "unwarranted" vision exist, wrests forth from "beyond" the façades of Paris sinister implications of impending disaster, chaos, and pervades the final encounter of Strether and Mme de Vionnet with "the smell of blood." Their relation has all along been based on Strether's "exorbitant" commitment to "save her" if he could. Here, the evocation of bloody sacrifice, eliciting a state of moral exorbitance, authorizes the intensity of the encounter, where Strether sees Mme de Vionnet as resembling Mme Roland on the scaffold, and where he moves to his most penetrating vision of the realm of moral forces in which she struggles. "With this sharpest perception yet, it was like a chill in the air to him, it was almost appalling, that a creature so fine could be, by mysterious forces, a creature so exploited" (II, 284). Strether, and James, have pierced through to a medium in which Mme de Vionnet can be seen as a child of light caught in the claws of the mysterious birds of prey. After this perception, when Strether speaks it is to say, "You're afraid for your life!"—an articulation which strikes home, makes Mme de Vionnet give up "all attempt at a manner," and break down in tears. This stark articulation, which clarifies and simplifies Mme de Vionnet's position and passion, puts her in touch with elemental humanity—"as a maidservant crying for her young man," thinks Strether—and with the ravages of time, finally differs very little from the exchanges of the Count and Countess Restaud in the passage I quoted from *Gobseck*. The Jamesian mode is subtler, more refined, but it aims at the same thing: a total articula-

6. *The Ambassadors* (New York: Scribner's, 1909), II, 274.

tion of the grandiose moral terms of the drama, an assertion that what is being played out within the realm of manners is charged with significance from the realm of the moral occult, that gestures within the world constantly refer us to another, hyperbolic, parabolic set of gestures where life and death are at stake.

There is a passage from James's 1902 essay on Balzac (he wrote five in all) which touches closely on the problem of melodramatic representation. A notable point about the passage is that it constitutes a reparation, for in his 1875 essay, in *French Poets and Novelists,* James had singled out the episode in *Illusions perdues* where Mme de Bargeton, under the influence of her Parisian relation the Marquise d'Espard, drops her provincial young lover Lucien de Rubempré, as an example of Balzac's ineptitude in portrayal of the aristocracy. The two women desert Lucien, whose dress is ridiculous and whose plebeian parentage has become public knowledge, in the middle of the opera, and sneak out of the loge. Aristocratic ladies would not so lose their cool, James argues in the earlier essay, would not behave in so flustered and overly dramatic a fashion. His view in 1902 is more nuanced, and shows an attempt to come to terms with the mode of representation we find in Balzac:

The whole episode, in "Les Illusions perdues," of Madame de Bargeton's 'chucking' Lucien de Rubempré, under pressure of Madame d'Espard's shockability as to his coat and trousers and other such matters, is either a magnificent lurid document or the baseless fabric of a vision. The great wonder is that, as I rejoice to put it, we can never really discover which, and that we feel as we read that we can't, and that we suffer at the hands of no other author this particular helplessness of immersion. It is *done*—we are always thrown back on that; we can't get out of it; all we can do is to say that the true itself can't be more than done and that if the false in this way equals it we must give up looking for the difference. Alone among novelists Balzac has the secret of an insistence that somehow makes the difference nought. He warms his facts into life—as witness the certainty that the episode I just cited has absolutely as much of that property as if perfect matching had been achieved. If the great ladies in question *didn't* behave, wouldn't, couldn't have behaved, like a pair of nervous snobs, why so much the worse, we say to ourselves, for the great ladies in question. We *know* them so—they owe their being to our so seeing them; whereas we can never tell ourselves how we should otherwise have known them or what quantity of being they would on a different footing have put forth.[7]

James's somewhat baffled admiration here seems to arise from a perception of "surreality" in Balzac's representation of the episode: the fact that its hyperbolic mode and intensity make it figure more perfectly than would an accurate portrayal of manners what is really at stake for the characters, and in their relationships. If reality does not permit of such self-representations, he seems to say, then so much the worse for reality. By the doing of the thing, we know the characters; we are, if not in the domain of reality, in that of truth.

James poses the alternative of judging Balzac's episode to be "either a magnificent lurid document or the baseless fabric of a vision," to conclude that we cannot tell which it is. This alternative, and the admission of defeat in the attempt to choose, strikes close to the center of the problem of melodrama. I would suggest that the melodramatic imagination writes magnificent lurid documents which are founded on the void, which depend for their validity on a kind of visionary leap. When Balzac pressures the details of reality, at the start of *La Peau de chagrin,* to make them yield the terms of his drama, when he insists that gestures refer to a parabolic story; or when he creates a hyperbolic version of Lucien de Rubempré's social defeat, he is using the things and gestures of the real world, of social life, as kinds of metaphors which

7. "Balzac," in *Notes on Novelists* (New York: Scribner's, 1914), p. 111.

refer us to the realm of spiritual reality, the realm of latent moral meanings. Things cease to be merely themselves, gestures cease to be merely tokens of social intercourse whose meaning is assigned by a social code; they become the vehicles of metaphors whose tenor suggests another kind of reality, which is the true object of attention. Likewise, discovery of Mme de Vionnet's affair with Chad is essentially a vehicle for discovery of her entrapment and exploitation by "mysterious forces," her victimization by life. I. A. Richards has given a global definition of metaphor as a "transaction between contexts," and in all these cases there is such a transaction: pressure on the primary context is such that things and gestures are made to release hidden meanings, to transfer their signification to another context.

Both Balzac and James weave a rich texture of metaphor in their prose, and the metaphors almost always create an expanded moral context for the narrative. But it is not a question of metaphoric texture alone; it is rather that to the melodramatic imagination, things are necessarily all in the nature of metaphor because things are not simply themselves, but refer to, speak of something else. If we consider in this light the implications of works like *The Beast in the Jungle* and *The Sacred Fount,* we realize that the more elusive the tenor of the metaphor becomes—the more difficult it becomes to put one's finger on the nature of the spiritual reality alluded to—the more highly charged is the vehicle, the more strained with pressure to suggest a meaning beyond. Melodrama may be a drama which is heightened, hyperbolic *because* the moral realm it wants to evoke is not immediately visible, and the writer is ever conscious of standing over a void, dealing in conflicts, qualities and quantities whose very existence is uncertain. The violence and extremism of emotion and moral statement we find in melodrama may correspond to the fact that they are unjustified, unfounded emotion and ethical consciousness, qualities that cannot be shown to bear any imperative relationship to the way life is lived by most people. To the uncertainty of the tenor corresponds the exaggeration, the heightening of the vehicle. To come at the question in other terms: a definition of melodrama might be analogous to T. S. Eliot's definition of "sentimentality" in his essay on *Hamlet*. Sentimentality he calls emotion in excess of the objective correlative which ought to embody emotion—that is to say, unfounded emotion.

But melodrama in Balzac and James seems to indicate not so much a failure to proportion objective correlative to emotion as the impossibility of doing so; it suggests a Promethean attempt to reach beyond the visible conditions of man's quotidian drama to its occult issues. My argument here has analogies with that of James Guetti in *The Limits of Metaphor*. He maintains that the work of Melville, Conrad and Faulkner shows ever more audacious and desperate attempts to understand and speak of a central "darkness" which is finally inexpressible, which can finally only be alluded to, can never become the center or object of the narrative that it claims to be.[8] It is, like Marlow's discovery in the heart of darkness, "unspeakable," and the whole narrative is a metaphor whose tenor is ineffable, a tenuous "as if" construction which can never say its meaning and its goal. *The Beast in the Jungle* is a perfectly parallel case, because the beast lying in wait for Marcher is finally nothing, nothingness, the void of his life, the very absence of event—yet this absence is of course charged with terrible and unspeakable meaning by the life lived in its terms, lived in order to reach it. I suppose that *The Sacred Fount* would be the ultimate development of a fiction in which the "lurid document" has become completely indistinguishable from the

8. See James Guetti, *The Limits of Metaphor* (Ithaca: Cornell Univ. Press, 1967).

"baseless fabric of a vision": the narrator's image of the world
may be either, and he cannot himself be sure which. All we
can say is that the lurid document, the highly colored repor-
tage of his perceptions, seems to be a function of the baseless-
ness of the vision: the more the melodramatic imagination
soars in flight, the more highly it charges the documentary
terms, the vehicles which must carry its message. And if *The
Sacred Fount* probably fails ultimately, it is because the vehicle has been overcharged, and can't bear the weight.

I am conscious that I have until now been using the word
"melodrama" without any attempt to justify it or define it
historically. I think that we all receive pretty much the same
connotations from the word: extravagant expression, moral
polarization, emotional hyperbole, extreme states of being.[9]
But it may be useful to dwell for a moment on the historical
esthetics of melodrama, which show in clear skeletal form
many of the elements I have been discussing in Balzac's and
James's fictional dramatizations, and can help to elucidate
the tropes that they employ, the metaphorical nature of their
enterprise, and particularly the way in which they use the
gestures of social reality to imply states of moral being.

Melodrama, most would agree, represents a degenerate
form of the tragic—a form of the tragic, we might say, for a
world in which there is no longer a tenable idea of the sacred.
It is also a popular form of the tragic, exploiting similar
emotions within the context of the ordinary. If we return to
someone like Guilbert de Pixerécourt, who reigned as king
of Parisian melodrama for some thirty years at the start of
the nineteenth century, we find a spectacular theatre exploiting extreme emotional states of being, which are often
represented by extreme physical states: most plays will have

9. A good description of the characteristics of melodrama is given by
Eric Bentley in *The Life of the Drama* (New York: Atheneum, 1964),
pp. 195–218.

a blind man, a mute, or someone dramatically mutilated. (How often do Balzac and James create invalids, and make illness a point of view?) Characters tend to express these extreme states in a language of polarized moral abstractions; they *say* their emotional condition, and the drama is a clear clash of the claims of goodness against the claims of badness. If the world at the start of a melodrama seems charged with moral ambiguities—suggested by such titles as *The Woman with Two Husbands* or *The Man with Three Faces*—these ambiguities are not inherent to ethics. They are rather appearances to be penetrated, mysteries to be cleared up, so that the world may bathe in the stark moral lighting of manichaeism—the final fixity of the Count and Countess Restaud, of Gilbert Osmond, of Kate Croy condemned to the solitude of her egotism. Ambiguities are cleared up by total expression: first of the characters to the audience, then of characters to one another. As much as in Greek tragedy, the audience must know where truth and justice lie. But the catharsis sought by melodrama comes less from pity and terror than from the total articulation and vigorous acting out of the emotions: the last act contains chases, duels, struggles which bring the physical release of violence, and clear statements of the victory of light over darkness. The hidden identities, mysteries, evils of melodrama are never the result of chance or fate, but of conscious plotting: evil is concerted, volitional—which is not to say that it is motivated. Indeed, the more it is unmotivated the more it becomes a pure product of will, demonstrating that the world is inhabited by a Satanism as real as it is gratuitous.

There further seems to me to be an underlying esthetic principle in stage melodrama which is even more pertinent to the fictional melodrama I have been discussing, and which is bound up with the very origin of the idea of melodrama. Melodrama of course originally meant drama accompanied by music, and this use of music seems to have begun in popular eighteenth-century pantomime, and a bastard form known as "pantomime dialoguée." Now the esthetics of pantomime, and a prediction of its centrality to modern theatre, are first developed in Diderot's seminal text, the *Entretiens sur Le Fils naturel,* where he justifies his "bourgeois drama." Diderot makes a major element of his new theatre the use of *tableaux,* groupings of persons on the stage, and the gestures of these persons, which will be expressive of the interrelationships and emotions of characters as they respond to an event. He describes the family tableau that should be formed with announcement of the son's death: like his favorite painter, Greuze, he is striving to catch in people's postures their qualities of being at a moment of maximal emotionalism. This announces a major break with French neo-classical canons, by which the serious theatre was an absolutely verbal medium, a clash of words where action and gesture were extremely restrained and formalized. Gesture becomes of primary importance since it can express more than words, it can represent the unsayable.

This new valorization of gesture seems to me important to an understanding of the melodramatic mode. What it implies is the total legibility of gesture as expression. To clarify this point, let me quote the stage directions for a bit of pantomime from *Le Chef Ecossais*—"The Scottish Chief"—by J. G. A. Cuvelier, another popular melodramatist. On stage are the Bard and the Chief's son, Linni:

The Bard smiles at him, and indicates approval. Then, taking on a character of severity, he tells him that more important subjects should occupy him; he shows him the clouds gathered far off on the mountain slopes in bizarre shapes; he tells him of the glory of Fingal and Ossian, whose images he thinks he sees in their airy palaces; thus he raises the thought of young Linni to the Godhead. The child crosses his arms, bows and worships.[10]

10. J. G. A. Cuvelier, *Le Chef Ecossais ou la Caverne d'Ossian: Pantomime en deux actes à grand spectacle* (Paris: Chez Barba, 1816).

Now all this is to be got across without words, through facial expression and gesture alone. This means that gesture must convey enormous amounts of signification. Gesture itself must be exaggerated, hyperbolic, irreal, charged with meaning beyond itself. And if gesture can be so meaning-full, its transcription, its writing down, becomes the process of revealing the latent meaning of everything, the sense of all the *animae* inhabiting a world totally invested with meaning. The totally significant and legible gestures of pantomime constitute a step toward a novelistic enterprise where transcribed gesture, the world described, will be totally significant and legible, and totally expressive of emotional and moral conditions.

Gesture has this same intense charge of meaning in Balzac and James because of its metaphorical ambitions. Its meaning comes, not from its place within a code of gestures which assigns meaning (which is the case in most eighteenth-century comedy of manners, or in Jane Austen, for example), but from its claim to express moral and emotional qualities beyond itself. The dandy De Marsay, refusing to recognize Lucien de Rubempré, lets his lorgnon fall "so singularly that it seemed to Lucien the blade of the guillotine" (IV, 624). In the tale *Facino Cane,* the old blind musician replies to the narrator with "a frightening gesture of extinguished patriotism and disgust for things human" (VI, 71)—an extreme example, because the gesture is so overcharged with meaning, meaning in excess of its vehicle, that the literal gesture is itself virtually obliterated by the meanings it implies. Another example would be Mme de Mortsauf's "forced smile" on her deathbed, in *Le Lys dans la vallée,* in which the narrator reads "the irony of vengeance, the anticipation of pleasure, the intoxication of the soul and the rage of disappointment" (VIII, 1003). Such a gesture is overdetermined, it produces not only meaning but super-signification. It suggests a world of such electrically charged interconnections and correspondences that everything is inhabited by meaning. With James, we may be tempted to think that gesture receives its charge from its social context; this is after all a classic view of James, but it really does not stand up to scrutiny. The social signification is only the starting point for the immense implications of Jamesian gesture. Take the moment in *The Wings of the Dove* when Densher is told by Milly Theale's gondolier, Eugenio, that Milly can't receive him—his, and our, first indication that a crisis, the crisis, has arrived. Eugenio

now, as usual, slightly smiled at him in the process—but ever so slightly, this time, his manner also being attuned, our young man made out, to the thing, whatever it was, that constituted the rupture of peace.

This manner, while they stood for a long minute facing each other over all they didn't say, played a part as well in the sudden jar to Densher's protected state. It was a Venice all of evil that had broken out for them alike, so that they were together in their anxiety, if they really could have met on it; a Venice of cold, lashing rain from a low black sky, of wicked wind raging through narrow passes, of general arrest and interruption, with the people engaged in all the water-life huddled, stranded and ageless, bored and cynical, under archways and bridges.[11]

The Jamesian prestidigitation is in full glorious evidence here. Eugenio's slight, *too* slight smile is the detailed gesture which indicates a larger manner which in turn indicates a "rupture of peace"—already the vocabulary is taking on strong coloration—and this rupture then becomes the passageway for a flood of evil, conjuring into existence a new Venice of storm, darkness, and suppressed violence.

Reflecting on this metaphorical usage in which gestures express qualities beyond themselves, we may be struck by the seeming paradox that the total expressivity assigned to ges-

11. *The Wings of the Dove* (New York: Scribner's, 1909), II, 259.

ture is in fact posited on the ineffability of what is to be expressed. Gesture is read as containing such meanings because it posits their existence, since it works as a metaphorical approach to what cannot be said. If we are often perilously close, in reading these novelists, to a feeling that the represented world won't bear the weight of the significances placed on it, this is because the represented world is almost always being used metaphorically, as sign of the occult moral world. The way the world is represented becomes the very process by which the moral occult is brought into existence, postulated as a true fact, the most important fact of human existence.

The melodramatic imagination is, then, perhaps a way of perceiving and imaging the spiritual in a world where there is no longer any clear idea of the sacred, no generally accepted societal moral imperatives, where the body of the ethical has become a sort of *deus absconditus* which must be sought for, posited, brought into man's existence through exercise of the spiritualist imagination. Balzac's and James's melodrama, and the development of the melodramatic mode from, say, Samuel Richardson to Norman Mailer, is perhaps first of all a desperate effort to renew contact with the sacred *through* the representation of fallen reality, to insist that behind reality, hidden by it yet indicated within it, there is a realm where large moral forces are operative, where large choices of ways of being must be made. I have called this realm the moral occult: it is occult in a world where there is no clear system of sacred myth, no unity of belief, no accepted metaphorical chain leading from the phenomenal to the spiritual, only a fragmented society and fragments of myths. Yet the most Promethean of modern writers insist that this realm does exist, and write their fictions to make it exist, to show its primacy in life.

We can conceive of the melodramatic imagination as coming into being during the later eighteenth century, with the final liquidation of a world and a society theoretically organized around sacred myth and sacred history, and the decadence of those literary forms—neo-classical tragedy and comedy of manners—which image a spiritual and socially unified community. That is, the melodramatic mode arises in an era which demands rediscovery of the spiritual within and behind a phenomenal realm which seems to have been deprived of possibilities for transcendence. Stage melodrama is one early response to this demand, the Gothic novel is another. With its exploration of mystery, horror, terror; its graveyards and catacombs, putrid corpses and bloody ghosts, the Gothic novel, as Lowry Nelson has argued, suggests a reassertion of the sacred in its most primitive form, as forces in the phenomenal world that must be propitiated, and to be propitiated must be recognized.[12] In his study entitled *The Gothic Flame,* D. P. Varma calls the Gothic enterprise a "quest for the numinous." [13] This seems to me accurate: books like *The Monk* and *Frankenstein* insist that life cannot be accounted for in terms of social manners and interpersonal conflict alone, that every step man takes on earth calls spirits from the vasty deep, which he must then reckon with. These spirits may of course be read as dwelling within man himself, in areas which the daylight and the social realm take insufficient account of. The Gothic castle itself, with its pinnacles and dungeons, crenellations, moats, drawbridges, spiraling staircases and concealed doors, can be read as a first draft of the Freudian model of the mind, the structure of consciousness and the unconscious, and their treacherous relationship. The numinous of the Gothic imagination is

12. Lowry Nelson, Jr., "Night Thoughts on the Gothic Novel," *Yale Review,* 52 (1963), 236.

13. Devendra P. Varma, *The Gothic Flame* (London: A. Barker, 1957), p. 211.

at one stage the unconscious, and this reading can, as I suggested earlier, be extended to Balzac and James as well: the melodramatic mode of utterance is a victory over the repression and censorship of the social reality-principle, a release of psychic energy by the articulation of the unsayable. One might say that the Gothic quest for renewed contact with the numinous, the supernatural, the occult forces of the universe, leads into the moral self.

The melodramatic imagination, I would argue, provides the very basis of the modern mind's conception of spiritual reality and moral conflict. We should recognize this mode as a central fact of the modern sensibility in that modern art —and I take Romanticism to be the genesis of the modern, of the sensibility within which we are still living—has typically felt itself to be constructed on, and over, the void, postulating meanings and symbolic systems which have no certain justification because they are backed by no religious hermeneutic and no universally accepted social code. The mad quest of Mallarmé for a Book which would be "the Orphic explanation of the earth," of Yeats for a synthetic mythology which would enable him to hold "in a single thought reality and justice," of Norman Mailer for dreams adequate to the moon —these are all versions of a reaction to the vertiginous feeling of standing over the abyss created when the necessary center of things has been evacuated and dispersed. The search to bring into the drama of man's quotidian existence the higher drama of moral forces seems to me one of the large quests of the modern imagination, and I think that the melodramatic mode as I have described it is an intensified, exemplary version of what most art, since the beginnings of Romanticism, has been about.

What seems to me particularly important in the enterprise of the social melodramatists—and here one should of course include many names beyond Balzac and James—is their dual engagement with the representation of man's social existence, the way he lives his life, and with the moral drama implicated by and in his existence. They write a melodrama *of* manners. On the one hand, they refuse any metaphysical reduction of real life, and refuse to reduce their metaphorical enterprise to the cold symbolism of allegory. They recognize, with Isabel Archer during her intense vigil, that "this base, ignoble world, it appeared, was after all what one was to live for" (II, 197). On the other hand, they insist that life does contain, dissimulated but present within reality, a moral occult which is the realm of eventual value, and this insistence finally makes them more nourishing than more "behavioristic" novelists who, from Flaubert onwards, have suggested that there are not more things on earth than can be represented exclusively in terms of the material world. The melodramatists refuse to allow that the world has been drained of transcendence; and they locate that transcendence in the struggle of the children of light with the children of darkness, in the play of ethical mind.

It comes down, finally, to that alternative between the "magnificent lurid document" and the "baseless fabric of a vision" which James posed about Balzac. To make the fabric of vision into a document, to make the document lurid enough so that it releases the vision, to make vision document and document vision and to persuade us that they cannot be distinguished, that they are necessarily interconnected through the chain of spiritual metaphor, that resonances are set up, electrical connections established whenever we touch any link of the chain, is to make the world we inhabit one charged with meaning, one in which interpersonal relations are not merely contacts of the flesh, but encounters that must be carefully nurtured, judged, handled as if they mattered. It is a question, finally, of that attention to the significant in life that James captured in a famous line of advice to young novelists: "Try to be one of the people on whom nothing is lost." [14] To be so sensitized an instrument, one upon whom everything leaves a mark, with whom everything sets up a correspondence, is not simply to be an observer of life's surface, but someone who must bring into evidence, even bring into being, its moral substance. So that the task of the writer is like that assigned by Balzac to the exiled Dante in his tale, *The Proscribed:* "he closed himself in his room, lit his lamp of inspiration, and surrendered himself to the terrible demon of work, calling forth words from silence, and ideas from the night" (X, 344).

14. "The Art of Fiction," in *The Future of the Novel,* ed. Leon Edel (New York: Vintage, 1956), p. 13.

DAVID THORBURN

Conrad's Romanticism:
Self-Consciousness and Community

It is not hard to imagine Conrad's reaction to my present enterprise. He distrusted critics, though their judgments afflicted him more intensely than he would acknowledge, and he was impatient especially with terms like Realism, Romanticism and Naturalism. Mere temporary formulas, he called them.[1] "There is even one abandoned creature," he once observed with something less than amusement, "who calls me a neo-platonist? What on earth is that?" [2]

I take these sentiments, and similar ones I've not mentioned, as an incitement to caution but not to silence. Resisting the small temptation to call Conrad a neo-Romantic, I want to focus, nonetheless, on certain qualities in his work that have come in recent years to be slighted or misunderstood.

The Conrad who emerges, or is permitted to emerge, from the thickets of recent scholarship is a modern writer first and last, profoundly "one of us," as the critics (remembering

1. In the Preface to *The Nigger of the "Narcissus,"* Collected Edition (London: Dent, 1947), pp. x–xi. Subsequent citations from Conrad's works will be incorporated in the text and will refer to this edition.

2. Letter of 28 August 1908, in *Letters from Joseph Conrad, 1895–1924,* ed. Edward Garnett (1928; rpt. New York: Charter Books, 1962), p. 214.

Lord Jim) are fond of saying. This Conrad is the political
prophet whose insights into imperialism and revolutionary
desperation constitute a text for our times; [3] he is a giant
in exile, as the subtitle of one recent book has it,[4] whose
acute sense of alienation measures the wintry afflictions of
the modern spirit. Conrad provides us with "new myths for a
profane civilization," according to another recent study.[5]
Agreeing, but in his own terms, Hillis Miller (in a suggestive
chapter) tells us that Conrad keeps company with the "poets
of reality," being a writer who follows nihilism to the very
heart of its darkness and "so prepares the way beyond it" [6]—
a road not taken, apparently, by Auden or Frost, neither of
whom is mentioned in Miller's account, but traveled decisively by five other poets of this century: Yeats, Eliot, Dylan
Thomas, Stevens, and William Carlos Williams.

With a few important exceptions,[7] the habit—or perhaps

3. See, for example, Eloise Knapp Hay, *The Political Novels of
Joseph Conrad* (Chicago: Univ. of Chicago Press, 1963) and Avrom
Fleishman, *Conrad's Politics* (Baltimore: Johns Hopkins Univ. Press,
1967).

4. Leo Gurko, *Joseph Conrad: Giant in Exile* (New York: Macmillan,
1962).

5. Claire Rosenfield, *Paradise of Snakes: An Archetypal Analysis of
Conrad's Political Novels* (Chicago: Univ. of Chicago Press, 1967). The
quoted phrase is the title of Rosenfield's fifth chapter.

6. *Poets of Reality* (Cambridge, Mass.: Harvard Univ. Press, 1965),
p. 1. Conrad's crucial place in the development of the modern novel
has, of course, been a recurring subject for critics. For interesting recent
contributions to this discussion, see Alan Friedman, *The Turn of the
Novel* (New York: Oxford Univ. Press, 1966), pp. 75–105; and Peter
K. Garrett, *Scene and Symbol from George Eliot to James Joyce:
Studies in Changing Fictional Mode* (New Haven: Yale Univ. Press,
1969), pp. 160–80.

7. Notably, Morton Zabel's chapters on Conrad in *Craft and Character in Modern Fiction* (New York: Viking, 1957) and three essays by
Ian Watt (to which I am particularly indebted): "Conrad Criticism and
The Nigger of the 'Narcissus,'" *Nineteenth-Century Fiction,* 12 (1958),
257–83; "Story and Idea in Conrad's 'The Shadow-Line,'" *Critical*

the need—of modern criticism has been to retrieve Conrad from the century in which he lived more than half his life and in which he published not only his two apprentice novels, *Almayer's Folly* (1895) and *An Outcast of the Islands* (1896), but also, among other, lesser things, *The Nigger of the 'Narcissus'* (1897), "Youth" (1898), *Heart of Darkness* (1899) and a substantial part of *Lord Jim,* which began to appear serially in *Blackwood's Magazine* in October 1899 and was published complete in 1900. That this rescue operation has increased our understanding of Conrad's achievement cannot be disputed. But as any Wordsworthian, not to say Freudian, knows, even the most loving eye half-creates the objects it perceives; and this seems to me clearly true of the purposeful, high-minded ardor with which modern scholarship has embraced Conrad.

The cost of transforming Conrad into an image of ourselves is greater, I think, than has been generally realized and affects both our understanding of his achievement as a writer of fiction and our sense of literary history. It has become easy and even fashionable for critics to smile with condescending tolerance at the anonymous reviewer of *Almayer's Folly* who predicted that Conrad "might become the Kipling of the Malay Archipelago." [8] But the fact is, this reviewer was responding with genuine alertness to an important aspect of Conrad's first book, and one that remained central in his fiction throughout his career. In his very subjects and in his dominant attitudes toward those subjects, Conrad was in fundamental ways a man of the nineteenth century; his affinities with the Romantic poets and especially, I think, with Words-

---

Quarterly (Summer, 1960), 133–48; "Joseph Conrad: Alienation and Commitment," in *The English Mind: Studies . . . Presented to Basil Willey,* ed. Hugh Sykes Davies and George Watson (Cambridge: Cambridge Univ. Press, 1964), pp. 257–78.

8. *The Spectator,* 75 (1895), 530.

worth are even stronger and more fundamental than his connection with, say, Kafka and other prophets of our disorder. To say this is not to deny Conrad's modernity but to qualify it by making two related assertions which will be my purpose to try to justify: first, that Conrad habitually relied on what must be called Romantic modes of story-telling and created fictional worlds in which alienation, despair, and human separateness are contained, however precariously, by a stoic Romanticism grounded in a sense of human sharing and continuity; and second, that the increasingly powerful argument for Romanticism itself as a modern tradition—the phrase is Robert Langbaum's—receives convincing, perhaps crucial support from Conrad's example.

Conrad's characteristic and recurring story is a clearly Romantic bildungsroman—"It is the Romantics," Goeffrey Hartman reminds us, "who first explored the dangerous passageways of maturation" [9]—a bildungsroman cast usually in the form of a voyage out into an uncluttered, elementary world that appears to promise self-discovery, growth, personal renewal. Conrad's protagonists leave the ordinary, the "civilized" world behind them, or think they do, and travel into primitive locales where they are tested, if not by a Nature alive with magical or demonic powers, at least by a Nature whose menace and strangeness retain something of the old enchantment. A man is judged partly by his willingness to try himself in these exotic places. "Nobody amongst us," says one Conrad narrator, "had any interest in men who went home. They were all right; they did not count any more. Going to Europe was nearly as final as going to Heaven. It removed a man from the world of hazard and adventure" (*Victory*, 23).

9. "Romanticism and 'Anti-Self-Consciousness,' " in *Beyond Formalism: Literary Essays, 1958–1970* (New Haven: Yale Univ. Press, 1970), p. 299.

Set over against this fledgling voyager are two (usually) older figures. The first is a character common not only in Conrad's fiction but in nearly all adventure stories. This is a companion or partner for the protagonist, a retainer-figure whose appearance and commitments are vaguely unlawful— he may be a peg-legged pirate like Stevenson's Long John Silver—and whose familiarity with the alien world in which his young accomplice moves is intimate and often professional. This companion plays the role of guide, teacher, and protector to the young man's hero, though he may also implicitly (and explicitly in some of Conrad's best fiction) menace the young man.

The second figure, also experienced where the young man is not, is the witness or observer, the teller of the story. Sometimes, as in "Youth" or *Heart of Darkness,* this teller is the young man grown older, looking back now in memory at the self he had been; elsewhere, as in *Lord Jim* or *Chance* or *Under Western Eyes,* this narrator describes not his own experiences but those of another. But in both versions the narrating voice is explicitly separated temporally and ontologically from the protagonist of the story, and this separation— which often determines both the shape and the meaning of Conrad's fiction—links the author of *Lord Jim* to the Romantic poets even more decisively than his fondness for exotic settings or his frequent reliance on variations of quest romance. It is striking, in fact, how closely Conrad's most characteristic works resemble what M. H. Abrams has identified as the greater Romantic lyric, a poetic form whose defining features are the play of memory across time and the juxtaposing of an older poet with his younger self.[10]

10. "Structure and Style in the Greater Romantic Lyric," in *From Sensibility to Romanticism: Essays Presented to Frederick A. Pottle,* ed. Frederick W. Hilles and Harold Bloom (New York: Oxford Univ. Press, 1965), pp. 527–57. Poems of this sort, Abrams tells us, "present a determinate speaker in a particularized, and usually a localized, outdoor

The central poems of the English Romantics and many
Conrad works focus especially on the extraordinary distance
between narrator and actor, between the active, unreflective
young voyager in his glad animal vitality and his older self,
wiser perhaps, but also passive, somehow diminished. Conrad's speakers are often more ironic about their younger incarnations, but Wordsworth is scarcely void of such irony—
the naive wanderer in "Resolution and Independence" is one
example. In any event, both writers are heavy with nostalgia,
and something more than nostalgia, over what the self must
yield up to experience. And in both there are clear intimations that this loss involves, particularly, a rare quickness, a
splendor or radical potency of being. The Conrad work that
develops this notion most fully—it is implicit nearly everywhere—is perhaps *Under Western Eyes*, that Dostoevskian
political fable, which twists (but not quite beyond recognition) the usual Conradian adventure plot but which preserves
and even extends the interior voyage of discovery that nearly
always in Conrad, as in the Romantic poets, parallels these
outer journeys. In *Under Western Eyes* the old teacher of

---

setting, whom we overhear as he carries on, in a fluent vernacular
which rises easily to a more formal speech, a sustained colloquy sometimes with himself or with the outer scene, but more frequently with a
silent human auditor. The speaker begins," Abrams continues, describing
ing Marlow as surely as Wordsworth or Coleridge, "with a description
of the landscape; an aspect or change of aspect in the landscape evokes
a varied but integral process of memory, thought, anticipation, and
feeling which remains closely intervolved with the outer scene. In the
course of this meditation the lyric speaker achieves an insight, faces up
to a tragic loss, comes to a moral decision, or resolves an emotional
problem. Often the poem rounds upon itself to end where it began, at
the outer scene, but with an altered mood and deepened understanding
which is the result of the intervening meditation" (pp. 527–28). This,
surely, is a remarkably complete description of the essential structure
of many of Conrad's first-person pieces, and especially of *Heart of Darkness*, which ends, just as the Romantic lyric does, by rounding upon itself, "at the outer scene, but with an altered mood."

languages who tells the story is, it is more than hinted, literally impotent, a kind of pathetic, unconscious rival for the
hand of Natalia Haldin. This narrator is a man whose passive skills as pedant and editor are meant to expose his inadequacy as a reporter of the violent, driven lives of the central characters. As the title suggests, the Western narrator
confronts the seething energies of this Russian story as an
outsider, an alien, at once attracted and repelled by what he
calls the "terrible corroding simplicity" of the characters in
his story, yearners after apocalypse who "detest the irremediable life of the earth as it is" (104). This narrator's profound
ambivalence toward his story—his strained groveling confessions of impotence consorting uneasily with condescending assertions of his superiority—this narrator's deep ambivalence measures and exposes a need he shares with nearly all
Conradian narrators: a need, which sometimes shades into
outright obsession, to thrust himself between the story and
the reader, to deflect attention away from the tale and toward
the teller, as if in this way to claim for himself, to absorb
into himself, the fierce living energies of the world he describes but cannot fully enter.

Conrad's fondness for profoundly self-conscious and self-
dramatizing narrators is usually seen as a mark of his modernity, as one of his clearest links with the self-absorption that
characterizes so much twentieth-century fiction. There seems
no question of Conrad's influence in the work of such novelists as Gide, Mann, and Faulkner, and he seems an equally
powerful presence for contemporary writers like John Barth,
Borges, Nabokov, and Doris Lessing. But what does seem
questionable is the assumption that the prominent self-consciousness of these writers is a phenomenon that begins, essentially, in our own century. Two things, especially, call
this assumption into doubt. There is, first, the disquieting
fact that from the moment of its birth, the novel as a form

seems given to a radical, mocking awareness of itself as artifice. *Don Quixote,* after all, is the most self-conscious of books
and is as obsessed as Nabokov's *Pale Fire* with the precariousness of human fictions.

> In order to test [his helmet's] strength and see if it was sword-
> proof, [Quixote] drew his sword and gave it two strokes, the first
> of which instantly destroyed the result of a week's labor. It
> troubled him to see with what ease he had broken the helmet in
> pieces, so to protect it from such an accident, he remade it and
> fenced the inside with a few bars of iron in such a manner that
> he felt assured of its strength, and without caring to make a sec-
> ond trial, he held it to be a most excellent helmet.[11]

Ian Watt's account of the rise of the novel seems relevant
here, for his description of the philosophic and social pressures that lie back of the novel makes clear that the genre's
commitment to what he calls "formal realism" involves at
least implicitly a nominalist attitude toward language, a
concern with the distance between words and real objects.[12]
If Watt is right, then the novel as a genre—its very existence
as a literary kind dependent upon its commitment to a par-
ticularizing, concretizing realism—would appear to be caught
from the very beginning in a continual crisis of self-doubt
and self-examination. "Words, as is well known," says the
narrator of *Under Western Eyes,* "are the great foes of reality" (3).

More important, if the existence of novels like *Don Quixote* and *Tristram Shandy* casts doubt on the facile assumption that self-consciousness is the special mark of our modern
literature, there is also the fact that the old notion of a radical

---

11. This passage from the first chapter of the *Quixote*—I have quoted
Walter Starkie's translation (New York: Signet-New American Library,
1964)—is, of course, merely a convenient distillation of what is perhaps
the novel's principal subject as well as the key to its structure.

12. *The Rise of the Novel* (1957; rpt. Berkeley: Univ. of California
Press, 1959), esp. pp. 9–34.

break or discontinuity between Romanticism and Modernism has been shown to be largely specious. In this respect as in others, criticism of fiction has not kept pace with the scholarship that has grown out of the study of poetry. In the work, especially, of Geoffrey Hartman, Northrop Frye, Robert Langbaum, M. H. Abrams and Harold Bloom, we are confronted with varying and powerful evidence for an essential continuity between the Age of Wordsworth and ourselves—and for a continuity based in part on a recognition of self-consciousness as a specially Romantic malaise.[13]

This second, Romantic perspective bears crucially on Conrad. The period in which Conrad began to publish was a period in which the exotic adventure story was a dominant

13. The general argument is summarized in Abrams' essay on the Romantic lyric: "The central enterprise common to many post-Kantian German philosophers and poets, as well as to Coleridge and Wordsworth, was to join together the 'subject' and 'object' that modern intellection had put asunder, and thus to revivify a dead nature, restore its concreteness, significance and human values, and redomiciliate man in a world which had become alien to him. The pervasive sense of estrangement, of a lost and isolated existence in an alien world, is not peculiar to our own age of anxiety, but was a commonplace of Romantic philosophy" (p. 546). Much of Frye's work argues for the continued dominance of Romantic myths and forms, but see especially the first chapter of his *A Study of English Romanticism* (New York: Random House, 1968). Robert Langbaum's *The Poetry of Experience* (1957; rpt. New York: Norton, 1963) is a seminal contribution to the subject, particularly his introduction, "Romanticism as a Modern Tradition," pp. 9–37. Harold Bloom's anthology of essays by various scholars, *Romanticism and Consciousness* (New York: Norton, 1970), contains several important papers which show (as Bloom says in a headnote, p. 1) that "subjectivity or self-consciousness is the salient problem of Romanticism, at least for modern readers." Bloom's own *Yeats* (New York: Oxford Univ. Press, 1970) is full of powerful and unsettling revaluations, many of which challenge the assumption that Romanticism and Modernism are discontinuous. Most of Hartman's scholarship is relevant here, but see especially *The Unmediated Vision* (New Haven: Yale Univ. Press, 1954) and "Romanticism and 'Anti-Self-Consciousness,'" cited above.

literary form. It was the period of Kipling, of Rider Haggard, of Anthony Hope (who wrote *The Prisoner of Zenda*) and, mostly notably, of Robert Louis Stevenson. We can perhaps recover something of the atmosphere of the period from Quiller-Couch's extravagant eulogy for Stevenson, who died in Samoa in the year preceding the publication of *Almayer's Folly:*

> Put away books and paper and pen. Stevenson is dead and now there is nobody left to write for. . . . [F]or five years the needle of literary endeavour in Great Britain has quivered towards a little island in the South Pacific, as to its magnetic pole.[14]

In direct and unambiguous ways in his less successful works, and in more complex ways in his major fiction, Conrad was clearly a part of this late nineteenth-century tradition of exotic adventure. Insofar as he freed himself from the triviality and mere novelty of this popular fiction, Conrad was not so much anticipating modern developments as returning to earlier, more problematic versions of Romantic subject matter. As recent critics have made clear in the case of Stevenson,[15] the essential premises of the adventure story originate in the defining pieties of High Romanticism. But they are in such stories, especially those written in the eighties and nineties, debased pieties now, so reduced in intensity and seriousness as to constitute not the visionary and *tentative* assertions of a Wordsworth, but the simplistic assumptions of the middle-brow reading public. It is one of Conrad's chief distinctions, though he is rarely honored for it, to have written in this popular mode and to have exploited pre-

14. "Robert Louis Stevenson," *Adventures in Criticism* (London: Cassell, 1896), p. 184. This essay originally appeared in *The Speaker,* 22 December 1894.

15. Edwin M. Eigner, *Robert Louis Stevenson and Romantic Tradition* (Princeton: Princeton Univ. Press, 1966), and Robert Kiely, *Robert Louis Stevenson and the Fiction of Adventure* (Cambridge, Mass.: Harvard Univ. Press, 1964).

cisely these tired and apparently exhausted pieties with a full conscious energy that renews their vigor and rediscover their high seriousness.

Considering such matters, I am tempted by a Spenserian fantasy in which the Damsel Romanticism is sustained and nourished by various writers through the nineteenth century but is captured, finally, and betrayed, by two sibling dragons, a Pre-Raphaelite and Rider Haggard. The damsel is rescued and restored to beauty by two knights, Conrad and Yeats. Conrad, of course, slays Rider Haggard; and Yeats, after a struggle, slays Christina Rossetti.

The virtues most unequivocally celebrated in adventure stories are typically masculine and active ones. Conrad's typical retainer figure, like many characters in Stevenson, Rider Haggard, Kipling, Marryat, Fenimore Cooper, even Hemingway, is courageous, loyal, skilled in his craft, and taciturn. His taciturnity is particularly emphasized. He speaks only when it is essential to the job at hand and then with quiet succinctness.

This emphasis is entirely consonant with the traditional expectations of the adventure mode, which, because it is focused on events, on action, comes almost inevitably to value deeds over words, men of action over men of eloquence and contemplation. Because of its (often simplistic) commitment to what are held to be the deeper, more elemental human realities, the exotic adventure yarn, always by implication and in many cases explicitly, involves a rejection of the civilized, the controlled, the artificial. Many of Stevenson's theoretical pronouncements about fiction are grounded in precisely such a rejection,[16] one consequence of which may be a bias

16. One example, from the essay "Pastoral" in *Memories and Portraits*, Vol. XIII of the Scribner's edition of Stevenson's works (New York, 1902), p. 238: "Novels begin to touch not the fine *dilettanti* but

not only against reflective characters, but also against characters who are able to express themselves in more than monosyllables.

Something of this bias survives powerfully in Conrad, although with even the simplest of Conrad's sailors, as with Wordsworth's rustics, one senses what Marlow says of Lord Jim: "He was not eloquent, but there was a dignity in this constitutional reticence, there was a high seriousness in his stammerings" (248). Conrad's boldest if least nuanced treatment of this theme is *The Nigger of the "Narcissus,"* where inarticulateness is the very mark of seamanly virtue, and where, conversely, to be talkative is to reveal one's unmanly wickedness. The novel dramatizes this idea most fully in the opposition of Singleton and Donkin. The former lives among the crew "taciturn and unsmiling" (41), his silence and simplicity the very source of his heroism. Symbolically named, Singleton belongs to a dying species of "voiceless men," a generation "inarticulate and indispensable" whose modern successors are no longer "strong and mute" because "if they have learned how to speak they have also learned how to whine" (25). Donkin embodies this new generation of whining complainers; he is a bad sailor, a conniving malingerer, and so a "consummate artist" (100) whose "picturesque and filthy loquacity flowed like a troubled stream from a poisoned source" (101). These matters are crystalized for us early in the novel when Donkin makes his first appearance in the fore-

---

the gross mass of mankind, when they leave off to speak of parlours . . . and begin to deal with fighting, sailoring, adventure, death or childbirth. . . . These aged things have on them the dew of man's morning; they lie near, not so much to us, the semi-artificial flowerets, as to the trunk and aboriginal taproot of the race." See also, in the same volume, "A Gossip on a Novel of Dumas's," "A Gossip on Romance," and "A Humble Remonstrance," pp. 315–58; and, from *Familiar Studies of Men and Books,* Vol. XIV of the Scribner's edition, "Victor Hugo's Romances," pp. 17–45.

castle: "A taciturn long-armed shellback, with hooked fingers, who had been lying on his back smoking, turned in his bed to examine him dispassionately, then, over his head, sent a long jet of saliva towards the door" (10).

More oblique than his shellback and less sure of himself, Conrad nevertheless is driven repeatedly in his fiction to juxtapose talkers and doers, to establish oppositions between men of pragmatic simplicity and men of seductive eloquence. There are particularly rich instances of such oppositions in *Lord Jim,* for example, where the shrill eloquence of Cornelius and the vivid rantings of Gentleman Brown contrast with the actions of taciturn men like the French Lieutenant and Captain Brierly. *Typhoon* gives us a semicomic version of a similar opposition, for in that story MacWhirr's ambiguous fraternity with his first mate Jukes is an alliance of unimaginative, even stupid competence with self-conscious and quavering intellection; an alliance between a captain "who found very little occasion to talk" (90) and his loquacious first officer; an alliance, appropriately, between a man who writes brief, dull letters and a man whose letters, however self-involved, are thoughtful and interesting. Again, in *Under Western Eyes* Conrad relies in a fundamental way on our latent distaste for certain kinds of eloquence. The reader's harsh judgment of Peter Ivanovitch, for example, is a consequence not primarily of his involvement in revolutionary activities but of the fact that he cheapened his heroic escape from Russia *by writing about it,* by trading in words upon his exploits. Similarly, Sophia Antonovna seems to Razumov more appealing than Ivanovitch because, despite her fanaticism, she is "stripped of rhetoric, mysticism and theories" (261). And Razumov himself, "a comparatively taciturn personality" (6), "a man of few words" (173), "a silent man" (255), appears least sympathetic during his return from Ziemianitch's stable when, walking in the Moscow streets, he compromises his essential nature by growing eloquent in betrayal, "holding a discourse with himself with extraordinary abundance and facility" (35). In such discourse Razumov justifies his decision to betray Haldin, and the glibness of his rationalization is offensive. Later in the novel, when the reader's sympathy has shifted almost wholly toward Razumov, one finds that his essential trait is again taciturnity; confronted by the furious and absurd eloquence of Ivanovitch and the imperceptive wordiness of the English narrator, Razumov's mute suffering is more appealing than any rhetoric.

One could multiply these examples, and consider each more fully; but I will end with the reminder that Donkin's most striking counterpart in Conrad's work, even more clearly a "consummate artist," is Kurtz in *Heart of Darkness,* who (we learn) is both a painter and a poet and whose distinguishing characteristic is his "magnificent eloquence." The deep ambiguity in Conrad's attitude to language as a means of illumination and insight but also as a source of delusion and treachery is focused in Kurtz—and in Marlow, himself an eloquent man, whose mingling of admiration and disdain and even terror at Kurtz's example is a dramatic mirroring of Conrad's own ambivalence.

The remarkable directness of Conrad's disapproval of Donkin's writerly loquacity, and, still more, his open and fully acknowledged ambivalence concerning Kurtz's dark eloquence help to distinguish him from writers like Kipling, Marryat, the early Stevenson. The books of these men implicitly attack artifice, intellection, language, without ever accepting full responsibility for such an attack; while in Conrad, as in the Romantic poets, the man's suspicion of art and of language, of the hesitations and limits of intellect, is translated into the artist's conscious subject matter.

We begin to close with that subject matter—with Conrad's

abiding Romantic preoccupation with the reaches and limits of language—in the character of Lord Jim, afflicted at the inquiry into his desertion by his acute sense of the inviolable integrity of any single moment of experience, undone (finally) by his discovery that the very pulse and intensity of experience passes away in the instant of its occurring:

He wanted to go on talking for truth's sake, perhaps for his own sake also; and while his utterance was deliberate, his mind positively flew round and round in the serried circle of facts that had surged up all about him to cut him off from the rest of his kind: it was like a creature that, finding itself imprisoned within an enclosure of high stakes, dashes round and round, distracted in the night, trying to find a weak spot, a crevice, a place to scale.   [31]

This compelling vision of a man caught in the imprisoning privacy of his own experiences defines one of Conrad's deepest fears, enacts one of this novel's crucial insights and, finally, begins to explain the fevered erratic shifting of the book's narrative form. Again and again in *Lord Jim* both Marlow and Jim himself will be caught in similar circumstances. Repeatedly, we see Jim gesturing with at best feeble success toward communication with other men. Just as he fails to explain himself at the inquiry, so he fails again in his long communing with Marlow at dinner after the first day of the hearing. Similarly, in his final interview with Jewel he discovers that he cannot explain why he must desert her. Again, in the final crisis on Patusan, Jim turns writer for a brief instant, once more undone by the recalcitrant privacy of the reality he lives but cannot fathom or describe:

It is . . . impossible to say whom he had in his mind when he seized the pen: Stein—myself—the world at large—or was this only the aimless startled cry of a solitary man confronted by his fate? 'An awful thing has happened,' he wrote before he flung the pen down for the first time; look at the ink blot resembling the head of an arrow under these words. After a while he had tried again, scrawling heavily, as if with a hand of lead, another line. 'I must now at once . . .' The pen had spluttered, and that time he gave it up. There's nothing more; he had seen a broad gulf that neither eye nor voice could span. I can understand this. He was overwhelmed by the inexplicable . . . [340–41, first and third ellipses added]

Marlow, too, like many Conrad characters and especially narrators, is overwhelmed, or nearly so, by the inexplicable. And the description of Jim trapped in an enclosure of the self and scrabbling in fevered bafflement to escape is also the very image of Marlow's condition. In *Lord Jim,* as elsewhere, the Conrad narrator's confessions of failure are so frequent they resemble a refrain.

All this happened in much less time than it takes to tell, since I am trying to interpret for you into slow speech the instantaneous effect of visual impressions.   [48]

I can't explain to you who haven't seen him and who hear his words only at second hand.   [93]

The blight of futility that lies in wait for men's speeches had fallen upon our conversation, and made it a thing of empty sounds.   [148]

That was all then—and there shall be nothing more; there shall be no message, unless such as each of us can interpret for himself from the language of facts, that are so often more enigmatic than the craftiest arrangement of words.   [340]

The list is far from exhaustive.

Marlow's characteristic diction, his persistent reliance on what might be called a vocabulary of uncertainty is intimately related to these explicit confessions of limitation and bafflement. In *Lord Jim,* as in *Heart of Darkness,* the famous adjectival insistence which has so disturbed Leavis and others is for the most part an essential aspect of the novel's mean-

ing.[17] For Marlow's fondness for vague, abstract adjectives—
one might call them Shelleyan adjectives—reinforces his
overtly stated conviction that his telling must fall short of
perfect truth. The drama of Marlow's rhetoric is a drama of
Romantic aspiration and failure, a drama in which vividly
precise scenic details are juxtaposed against an abstract commentary which continually calls that scenic vividness into
question or which insists on its radical incompleteness. "I
cannot paint / What then I was," cries Wordsworth in *Tintern Abbey,* though he tries in the very next phrase, resorting
to a metaphor whose tentative, problematic quality is especially clear because it follows upon this confession of limitation and failure. "The sounding cataract / Haunted me like
a passion . . ." Marlow's eloquence, like Wordsworth's, is
driven, tentative, self-doubting: a harsh, earned eloquence
which registers, above all, a fundamental humility.

Something of that humility, though a touch of artist's pride
as well, is present, too, in Marlow's explicit awareness of the
fact that there is a sense in which Jim's very existence depends upon his skill as a narrator.

I am telling you so much about my own instinctive feelings and
bemused reflections because there remains so little to be told of
him. He existed for me, and after all it is only through me that
he exists for you. I've led him out by the hand; I have paraded
him before you. [224]

In this representative passage, as in Wordsworth's most characteristic lyrics, the reader is required to bear in mind simul-
taneously two distinct moments of time: first, the moment of
the experience itself, and second, the *now* of Marlow's telling

17. My argument here parallels in part that of James Guetti, who
sees Marlow's troubled narrative in *Heart of Darkness* as Conrad's way
of dramatizing "the failure of imagination." See his *The Limits of
Metaphor* (Ithaca: Cornell Univ. Press, 1967), pp. 46–68.

about that experience. Repeatedly through the novel, and in many other stories and novels, Conrad maintains, insists upon, this double perspective; repeatedly, as we hear about Jim we are forced also to attend to another and essentially separate story, the story of Marlow's attempt to communicate. Virtually all the impressionist strategies to which Marlow has recourse during his narrative—the jumbled, digressive chronology; the breaks in the story when Marlow interrupts himself to address his listeners or merely to pause reflectively; his persistent admissions of inadequacy; the adjectival diction— all these strategies serve not simply to show us, in the words of one of the novel's admirers, "how hard it is to know, and how hard to judge; and how hard even to separate the two processes." [18] They serve also to transform Marlow from a mere narrative convenience to a credibly evoked human being whose hesitations and desperate involvement in the task of understanding and narrating constitute *in themselves* a compelling drama, which rivals the more traditional story of Jim's adventures.

Marlow explicitly acknowledges the existence of this second story when he says that he finds himself caught in his "own instinctive and bemused reflections"—caught, that is, not in Jim's anguished career of failure, but in his own parallel anguish in this drama of the telling. Auden's elegy for Yeats addresses such anguished tellers: "Sing of human unsuccess / In a rapture of distress." And a line from Faulkner, Conrad's greatest successor in the uses of this drama of the telling, is relevant, too. This is the line in *Absalom, Absalom!* in which General Compson, Quentin's grandfather, defines language as "that meager and fragile thread by which the little surface corners and edges of men's secret and soli-

18. Lawrence Lerner, "Joseph Conrad," in *The Novelist as Innovator,* ed. Walter Allen (London: British Broadcasting Corporation, 1965), p. 84.

tary lives may be joined for an instant now and then before sinking back into the darkness." [19]

Faulkner expresses here a very Conradian and Romantic faith in language, in art, as an agency of community, as a fragile but genuine counterforce to the secrecy and solitariness of the human circumstance. And this faith, however embattled, may distinguish the Romantic self-consciousness from the modern or the contemporary. This distinction, surely, is one of degree, not of kind, but it seems to me significant, if only because it joins Conrad's characteristic awareness of the gap between language and reality to the Romantic agony rather than to its contemporary versions.

Consider this great, bitter poem by J. V. Cunningham:

> Time will assuage.
> Time's verses bury
> Margin and page
> In commentary,
>
> For gloss demands
> A gloss annexed
> Till busy hands
> Blot out the text,
>
> And all's coherent.
> Search in this gloss
> No text inherent:
> The text was loss.
>
> The gain is gloss.[20]

The final pun is brilliant and terrifying: the gain is gloss—it is dazzling, remarkable; but it is all gloss, it is *mere* gloss,

---

19. *Absalom, Absalom!* (1936; rpt. New York: Modern Library, 1951), p. 251.

20. "To the Reader," in *Quest for Reality: An Anthology of Short Poems in English,* ed. Yvor Winters and Kenneth Fields (Chicago: Swallow Press, 1969), p. 168.

it includes nothing of the thing itself. Cunningham's resentment is contained by the terrible concision of the dimeter
line, by the enclosing rimes, by the icy finality of his concluding pun. He is not desperate but coldly imprisoned. There
is space here for bitterness and for tough, angry wit. But to
struggle would be pointless. Cunningham's attitude is perhaps mirrored in the weary half-silences of Beckett or in the
mad ingenious puzzles of Nabokov. But Conrad, like the
English Romantic poets, holds to a meager but partly sustaining faith in the power of language to make sense of the world
and, however imperfectly, to recreate it. "I cannot paint /
What then I was." But I will try and I will come close. Conrad's narrators, like Conrad himself, are perpetually dissatis-
fied, obsessed by failure, driven repeatedly to renew their
struggle, to tell the story in a new way or to investigate the
facts yet one more time. Their emblem might be the moving
and characteristically Romantic conclusion to Coleridge's
brief preface to *Kubla Kahn,* in which the poet tells us that
he wrote the fragment which survives immediately on waking
from an opium dream and that an interruption by "a person
on business from Porlock" kept him from completing it.
"The author has frequently purposed to finish" the poem,
Coleridge says, and quotes a line from Theocritus which he
has adapted for his purpose and which translates as: "I will
sing a sweeter song tomorrow." To this Coleridge adds a mor-
dant line of his own: "But the tomorrow is yet to come."

Faulkner's menaced but surviving faith in the word as a
fragile thread which may in some degree join men together,
deny their separateness, implies that a sense of Other may
help to rescue the Romantic desperation about language from
total absorption or dissolution in the Self. The agony of the
Conrad narrator is two-edged: like the speaker in a number
of English Romantic poems, this narrator is constantly being

drawn inward and through time toward the world of his reminiscence, and also outward, toward his auditors or readers. He is not, that is, characteristically engaged simply in the act of recreating or rediscovering for himself that younger self or past time which is the object of his remembering; he is also, and crucially, engaged in the equally difficult task of bringing that world and that younger self into contact with those who read or listen to him. "It is certain," said Novalis in a passage so important to Conrad that he used it as the epigraph to *Lord Jim* and again in a crucial moment in one of his autobiographical books,[21] "It is certain that my conviction gains infinitely the moment another soul will believe in it."

Now all narrators are implicitly surrogates for the artist and all are implicitly engaged in an act which mediates between the tale and its intended audience. But in Conrad and in the Romantic poems that most closely resemble his fiction this mediating role has a special urgency. The gesture of community implicit in any teller's decision to relate a story is acknowledged and lifted to particular prominence by Conrad's insistent habit of setting the scene in which the telling occurs, of introducing auditors who converse with the narrator and even (as in *Lord Jim*) receive letters from him. This procedure has its parallel in Wordsworth's habit of addressing particular speakers in a number of his poems, his sister Dorothy and Coleridge especially. The whole of the *Prelude* is addressed to Coleridge, and it is more than an interesting trifle that at crucial moments in the text Wordsworth will speak directly to him, reaching out, one feels, for a friend's consoling and encouraging sympathy. Coleridge, too, has some important poems—including *To William Wordsworth* and the *Dejection Ode*—in which the speaker implicates a particularized auditor in the spiritual anguish he

21. In *A Personal Record*, p. 15.

is evoking. These, as in Conrad, are clearly gestures of inclusion and sharing—very often in the poets accompanied by exclamation points intended to emphasize the fervor and sincerity of the speaker's need for spiritual company. They are gestures designed to create an alliance of shared feeling that will bind the speaker and his sense of what is important and humanly true to the validating sympathies of another person. The conclusion of *Tintern Abbey,* in which Wordsworth turns finally to the figure of his sister for whatever consolation he can tentatively find in her human presence and in her resemblance to his younger self, is a specially clear and resonant example of this crucial Romantic and Conradian procedure.

Wordsworth's sister serves in the poem especially as an assurance of continuity—the continuity not simply of blood but of those glad animal movements which Wordsworth had experienced in youth and inevitably lost but whose reappearance in his sister gives proof that human beings resemble one another, share essential qualities. Conrad, too, is deeply interested in the continuities between young and old, and his most characteristic situation involves, as I suggested earlier, a meeting or a joining together of two characters, one young and inexperienced, the other (usually) older whose role is that of guide and teacher. This recurring relationship might be called the adventure partnership because it is found in some form in nearly all adventure fiction and because it dramatizes, or assumes, an alliance between the young hero and the retainer figure.

The importance of such alliances in Conrad's work can be seen with particular clarity in *The Mirror of the Sea.* This uneven autobiographical book concerns the traditions of seafaring and contains several chapters which speak with a charming grandiloquence about sailing ships and maritime history. These generalizing passages are intended to place

Conrad's personal experiences in the context of a long tradition of common struggle and achievement. But in *The Mirror of the Sea,* as in his great first-person fiction, Conrad's interest in this theme goes beyond such abstraction and is realized dramatically in the relationships between young seamen and their more experienced elders. Nearly all of Conrad's personal anecdotes in *The Mirror* focus a scene between his younger self and an older figure, usually a sailor, the most memorable of whom is Dominic Cervoni, *padrone* of the *Tremolino* on which Conrad tells us he sailed in the adventure which began his manhood. These recurring scenes between youth and age enact a ritual of continuity, dramatize the theme of solidarity and human dependence about which other passages in *The Mirror* speak only abstractly. Aboard the *Tremolino,* for example, pursued by their enemies, Conrad and Dominic discover that their ship has been sabotaged by one of the crew. "The experience of treachery" overwhelms the young Conrad, and "on the verge of tears" (175, 176), he finally stammers out his fear of capture. It is the older, more experienced Dominic who reassures him and gives him back his courage, as MacWhirr's stolid presence saves Jukes in *Typhoon,* and as Ransome's calm certainty forces the new captain in *The Shadow-Line* to accept the responsibilities of his command.

As I have just implied, the relationship between Conrad and Dominic Cervoni provides a simplified version of a recurring Conradian pattern. As Dominic helps the young Conrad, so Marlow becomes for Lord Jim "an ally, a helper, an accomplice" (93). The ache for human contact, for a sharing of solitudes, is the novel's obsession. "I don't know how old I appeared to him—and how much wise," Marlow observes with pain. "Not half as old as I felt just then; not half as uselessly wise as I knew myself to be." And adds that he is drawn to Jim by more than "the fellowship of the craft," by the strength of "the feeling that binds a man to a child" (128, 129). Though all his people are orphans, Conrad remains one of the great portrayers of the anguished impotence of fatherhood. One of his great subjects is the frustration of maturity's useless generosity toward the young.

But Jim does more than frustrate Marlow. He also threatens him.

He was the kind of fellow you would, on the strength of his looks, leave in charge of the deck—figuratively and professionally speaking. I say I would, and I ought to know. Haven't I turned out youngsters enough in my time . . . I tell you I ought to know the right kind of looks. I would have trusted that youngster on the strength of a single glance, and gone to sleep with both eyes— and, by Jove! it wouldn't have been safe. There are depths of horror in that thought.   [44, 45]

It is a small enough faith to hold to the notion that one's practiced eye can distinguish between reliable and unreliable men, but it is a faith necessary to such a man as Marlow. If he can be mistaken about Jim, then he could have been mistaken about all the other young men whose training into seamanship and manhood has been Marlow's job in life. This hard truth contains "depths of horror" not because it undermines Marlow's confidence in his ability to judge a man— that is a mere blow to one's self-esteem, and can be borne— but because there can be no partnership in hazard if your companion is not to be trusted. To lose one's partner is to confront what Decoud, in *Nostromo,* confronts on the Golfo Placido: the dissolution of human community and (therefore) the dissolution of the self. Jim's desertion of an imperiled humanity, that is to say, threatens to expose as fraudulent, as mere illusion, that sustaining partnership of "shared solitude" between sailors, that fellowship of trust and mutual effort whose existence is, for Marlow and also for Conrad, one of the "few simple notions you must cling to"—I am quoting

Marlow—"if you want to live decently and would like to die easy" (*Lord Jim,* 43).

If Marlow is the wise elder in *Lord Jim,* he is the young hero in "Youth" and *Heart of Darkness.* In this role Marlow closely resembles Jim himself, the protagonists of *The Secret Sharer* and *The Shadow-Line,* and the biographical Conrad as he appears in a series of moving and subtle vignettes with senior officers, maritime examiners and older relatives and companions in both *The Mirror of the Sea* and *A Personal Record.* In all these works, and in others, too, Conrad studies one of his fundamental subjects—the continuities and distances between youth and age, showing us wise elders, and some not so wise, attempting to pass on their knowledge (or sometimes their madness) to younger men, and showing us younger men as sometimes eager, sometimes hostile learners. In the best of these books Conrad projects a world, very like Wordsworth's, in which we discover our saving connections with the human community almost by accident and in the least likely of men.

In *The Shadow-Line,* for example, perhaps Conrad's subtlest adventure story, the exterior simplicities of the retainer figure have been wholly discarded. The hero's first partner, or ally, is Giles, a placid, garrulous, somewhat pompous old captain "with a greaty shiny dome of a bald forehead and prominent brown eyes" (11). In the wry, incisive comedy of the first chapter, this unlikely partner forces his wisdom upon a bored and disrespectful junior, whose indifference nearly causes him to lose his first command. Later, aboard ship and betrayed by the previous captain who has sabotaged the vessel's medical supplies, the young hero has need of another partner, and he, too, scarcely resembles the traditional adventure retainer. No romantic outlaw with a maimed leg like Long John Silver, this figure's disablement is internal: he is Ransome, the ship's cook, and he has a bad heart. But in the great crisis aboard ship, with the entire crew struck down by fever, Ransome is a prodigy of energy and endurance; he becomes the embodiment of the indispensable man, "unfailing" (105) and faithful, the "consummate seaman" (126) who "noticed everything, attended to everything, shed comfort around him as he moved" (121).

In the ship's final desperate run into port only the captain and Ransome are able to sail the vessel, and in this vision of two men struggling together to survive calamity and further bound in a fraternity of weakness—Ransome's weak heart the physical emblem of his captain's moral incertitude—lies one of Conrad's recurring and deepest metaphors. In *The Shadow-Line* the rest of the crew lie helpless and semiconscious on the decks as these partners in adventure work alone to save them. Earlier, the story has provided a comic prefiguring of this climactic moment when Giles, in the scene in the sailors' home, attempts to protect the narrator from the petty hostilities and machinations of the house steward. In *Typhoon* Jukes and his captain, contending with the fierce hostility of the storm, are thrown together in a literal embrace that symbolizes this same vision of human partnership beseiged and in danger but finally surviving. And in a similar way, Dominic and the young Conrad aboard the *Tremolino*, in flight from enemies and betrayed by one of their fellows, must confer in secret about their betrayal and remain silent lest their unwilling crew mutiny rather than risk the perils of escape. In all these moments, and consummately in *Heart of Darkness*, Conrad wrests from the conventional adventure partnership an enduring image of human community collapsed to its very limits and threatened, though not always undone, by annihilation.

Captain Giles, like Jim's Marlow, is a benign figure, who actively seeks to help his young colleague. In *Heart of Darkness* and *The Secret Sharer* this kindly elder is radically transformed and, although inescapably the hero's accomplice and partner, becomes also his enemy. Our communion extends, Wordsworth tells us in poems like "Michael" or "The Old Cumberland Beggar" or "The Idiot Boy," to the very edges of the human, to old men walking who seem scarcely alive, to leech-gatherers who are allied more closely to inanimate nature than to our human quickness. Just so, says Conrad in *Heart of Darkness* and *The Secret Sharer,* our communion extends, whether we like it or not, even to murderers.

"I accepted this unforeseen partnership," Marlow says of Kurtz, "this choice of nightmares" (147). "I . . . remained loyal to Kurtz to the last" (151). For part of the journey, on the trip back up river on his ancient steamer, Marlow is bound to the dying Kurtz in a kinship ignored and distrusted by the other "pilgrims." During this time Marlow holds in his hands "[a]ll that had been Kurtz's . . . : his soul, his body, . . . his plans, his ivory, his career" (155). And in these days of isolated communion Marlow and Kurtz enact together a terrible drama of human fellowship. It is a fragile and imperiled fellowship, threatened by the hostile pilgrims and by the warlike natives dancing along the shore; and undermined still more by Kurtz's depraved hallucinations of power and grandeur and by Marlow's fear and contempt for this "hollow sham" (147). But its intensely fragile, precarious character also signals the desperate vigor of those human needs which call such fraternity into life:

I looked ahead—piloting. 'Close the shutter,' said Kurtz suddenly one day; 'I can't bear to look at this.' I did so.

One morning he gave me a packet of papers and a photograph— the lot tied together with a shoe-string. 'Keep this for me,' he said.

One evening coming in with a candle I was startled to hear him say a little tremulously, 'I am lying here in the dark waiting for death.' The light was within a foot of his eyes. I forced myself

ırmur, 'Oh, nonsense!' and stood over him as if transfixed.
[148-49]

It is a radical and profound vision of community, reduced as so often in Conrad to the smallest possible unit, and imperiled, as I have said, by many things. But still it survives. Marlow is moved, partly by inner necessity, to compassion and even devotion, and Kurtz to asking tremulously for them. Like Leggatt and the young captain of *The Secret Sharer,* but with even greater difficulty, Kurtz and Marlow are partners in a great adventure which measures the hero against an outlaw-accomplice, a companion in hazard of whom the hero must finally say, with Kurtz's harlequin disciple, "Oh, he enlarged my mind!" (140).

Conrad's unending interest in this drama of unexpected fraternity, in these rituals of sharing and continuity that are sometimes chosen, more often forced upon us, exposes the stoic, earthbound side of his art, a side of his work finally more important than the anarchic, exotic elements to be found in the Russian maelstrom of *Under Western Eyes* or in the ambiguous savage (but also hollow) transcendence achieved by Kurtz in *Heart of Darkness*. This pragmatic, profoundly Wordsworthian side of Conrad is perhaps distilled for us in a remark he once made in response to an anecdote of Edward Garnett's: "Yes dear Edward. But have you ever had to keep an enraged negro armed with a razor from coming aboard, along a ten-inch plank, and drive him back to the wharf with only a short stick in your hands?" [22]

Subjecting the exotic (and innocent) imagination to the test of real experience, this remark illuminates Conrad's characteristic revision of the typical adventure plot. The hero in conventional adventure, escaping the confines of the ordinary world, escapes also from his human limitations. In Conradian adventure, of course, the hero, "housed in a dream, at dis-

22. *Letters from Joseph Conrad,* ed. Garnett, p. 12.

tance from the Kind" like the younger self Wordsworth describes in *Peele Castle,* escapes into an unfamiliar universe only to be confronted with the fact of his error and weakness, with the sure and terrible limitations of his humanity, and with his need for other men.

From these inevitable disillusionments Conrad turns, as Wordsworth does, to such consolation as there is in what the Russian zealots of *Under Western Eyes* are said to scorn: "the irremediable life of the earth as it is." And to what Dennis Donoghue has called "the ordinary universe." [23] This is a place in which elemental necessities join men to one another, a place in which men are not entirely cut off from their kind because they share similar feelings, fear death and want to keep living, ally themselves together when they must, and carry on long continuities of labor and struggle. In such an earthbound world, the poet or novelist discovers that one of his central tasks is to preserve in the memory of other men what he and those he has known have felt and have done. Conrad praises Frederick Marryat on these grounds. "History preserves the skeleton of facts," Conrad remarks, ". . . but it is in Marryat's novels that we find the mass of the nameless, that we see them in the flesh, that we obtain a glimpse of the everyday life and an insight into the spirit animating . . .

23. *The Ordinary Universe: Soundings in Modern Literature* (New York: Macmillan, 1968). Emphasizing what Randall Jarrell calls "the dailiness of life," Donoghue claims for certain modern writers, including late Romantics like Yeats and Rilke, what I am claiming for Conrad. For this antiapocalyptic side of Romanticism, see also Lionel Trilling, "Wordsworth and the Rabbis," in *The Opposing Self* (1955; rpt. New York: Compass Books-Viking, 1959), pp. 118–50; Richard Ellmann's essay on Auden, "Gazebos and Gashouses," in *Eminent Domain* (New York: Oxford Univ. Press, 1967), pp. 97–126; Gordon Haight's introduction to *Adam Bede* (1948; rpt. New York: Holt, Rinehart and Winston, 1961), pp. v–xviii, which sees this side of Wordsworth as the poet's primary legacy in George Eliot's work; and Karl Kroeber, "The Relevance and Irrelevance of Romanticism," *Studies in Romanticism,* 9 (1970), 297–306.

[that] crowd of obscure . . . [seamen] who knew how to
build for their country such a shining monument of memories" ("Tales of the Sea," *Notes on Life and Letters,* 53–54).
And Conrad sees his own writing in terms of this commemorative mission: "After all these years," he says in *A Personal
Record,* "each leaving its evidence of slowly blackened pages,
I can honestly say that it is a sentiment akin to piety which
prompted me to render in words assembled with conscien-
tious care the memory of things far distant and of men who
had lived" (10).

A similar piety lies behind Wordsworth's special interest
in beggars and wanderers, in leech-gatherers and solitary
reapers. The reaping girl is a symbol, enigmatic and rich, of
elemental human continuities. Geoffrey Hartman has written
of this commemorative aspect of Wordsworth's verse, linking
his characteristic poems with a form of writing called the
nature-inscription, in which natural objects and man-made
ones like tombs or statues are inscribed with verses intended
to commemorate some human or natural event.[24] Many of
Wordsworth's lengthy titles suggest a similar specifying or
commemorating impulse. "Lines left upon a Seat in a Yew-
Tree, which stands near the Lake of Esthwaite, on a desolate
part of the shore, yet commanding a beautiful prospect."
"Elegiac Stanzas, suggested by a picture of Peele Castle, in a
storm, painted by Sir George Beaumont." "Lines Composed
a Few Miles above Tintern Abbey, on revisiting the banks
of the Wye during a tour, July 13, 1789."

The charming, extravagant particularity of such titles answers in part Wordsworth's deep need to mark, to preserve,
the experiences he describes. The emotional states evoked in
the poems draw sustaining weight and credibility from the
earthbound precision of these titles. I felt this, Wordsworth

24. "Wordsworth, Inscriptions and Romantic Nature Poetry," in
Beyond Formalism, pp. 206–30.

says, at this particular place, two miles from that place, on this particular day in this particular year.

Conrad's extended efforts "to make us see," to give us characters who (as he said in a splendid letter) "will bleed to a prick, and are moving in a visible world" [25] parallels this Wordsworthian precision. And so does his compulsive need, in the prefaces to his novels, to insist on the real, autobiographical and historical origins of his stories and his characters. Don't disbelieve these characters, Conrad almost pleads with us in these Author's Notes. They really existed, I knew them, or read about them; or—sometimes—I *am* these characters. The powerful, recurring note of elegy in both Conrad and Wordsworth is part of this impulse to set down, to preserve, experiences or insights or stories that would otherwise be lost.

This impulse to memorialize and to connect things far distant and men who have lived is explicitly acknowledged in the Preface to the *Lyrical Ballads* and in several places in Conrad's nonfiction, most notably in his Preface to *The Nigger of the "Narcissus."* Commonly regarded as a manifesto of Modernism, Conrad's essay is often quoted for its line about making the reader see, but rarely looked at more closely.

Near the conclusion of his Preface Conrad elaborates a surprising definition of the artist. In an extended analogy, he compares the writer to "a labourer in a distant field" whose exertions are at once ordinary and vaguely mysterious. We who observe this laborer, Conrad says, are not desperate to understand him; our attention to his work is accidental, a leisurely interval as we lie "stretched at ease in the shade of a roadside tree." But "after a time," Conrad continues, we may

25. *Joseph Conrad: Letters to William Blackwood and David S. Meldrum,* ed. William Blackburn (Durham: Duke Univ. Press, 1958), p. 156.

begin to wonder languidly as to what the fellow may be at. We watch the movements of his body, the waving of his arms, we see him bend down, stand up, hesitate, begin again. It may add to the charm of an idle hour to be told the purpose of his exertions. If we know he is trying to lift a stone, to dig a ditch, to uproot a stump, we look with a more real interest at his efforts; we are disposed to condone the jar of his agitation upon the restfulness of the landscape; and even, if in a brotherly frame of mind, we may bring ourselves to forgive his failure. We understood his object, and, after all, the fellow has tried, and perhaps he had not the strength—and perhaps he had not the knowledge. We forgive, go on our way—and forget.

And so it is with the workman of art.   [xi]

The odd mingling of pessimism and charity that marks this passage is clearly more purely Conradian than modern. So too with the disquieting modesty—it is perhaps just honest realism—implicit in the assumption that literature is an activity that engages most people only in their leisure moments. More centrally, the very terms of Conrad's analogy have an old-fashioned, distinctly "unmodern" character. For Conrad's comparison of the writer to a worker in a field, his identification of ordinary human work with the enterprise of art—this runs counter to symbolist and post-symbolist notions of the artist as a man isolated from his fellow men, relying (like Joyce's artist-hero) on silence, exile, and cunning to get his work done. Resisting the idea of the artist's alienation, grounding itself instead in an unstrident sense that we all belong to a fraternity of failure, the Conrad passage is not easily compatible with such (by now) standard versions of the role of art and the artist as these, which I take from the table of contents of Ellmann and Feidelson's *The Modern Tradition:* [26] "Art as Ascetic Religion" (Flaubert), "The Poet as Revolutionary Seer" (Rimbaud), "Art as Aristocratic Mystery" (Mallarmé), "Poetry as a Game of Knowledge" (Auden).

26. New York: Oxford Univ. Press, 1965.

If we look to place Conrad's laborer in more congenial company, we must go back to the Romantics, and particularly, I think, to Wordsworth. The passage I have quoted, in fact, is something near to a prose paraphrase of that recurring Wordsworth lyric in which a halted traveler looks across a rural distance at another human figure who is bent to the landscape, doing the work of survival. Acknowledging the physical and other distances that separate him from the figure he is observing, the watcher's meditation (like Conrad's paragraph) is at the same time an assertion of the bonds between them; and however weighted with a sense of loss or partialness, it is an act of community.

These parallels are scarcely fortuitous, for there is a definitive kinship between the whole of Conrad's Preface and Wordsworth's earlier, more systematic one. Both distinguish art from science; both speak of the need to revitalize a language which has (in Conrad's words) been "defaced by ages of careless usage." Both affirm art as a bringer of truth. But their most important agreement is their joint definition of the artist's mission.

The poet, says Wordsworth, is one who "binds together by passion and knowledge the vast empire of human society, as it is spread over the whole earth, and over all time." Conrad's version of this troubles the modern ear, and emphasizes the specially Romantic virtue of sincerity:

To snatch in a moment of courage, from the remorseless rush of time, a passing phase of life, is only the beginning of the task. The task approached in tenderness and faith is to hold up unquestioningly, without choice and without fear, the rescued fragment before all eyes in the light of a sincere mood. . . . In a single-minded attempt of that kind, if one be deserving and fortunate, one may perchance attain to such clearness of sincerity that at last the presented vision of regret or pity, of terror or mirth, shall awaken in the hearts of the beholders that feeling of unavoidable solidarity; of the solidarity in mysterious origin, in toil, in joy, in hope, in uncertain fate, which binds men to each other and all mankind to the visible world.   [x]

I find even the ornateness of that statement moving, and yet another measure of Conrad's decisive allegiances with the century of Wordsworth.

MICHAEL G. COOKE

Modern Black Autobiography
in the Tradition

Introduction: Autobiography

In terms of literature, Jung's antinomian law, "that the real picture consists of nothing but exceptions to the rule," [1] may have been framed for autobiography. Paradox inheres in the form, which calls for personal uniqueness and yet depends on a cogent general category—the definition of self achieved by one autobiographer must be both genuine and inimitable, and cannot lend itself to use by others without leading to a certain forgery. Critically speaking, we can be sure when generality has been taken too far, as in Gibbon's refusing to discuss "the first consciousness of manhood" on the grounds that this "very interesting moment of our lives" "less properly belong to the memoirs of an individual, than to the natural history of the species." [2] But we are equally sure that generality cannot be wished away. Even the prototypal professor of uniqueness, Jean-Jacques Rousseau, continually ascends to generality, though he finds it shaky

1. Carl Jung, *The Undiscovered Self*, trans. R. F. C. Hull (New York: Mentor Books—New American Library, 1958), p. 17.

2. Edward Gibbon, *The Autobiographies*, printed verbatim from hitherto unpublished mss., ed. John Murray (London: J. Murray, 1896), *Memoir B*, p. 150.

ground. Rousseau's example provides a vivid instance of the
paradox of autobiography: that in its presumption of uniqueness it is frustrated by the demands of philosophy, while remaining impotent in its conceptual and expository needs
unless it has the philosopher's tools at its command. It is
this state of being at odds with itself that I would like to
study here, with a view to showing that at least three modern
black writers have achieved happy resolutions of the autobiographical paradox, making evolutionary contributions to
the form of western autobiography.

It is important to maintain a distinction between what may
be autobiographical and autobiography proper, akin to the
distinction between the poetical and poetry. In another context, a recent writer on spiritual autobiography addresses
himself to this point: "Donne's record of his illness in *De-
votions upon Emergent Occasions* is a splendid example of
autobiographical material essential yet subordinate to a
work's main scheme; personal experience is assimilated into
what is, in effect, an extended homily" on the human condition.[3] Perfect obedience to memory and candor would
yield something richly autobiographical, but less than autobiography, just as the most eloquent profession of the meaning of one's life or reflections upon it would constitute more
of a credo than an autobiography. The form entails simultaneous, if conflicting, obligations to narrative and to analysis
and exposition. The essential thing in realizing this form is
that the work of memory, the material truth, not only must
contain an essential informing truth as an available element,
but must convey it as an explicit and active one. (The lack of
an informing truth as a principle of coherence keeps such
modes as the diary or journal or travelogue or memoir at the
level of the autobiographical, and has the same effect on many

3. George Starr, *Defoe and Spiritual Autobiography* (Princeton:
Princeton Univ. Press, 1969), pp. 33–34.

poems and novels, from Byron and Gottfried Keller to Conrad, Proust, and Joyce.)

The skepticism usually aimed at the autobiographer's reliability will not take us very far.[4] At least not if autobiography, as a literary form, incorporates an honorable selection and proportion of facts, and a plausible (not definitive) human judgment, *without being defined by them.* Individualizing articulation is the very spirit of the form. Barring a selection of data or an interpretive bias so flagrant as to involve autobiographer and reader in a cynical disregard of literary integrity, the point of autobiography is how shape and significance can be found in, or given to, the amorphousness of experience, how the abstraction of the "I" can be identified and realized.

And the overriding concern comes to center on the style of the autobiography, taking style to mean not sentence structure and vocabulary, as Roy Pascal seems to do,[5] but the whole complex of resources, of selection, proportion, sequence, and recurrence, as well as those verbal, rhetorical, logical, structural resources whereby the work at once appre-

4. Dr. Johnson, of course, thinks the "subjective" individual more, not less, reliable than the "objective" observer in matters of information and interpretation of his life. So does De Quincey. The mistrust of the autobiographer's motives and judgment seems to have sprung up in our century, but it is worth noting that it does not pass unchallenged; in his essay on "Finding a Poem" W. D. Snodgrass writes: "the only reality which a man can ever surely know is that self he cannot help being, though he will only know that self through its interactions with the world around it" (*Partisan Review,* 26 [Spring 1959], 283). Besides individual witnesses, there is an essential argument against skepticism, in that autobiography is both objective and subjective, and allows the autobiographer to turn the outsider's skepticism upon himself with the genuine possibility of a balanced view embodying the best of both perspectives. Otherwise, we must suppose him proceeding from subjectivity to objectivity, which is in turn subjectivity, and so on endlessly, in a maze of multiplying reservations that baffle expression and response.

5. *Design and Truth in Autobiography* (Cambridge, Mass.: Harvard Univ. Press, 1960), p. 79f.

hends and expresses its subject. In spite of his best efforts, then, Gibbon's treatment of the first consciousness of manhood, by its very idiom and its obliqueness, becomes as perspicuous as that of Rousseau or Yeats or Dylan Thomas. For in effect style in autobiography distinctively entails not just the representation of the self in language, but the giving over of the self to language. Anyone with enough energy and reflection to do an autobiography goes beyond a reporting into a realization of the self through the instrumentality of language.

It is no mere coincidence that autobiography first cuts its own stream in the literary landscape toward the end of the eighteenth century, or as a sign of the Romantic movement. Formally, or generically speaking, autobiography may be associated with the dissolution or permutation of genres in the romantic period: *The Prelude* is a lyrical-epical-philosophical-mystical-descriptive-travelogue-autobiographical poem. Further, autobiography feeds on the experimental or deferential arrogance of the age; the self is the source of the system of which it is a part, creates what it discovers, and although (as Coleridge realized) it is nothing unto itself, it is the possibility of everything for itself. Autobiography is the coordination of the self as content—everything available in memory, perception, understanding, imagination, desire—and the self as shaped, formed in terms of a perspective and pattern of interpretation. Autobiography readily engrafts itself on, or insinuates itself into what once had been generically simpler statements. The result of such multiplicity is both great hazards and great possibilities, the event again depending least on the intention of the writer, something shared equally by Gibbon and Rousseau. De Quincey poignantly indicates the autobiographer's anxiety in his *Autobiographic Sketches,* where he deprecates the mere "amusement which attaches to any real story," while remaining uncertain how to blend "intellectual impulses" and "absolute frankness" so as to produce the "deep, solemn, and . . .even . . . thrilling interest" which should bind together all the elements of the work.

What De Quincey is concerned about (and it should be observed that he is not speaking as a novice autobiographer) is the difficulty of finding a definition of his subject, *and* a congruent form. This indivisible difficulty may be taken as the essential one for autobiography. The way it is met, by the same token, would go far toward establishing the essential quality of an autobiography or of an era in autobiography.

The problem of establishing a subject and form gives special interest to the rewriting of autobiographies. Rewriting has been taken up on stylistic grounds, as in Ian Jack's study of De Quincey,[6] but unaccountably not as a characteristic or essential issue for autobiography, not even in John Morris' *Versions of the Self.*[7] For whether the restlessness that brings a man back to recast his image and form be psychic or critical, the stages of his self-presentation have to be tied up with a question of identity; the autobiographer loses clarity and authority even as he multiplies himself. One's autobiograph*ies* constitute an anomaly, though autobiography, as Wordsworth and Malcolm X in different ways have shown, may be generated out of a subject's knowing struggle for identity, by stages, or his undergoing a conscious evolution of self-conception.

The problem of the self and time is paramount for autobiography.[8] It compounds the problem of conceptual unity if the "self" alters in time, or alters its formulation. And yet

6. "De Quincey Revises His *Confessions,*" *PMLA,* 72 (1957), 122–46.

7. New York: Basic Books, 1966. See in particular p. 10, where the question is rather narrowly conceived, and set aside.

8. That is, with the exception of one suspicious subcategory, utilitarian or applied autobiography, exemplified by Bunyan, Franklin, Vico, and perhaps St. Augustine, who show little susceptibility to the internal material doubts which autobiography as such has been heir to.

no autobiography can be exempt from the force of its moment. As the selection of material can raise questions as to content, so the choice of time implies questions as to conception. How and what is written depends on the *when* of the writing. It is of particular interest, then, to see Edward Gibbon, habituated to neo-classical discipline and elegant practicality, going through the labyrinth of self-description. Both the tidiness of hand and the polished statement of each of the six versions of his *Autobiography* profess a clear decision and power as regards the portrayal of "the historian of Rome"; but the succession of versions, so obscure in its patternlessness, critically weakens the foundations of assurance on which the individual versions seem to rest. Indeed, *Memoir C,* which describes itself most impersonally as "the narrative of my literary life" (257), exhibits an unusual, if not uniform, degree of frankness and copiousness concerning a host of subjects: his "estate," as to which he is so reticent in *B;* the misdemeanors on his second visit to Lausanne; his desire for power and authority, especially in relation to his father, whose death is used as a motif and epoch here; his relationship with Deyverdun and his attitude toward women; and the predominance of pragmatism over affection in his makeup.

It seems at least statistically clear that the form of autobiography proved for Gibbon more recalcitrant than the form of his immortal history, for which he needed no more than three revisions of the initial chapters to hit his stride. The problem was in part one of settling on the attitude to take toward his subject and his audience, but it was probably first a problem of identifying his subject and his purpose. In short, the problem of autobiography unwittingly experienced by one whose habits of assurance, while evidently baffled, were strong enough to withstand the radical threats conveyed by the very form he adopts in what one may call his composed egotism. It is possible to extrapolate from the whole set of Gibbon's autobiographies, or would-be autobiographies, a basic concern with survival and security, generated by an ill-concealed intuition of the precariousness of life, personal freedom, and social expectations. But none of this is explicit or reliable, and it is not, by way of anticipation, till we come to Richard Wright's *Black Boy* that we find an achieved autobiography dealing centrally with these issues.

If Gibbon willy-nilly demonstrates the perennial problem of autobiography, it will be profitable to glance at the terms of success discovered by various exponents of the form, as a background for the scrutiny of Wright, Malcolm X and Eldridge Cleaver. For this purpose I should like to consider the original version of De Quincey's *Confessions of an English Opium Eater,* Newman's *Apologia pro Vita Sua,* and Yeats's *Reveries over Childhood and Youth,* as somehow typifying the periods in which they were written, and yet also as necessarily singular illustrations of the possibilities of success in autobiography.

De Quincey, Newman, Yeats

Things were to change by the time he got to the revised version, but De Quincey in 1822 had had neither time nor occasion to think better of the adventure of the original *Confessions of an English Opium-Eater.* A half-jocular hubris marks the work, which is ultimately less a confession than an exploration and appropriation of uncharted psychological territory. The revised version is more informative, but at the cost of becoming prolix, choppy and either sermonizing or polemical; [9] the original seems genuinely coherent and philosophical, provided we recognize the perversity of its confes-

9. See John Jordan's judicious summary in his introduction to *The Confessions* (New York: Everyman's Library, 1960), pp. x–xii. As a *book,* rather than a storehouse, I think the first version merits the palm.

sion. The sense of guilt, of reconciliation with the community, works only as an opening ploy to indulge the reader's self-importance and tranquilize his fear. The sense of avowing a position is the implicit one, and becomes salient in two ways. The first of these is negative, in the impugning of standard authorities and orthodoxies in the academy, in medicine, in a system of morality which has become" inhuman," and even in the social assumptions concerning wine; the second is positive, and takes the form of establishing his own credentials and authority as a philosopher of the "inner eye and [the] power of intuition for the vision and mysteries of human nature." The language of the text suggests that the vision is both apocalyptic and natural; opium is associated with Eden at its best and at its worst (it is ambiguously described as "insufferable splendour"), and again with dreams which are themselves associated with infinity, with childhood, and with unexceptionable figures like Dryden and Fuseli; so that myth and memory and art alike sanction it. In this respect the *Confessions* become an informal or dramatic trial of De Quincey's aborted *magnum opus, De Emendatione Humani Intellectus.*

No one needs to be reminded of De Quincey's incessant concern with the reader's reactions in the original *Confessions.* A note De Quincey added to the original preface gives a clear indication of why this is so:

I feel [our own age] to be, more emphatically than any since the period of Queen Elizabeth and Charles I, an intellectual, a moving, and a self-conflicting age: and inevitably, where the intellect has been preternaturally awakened, the moral sensibility must soon be commensurately stirred. The very distinctions, psychologic or metaphysical, by which, as its hinges and articulations, our modern thinking moves, proclaim the subtler character of the questions which now occupy our thoughts. Not as pedantic only, but as suspiciously unintelligible, such distinctions would, one hundred and thirty years ago, have been viewed as indictable.[10]

It is necessary to stress the way De Quincey's manner, while it involves playing up to the reader, intrinsically serves as a way of playing on him. The author's pious protestations that the will to be "useful and instructive" alone has made him remove the "decent veil of drapery" from his miserable experience is pious equivocation. The veil is really removed from unknown and hence uncomfortable regions of the human mind, of which De Quincey by "chance" or "accident" —key terms recurring throughout—has been the Columbus. The function of the autobiography is to map out this region, authenticate it, and annex it to the kingdom of humanity. The articulation of the life takes place in terms of the personal capacities and external circumstances which have equipped De Quincey for the task of emending the picture of the human mind. In this sense, the *Confessions* modulate into apologia and beyond that into radical missionary work for "the church of opium."

The peculiar interplay of chance and teleology in the career exhibited in the *Confessions,* and the temper of self-seeking and apostolic self-justification which informs it (De Quincey founds the "church of opium") bear a strong enough resemblance to Rousseau's *Confessions,* Wordsworth's *Prelude,* and Coleridge's *Biographia Literaria* to be thought of as Romantic. A certain buoyancy in the face of a situation problematical on the subjective as well as public levels marks all of these works, and is especially striking in the case of Coleridge, who, in the autobiographical context, surpasses

10. "De Quincey's Additions in 1856 to his Original Preface of 1822," *Confessions of an English Opium-Eater,* rev. and enl. ed. of 1856, in *The Collected Writings of Thomas De Quincey,* ed. David Masson, III (Edinburgh: A. & C. Black, 1890), 216.

himself in personal and philosophical daring.[11] In this light one is tempted to say that a concentration on the collapse of certitudes as a stimulus to Romanticism goes awry; a degree of courage and resiliency and resourcefulness in coping with incertitude seems to merit stronger emphasis. Certainly an almost evolutonary change can be recognized in the way autobiographers like Newman or Mill or Gosse or Pattison or F. W. H. Myers or even Tennyson, in the Victorian era, see themselves and the world in terms of the need for authority, with the self-generating philosophy of High Romanticism fading into improbability.

To deal in particular with Newman, it is hard to agree with Pascal that the *Apologia* does not enable us "to perceive and feel the driving forces in the man, the genetic sources of the personality, the numerous potentialities in him which ultimately led to [the] great decision of Newman's life" (*Design and Truth,* p. 100). The very contrary would seem true, unless one can indifferently pass by such lines as the following:

If I looked into a mirror, and did not see my face, I should have the sort of feeling which actually comes upon me, when I look into this living busy world, and see no reflexion of its Creator. . . . I am far from denying the real force of the arguments in proof of a God, drawn from the general facts of human society and the course of history, but these do not warm me or enlighten me; they do not take away the winter of my desolation, or make the buds unfold and the leaves grow within me, and my moral being rejoice.[12]

A salient feature of Newman's apologetics, for all its institutional and analytical tendencies, is its saturation with his

11. This point is developed by M. G. Cooke, *"Quisque Sui Faber:* Coleridge in the *Biographia Literaria," Philological Quarterly,* 50 (April, 1971), 208–229.

12. *Apologia pro Vita Sua,* ed. A. Dwight Culler (Cambridge, Mass.: Riverside ed., Houghton Mifflin, 1956), p. 230.

"private thoughts and feelings," or, to use another phrase of his, his capacity for "identifying" himself (p. 229) with authority. The pattern of the book follows a progression from personal to institutional authority, from national to catholic authority, from legitimate to infallible authority, where finally and alone true rest is possible. But Newman's impulse toward identifying himself with authority goes hand in hand with an impulse toward "vindicating it," so that the liveliest communication exists continuously between the poles of personalty and logic, and indeed, though Newman declares "it is not . . . easy . . . to wind up an Englishman to a dogmatic level," between personality and dogma when the dogma will not let him down and leave him, as did the Anglican divines, "in a humour" to "bite off [somebody's] ears." The crystallization of Newman's need for authority and dogma seems to have occurred around a typically nineteenth-century trauma: the humiliation and bafflement of death.

The truth is, I was beginning to prefer intellectual excellence to moral; I was drifting in the direction of the Liberalism of the day. I was rudely awakened from my dream at the end of 1827 by two great blows—illness and bereavement.

The "influence of a definite Creed," and "impressions of dogma" which were never "effaced or obscured" had been felt more than a decade before, in 1816, and "the doctrine of Tradition" had been grasped as a principle from Dr. Hawkins five years before, in 1822; but the critical point arrives in 1827, as just described. The crisis, of course, is not one of mutual exclusion as between intellectual and moral excellence, but of "preference." Intellectual excellence becomes more of an instrument than an ideal. If the *Apologia* exhibits Newman's need for authority, it also exhibits a true fastidiousness about the subject in the all but scrupulous deliberations which attended his acceptance of authority. Newman himself observes that "to reconcile theory and fact is almost an instinct of the mind," and it seems proper to treat his description of one change as normative:

The process of change [from liberalism] had been slow; it had been done not rashly, but by rule and measure, "at sundry times and in divers manners," first one disclosure and then another, till the whole evangelical doctrine was brought into full manifestation.

I would only suggest that not intellectuality but the subjective importance of authority is the ground of these deliberations, a paradox only compounded when Newman, quite justly, links acceptance of authority with "bold unworldliness and vigorous independence of mind." The phrase is applied to Thomas Scott of Aston Sandford, but Scott is used as a model by Newman, and his "independence," which takes the form of just acts of obedience to the right institution—"he followed truth wherever it led him" [13] —must be set against the independence of the man who, "at an unseasonable time," tries to carry "a reformation of an abuse, or the fuller development of a doctrine, or the adoption of a particular policy (p. 244). Newman's suspicion of such unqualified independence is noteworthy and may be treated in his own words:

Knowing that there is no one who will be doing anything toward [his objective] in his own lifetime unless he does it himself, he will not listen to the voice of authority, and he spoils a good work in his own century, in order that another man as yet unborn, may not have the opportunity of bringing it happily to perfection in the next. He may seem to the world to be nothing else than a bold champion for the truth and a martyr to free opinion, when he is just one of those persons whom the competent authority ought to silence; and, though the case may not fall within that

13. *Apologia,* p. 25.

subject-matter in which that authority is infallible, . . . it is clearly the duty of authority to act vigorously in the case.

[p. 245]

The introduction of the purpose clause—*in order that* another man . . . may not have the opportunity of bringing it happily to perfection"—where a result clause might seem more fitting, perhaps strikes an ominous note, but the argument for authority in terms of prudence or pragmatism is too gracious to arouse suspicion on that score. Basically it extends, and does not define Newman's position. Its prime effect is to deepen our understanding of Newman's panoptic devotion to authority, the quest for which almost comes to seem the essential feature of his "history of [him]self." I have suggested that such a quest marks him as a man of his time. What singles him out withal is the consciousness of the quest, the intricacy of its articulation, its eloquence, and the achievement of personal authority by the expression and satisfaction of his greatest needs and powers in terms of Authority.

If in retrospect the creation or discovery of spontaneous authority might seem to characterize De Quincey as a Romantic autobiographer, and dedication to formal authority to characterize Newman as Victorian, nothing could be more telling for twentieth-century developments than the way Yeats circumvents the awful authority of "God," whom he takes his Grandfather for, in *Reveries over Childhood and Youth.*[14] This is not to suggest that Yeats is taking a stand

14. The course of autobiography, though it encourages the recognition of time boundaries, may be rather evolutionary than otherwise, with various stages of development occurring together, and without loss of validity or viability for precedent forms, because others subsequently come to the fore. H. G. Wells may be regarded as Victorian in his "idea of the modern world-state," but modern in his sense of "the planless casualness of our contemporary world." And Edwin Muir shows what can still be done with autobiography in explicitly religious terms.

in direct relation to Newman; rather his stand freely lends itself to comparison with Newman's and furnishes important help toward understanding the evolution of autobiography.

On the surface, the *Reveries over Childhood and Youth* would seem to be little more than random "recollections of relatives and friends," [15] but there are good grounds for taking it as an integral work following quite original lines of organization. It is true that the opening statement as it were helplessly confesses a lack of order or relation in memory, and hence the impossibility of ordering and understanding experience. But this statement turns out to work more as a symbol than as description: "My first memories [Yeats writes] are fragmentary and contemporaneous. . . ." [16] But he immediately adds a metaphor of intellection: "as though one remembered some first moments of the Seven Days." In this way he makes the experience available to us by an imaginative act that seems to be widely possible; it is "one" who remembers, not "I." Further elaborating and, let me stress, interpreting this obscure experience, Yeats writes: "It seems as if time had not yet been created, for all thoughts connected with emotion and place are without sequence." In fact, time signals are plentiful enough in the writing, though occurring at random and not in such a way as to provide or permit the kind of assurance we are likely to feel about a work where we can set up its narrative progression (I mean, it is easier to think one knows *The Faerie Queene,* Bk. I, than *The Prelude,* Bk. I, simply in terms of ease of narrative connection). But the nullifying of time is not just incidental to Yeats's "first memories"; it informs *all* his memories, the *Reveries* being organized in discontinuous sections to reveal the fact that his entire experience, or perhaps his grasp of his experi-

15. Pascal, *Design and Truth in Autobiography,* p. 8.
16. *The Autobiography of William Butler Yeats,* (New York: Collier Books, 1971), p. 1.

ence, is "fragmentary and isolated and contemporaneous."

On the whole this might seem to describe only the effect and not the thesis of the presentation; but I would suggest that the final paragraph of the *Reveries* functions as a retro-active thesis, which carries us irresistibly back to the sense of aboriginal beginning, making this sense endless and ex-plaining the absence of narrative progression and the nullify-ing of time:

When I think of all the books I have read, and of the wise words I have heard spoken, and of the anxiety I have given to parents and grandparents, and of the hopes that I have had, all life weighed in the scales of my own life seems to me a preparation for something that never happens.[17]

In effect, the replication of the Seven Days in his own world, Yeats's version of the primary imagination, has not come about, so that we are left with an uncreated, and hence in literary terms an unorganized world, but also at the same time an adequate conception of this uncreated state, and even a sort of representation of it. Yeats is clear about his unclarity. Indeed, the number of sections in the *Reveries,* thirty-three, seems to me meant to suggest the Christological age, with the revealing difference that for Yeats whatever is in preparation "never happens." This suggestion in fact ap-pears to be strengthened by the title of the second part of Yeats's *Autobiography,* namely "The Trembling of the Veil." The analogy may be considered as clear, and as ob-

17. Richard Ellmann, pointing out that *At the Hawk's Well* ends on the same note as the *Reveries,* insists on the biographical fact that "a great deal had happened" (*Yeats: The Man and the Masks* [New York: E. P. Dutton, 1948], p. 216). But this ignores the difference between "happening" and "becoming," between experienced event and con-ceived or identified reality. By the same token, Joseph Ronsley's stress on "self-assertion" in the *Reveries* seems to ignore the indecisive and inconsequential quality of the gestures of self-assertion (*Yeats's Auto-biography: Life as Symbolic Pattern* [Cambridge, Mass.: Harvard Univ. Press, 1968], pp. 50 f).

scure, as the answer to the question: And what rough beast
. . . slouches toward Bethlehem? Yeats assembled his *Autobiography* with a running spontaneity but also with a retro-
spective calculation; and it is one of the happy effects of
his agnosticism that leaving the final section on "The Bounty
of Sweden" unshaped fits both his whimsy and his design.
For the "autobiographical muse," far from "betraying"
Yeats and "abandoning him to ultimate perplexity as to the
meaning of his experiences" (Ellman, *Yeats: Man and Masks,*
p. 2), seems instead to have clarified for him the elusiveness
of any such meaning, no matter how diligently he sought
it.

Yeats's achievement in autobiography, a considerable one,
is to have invented a sort of mosaic or pointillist form which
both represents and controls incertitude of mind, and futility of action. From H. G. Wells to Bertrand Russell and
Norman Podhoretz one still finds more or less plausible pre-
tensions to philosophy or to power, but what Yeats implies
and Wells himself declares, a sense of "planless casualness"
in the modern world, feels truer in the first place, and proves
stronger and deeper in literary experience: one may quickly
cite, for example, Frank Budgen's *Myselves When Young*
and Goronwy Rees's *A Bundle of Sensations.*[18] In this regard,
the work of modern black autobiographers emerges with
singular force. In this work, the sense of a perennially
emergent or explosive universe is made palpable, the sense
of personal encumbrance urgent and ubiquitous, while the
sense of the self as not only finding itself but somehow
thriving (not just making it) in the flux also comes through.
The presence of Yeats by itself will indicate that this is a cultural, and not just a black pattern; anyone who recalls Hemingway's *Green Hills of Africa* or H. M. Tomlinson's *The
Sea and the Jungle* will find this point driven home.

18. Well treated by Morris, *Versions of the Self,* p. 11.

Wright, Malcolm X, Cleaver

The three writers, Richard Wright, Malcolm X, and Eldridge Cleaver, at once become the environment it has been my concern to outline, and become their own men. They demand to be read for something more than what Gottfried Keller deigned to praise Rousseau for, a certain confessional shock-value. With *Black Boy*,[19] Wright, who does not fail to suggest the high security he attained in terms of "the external drama of life" (*BB*, 112), surpasses all writers I know in the naturalistic, non-Kafkaesque evocation of the physical dimensions of incertitude, its simple separation from the operations of interpretive reason and purposive will. Accident becomes substantive almost; as Wright says, "anything might happen" (224). Flogging, fighting, theft, death or threats of death, and above all the endless disorientation of moving and flight spread through the narrative so far as to become symbols, and finally round into the status of things, comparable to the litanies of objects that dot the early pages of the work. They are part of Wright's world, like trees. He breathes the atmosphere they exude, and escapes from them only by a kind of homeopathic experiment. "The thirst for violence . . ." he says, "was in me, for intrigue, for plotting, for secrecy, for bloody murders," but it is his first calculated, as opposed to reflexive, wrongdoing, stealing for money, that breaks him free.

This act, though, seems rather instrumental than essential to Wright's freedom. What saves him from the fascination of the physical is first his intuition of "the drama of human feeling," the inquisitive shaping mind and sensitivity of the artist whose external story (how and when I wrote what, and what then) is never told. Appropriately enough, this inner self is continually represented by Wright in metaphors, and

19. Richard Wright, *Black Boy: A Record of Childhood and Youth* (Cleveland and New York: World, 1945).

particularly in metaphors of a journey marked by an obscure destination and a threatening fate (187).

A spontaneous conviction of the essential being and the coercive impress of the physical state form two main threads of which *Black Boy* is woven. It is significant that Wright does not finally take in the coercive physical state until well past the mid-point of the work, where he calls himself "a black boy in Mississippi"; the phrase may be glossed, for posterity: a black boy in Mississippi is as good as a born slave, and at that a difficult rather than a quiescent one, to be carefully excluded from every good but work. And by this point Wright's personal metaphor, the leitmotif of travel, is well enough established to oppose this formula and suggest that he will have his "own strange and separate road" (140).

The personal and the public definitions do not meet without some turbulence, reflected in the continual revision of their relationship. Wright gives his life the character of something externally "shaped" (124) and determined, while also fluid and as it were arising by a creative capacity and response in himself. Perhaps a basic doubtfulness finds expression in the presence of a crepuscular light at key moments: the shopping episode, the selling of KKK papers, the threatened flogging by his Uncle to put him in his place. Certainly the definiteness with which Wright summarizes his existence in the light of his "mother's suffering" or "the white death"—his blinding phrase for the social syndrome which used to culminate in lynching—is of more local than general validity. The two do not chime together, a fact which provokes a distracting curiosity about the relation of his home life to the effect of Mississippi on him (111, 112, 165, 181, 190, 192); and neither allows for the reality of his "undreamed-of shores." A genuine duality arises here, I think, and it picks up Wright's knowing presentation of his swings

between wild activity and paralysis, as well as his consciousness of being "strongly tender and cruel, violent and peace-
ful" (112). The principle of reconciliation in this case does
not appear. What Wright gives us instead is a distillation
from the very solidity and at the same time disorder of his
experience. Twice, at points of wide survey, he sets up the
issues of his life in abstract terms. "At the age of twelve,"
he tells us, he formed "a conviction that the meaning of living came only when one was struggling to wring a meaning
out of meaningless suffering" (112). And then the grown man
writing his autobiography, pronounces that men "if . . .
lucky . . . might win some redeeming meaning for their
having struggled and suffered here beneath the stars" (285).
Even if the similarity in idiom is an accident of the time of
writing, the similarity in situation remains to give weight
to the problem of knowledge in the text. The bombardment
of the mind by multifarious data stands out in *Black Boy*,
and that may indicate the upshot of the mind's learning to
struggle toward *the* definition which will comprehend this
or that definition arising along the way. One struggles with
everything or risks getting caught off guard. But by the same
token the struggle, oblique or dormant as it can be, in part
limits the possibilities for ultimate resolution of particular
issues. There comes to mind the picture of Wright threatened with a more or less arbitrary flogging and refusing to
give in. The threat, you will recall, is common in the book,
and is never really overcome; one source of hope appears,
as Wright's reaction, at first hysterical, modulates toward the
cold resentment and clear-eyed strength of the clash with his
uncle. This scene, unlike, say, Wordsworth's hike toward
sunrise on Mt. Snowdon, does not furnish any kind of prac-
tical-symbolic solution to a basic question of being. But a
solution need not preoccupy us. The emergence of the ques-

tion against enormous odds is itself noteworthy, and Wright's portrayal of its ubiquitous physicality appears both cogent and distinctive.

The Autobiography of Malcolm X, [20] because of the circumstances under which it was produced, does not entirely lend itself to the stylistic approach I have been following. But the rhythm of the work gives legitimate grounds for comment on Malcolm X's response to changeableness, and his capacity for definition, two of the very issues which Wright so graphically raises. Though he is not above interpreting particular events in what might seem an arbitrary light (Allah made him fight Bill Peterson a second time, to end his "fight career"), the distinctive feature of the *Autobiography* is its naturalistic use of time, the willingness to let the past stand as it was, in its own season, even when later developments, of intellect or intuition or event, give it a different quality. It is, I would surmise, on such grounds that C.W.E. Bigsby calls Malcolm "a naif of stunning integrity." [21] Malcolm goes through a series of virtual incarnations, starting with the name Malcolm Little, and becoming delinquent, prize student, Shorty's "homeboy," Detroit Red, Satan, convert to Muslimism and so Malcolm X, ex-Muslim founder of the Muslim Mosque, Inc., and finally the follower of the orthodox Islam, El-Hajj Malik El-Shabazz. But not quite finally. The changes at first take place ad lib, but by the end it is clear that, though he does not seek change, Malcolm, seeking truth and his own best humanity, will not flinch from its demands. He may not have a stable position, but the interview with Africa's most respected American ambassador (who is white) clearly images a deeper stability of

20. Malcolm X, *The Autobiography . . . With the assistance of Alex Haley,* intro. by M. S. Handler (New York: Grove Press, 1965).

21. "The Black American Writer," in *The Black American Writer,* ed. C.W.E. Bigsby, Vol. I, *Fiction,* (Baltimore: Pelican Books, 1971), p. 21.

intellect and of spirit. The atmosphere in which the *Autobiography* operates is remarkably practical and quick-moving; its genius springs from being so and at the same time remarkably responsive to crystallizations of meaning, as Malcolm X avoids Richard Wright's anxieties without trying to evade his problems. In historical terms, a measure of this performance can be gained by reference to Bunyan and Wordsworth, since Malcolm X has written a distinctively modern conversion narrative without, like Bunyan, subordinating the intensity of particular stages of his life, and has depicted a wholeness of personality which accommodates unpredictable turns, like Wordsworth, but which does not suggest even an inscrutable teleology.[22]

On the surface Cleaver's *Soul on Ice* [23] seems as thoroughly given over to analysis as *The Autobiography of Malcolm X* to narrative. But I would propose that Cleaver's is really a highly eclectic style which, combined with an ingenious organization of diversified elements, produces in effect the autobiography of a mind, from the birth of an almost savage self-consciousness ("Prior to 1954 we lived in an atmosphere of novocain") to the spiritual projection of a wide human contact founded on self-sacrifice, self-understanding, compassion, reverence, and hope. In the sequence of items, political, sociological, psychological, epistolary, dramatic, analytical, narrative, journalistic, critical, we may be equally encounter-

22. In these terms one finds little basis for Richard Gilman's judgment of the *Autobiography:* "Its way of looking at the world, its formulation of experience, is not the potential possession . . . of us all; hard, local, intransigent, . . . it remains in some sense unassimilable for those . . . who aren't black" ("White standards and Negro Writing," in Bigsby, *Black American Writer,* p. 35). To the contrary, as James M. Cox observes, " 'The Autobiography of Malcolm X' is somehow one of the great imaginative works of the last decade" ("Autobiography and America," *Virginia Quarterly Review,* 47 [Spring, 1971], 252).

23. Eldridge Cleaver, *Soul on Ice,* intro. by Maxwell Geismar (New York: McGraw-Hill, 1968).

ing a raw source of experience and knowledge ("The Allegory of the Black Eunuchs"), the highly formal or formulaic
product of experience and reflection ("The Black Man's
Stake in Vietnam" or "The Primeval Mitosis"), the account
of participation in typical social patterns and the discovery
of their implications ("A Day in Folsom Prison"), or soul-
searching love-letters. The thing to recognize here is that
each is part of Cleaver's "adventure in discovery," as record,
or as stage. Cleaver explicitly identifies political and autobiographical concerns from the start:

> Nineteen fifty-four . . . is held to be a crucial turning point in
> the history of the Afro-American—for the U.S.A. as a whole—
> the year segregation was outlawed by the U.S. Supreme Court.
> It was also a crucial year for me.

The identification gets even clearer later on: "We are a
very sick country—I, perhaps, am sicker than most" (p. 16).
But that identification is not complete, or at least not deter-
ministic. In substance *Soul on Ice* develops Cleaver's knowledge that "instead of simply *reacting* [he] could *act*" (p. 5),
and beyond that his knowledge of the way to act with
strength and grace, so as to benefit others. In *Soul on Ice* we
see combined two major possibilities of autobiography isolated by James M. Cox: Franklin's model act of self-making,
and Thoreau's model act of self-possession.[24]

The title of the opening chapter, "On Becoming," sets the
keynote of the work, reducing to the status of details, rather
than implicit laws of being, the facts Cleaver cites at the
beginning of the second letter from prison:

> I'm perfectly aware that I'm in prison, that I'm a Negro, that I've
> been a rapist, and that I have a Higher Uneducation. . . . [But]
> I could just as easily . . . [mention] that I'm tall, that I'm
> skinny, that I need a shave, that I'm hard-up.   [pp. 18–19]

24. "Autobiography and America," p. 265.

Obviously Cleaver does not anticipate becoming an elected official, or even a registered voter; his commitment to becoming may in fact prolong his stay in prison. What he has in mind is the kind of man he is "going to be," and his response to Thomas Merton's *The Seven Storey Mountain* makes plain his attempt to digest everything, books, people, ideas, events, toward this end of becoming:

I was tortured by that book because Merton's suffering, in his quest for God, seemed all in vain to me. At the time I was a Black Muslim chained in the bottom of a pit by the Devil. Did I expect Allah to tear down the walls and set me free? . . . I wished that Merton had stated in secular terms the reasons he withdrew from the political, economic, military, and social system into which he was born, seeking refuge in a monastery.

Despite my rejection of Merton's theistic world view, I could not keep him out of the room. . . . Most impressive of all to me was [his] description of . . . Harlem.   [p. 34]

The passage Cleaver goes on to cite from *The Seven Storey Mountain* graphically and poignantly sets forth the repression and waste of "inestimable natural gifts, wisdom, love, music, science, poetry" in Harlem. Its value to Cleaver is manifold. Even where he "rejects" it, it helps to solidify his own political bent. And he candidly uses it to replenish his "flame of indignation," in that Merton confirms all he himself knows of the formidable threats to becoming, and so gives as much of an impetus to Cleaver's aims as Muhammad Ali or the Bibilical story of Lazarus.

It is, we may observe, this "flame of indignation" which swells to illuminate the "fundamental revolution and reconstruction" posited and promoted in "Rallying Round the Flag," "The Black Man's Stake in Vietnam," and "Domestic Law and International Order." By the same token, with a reversal of perspective the political generalities of these chapters yield to the "Prelude to Love," where the eroticospiritual way to "renew and transform" society (p. 190) is initiated. If anything is straightforward, simple and clear about "The Allegory of the Black Eunuchs," it is that Cleaver dramatizes in it the elimination of the old Negro, the Infidel as to the future, from the "sight" and "lives" of the "young, strong, superlative Black Eunuchs" (taking Eunuch as antithesis of the degraded stud). The new man, then, meets the present problems elaborated in "The Primeval Mitosis" and "Convalescence," and the positive forward movement of the section comes to its culmination in the solemn address "To All Black Women, from All Black Men," which combines a moving immediacy with an almost religious sense of assembly, a grave theory of history, and a sacred principle of action to create an atmosphere of atonement and exalted promise. If this falls short of loving "all mankind," it yet achieves a great deal; Cleaver's ability to speak so profoundly for all black men gives a fair measure of how far he has come, or how much larger he has become, since awaking to himself in felonious rage. And *Soul on Ice,* formally so singular, seems impeccably designed to show not so much the process as the elements of this becoming. Read just as Cleaver's opinions, it loses much of its life, because his opinions are infused with his autobiography, and practically inseparable from it.

"The self," Wallace Stevens has written,

> is a cloister full of remembered sounds
> And of sounds so far forgotten . . .
> That they return unrecognized. The self
> Detects the sound of a voice that doubles its own.
> In the images of desire, the forms that speak,
> The ideas that come to it with a sense of speech.

And autobiography, on this reading, must be something like a means of gaining access to the cloister, gaining knowledge of its lines of communication, its manners and laws and ideals, gaining perspective on these, and having withal the gift to tell the story justly both as to content and form. Generically, it seems to me, autobiography makes exceptional demands of originality, though remaining susceptible to the spirit of periods, and though subject to the pull of generality. Limits can be recognized for it; at least the idea of a surrealist painting as a "symbolic autobiography" [25] at best confuses the object autobiographical with autobiography proper, and perhaps actually mistakes the autobiographical implications of any personal gesture for a finished, reflective autobiography.

But if, instead of wondering where the genre might go, one asks about its recent history, there arises a legitimate question that nevertheless can only be answered by conjecture: why has the black writer so far flourished in the field of autobiography? First, I conjecture, as a part of a broad literary advance, encompassing the essay, the novel, drama, poetry. Second, because the genre of late seems peculiarly answerable to the explosive patterns of modern life, and the black writer may, by nature of his historical disadvantages, have a singular advantage in handling these patterns. Third, because the ubiquity of technology (as of institutional formulas) seems to have threatened to deface our humanity, and autobiography lends itself so well to a rediscovery that proceeds from the ego out—here the genre stands in opposition to a positive threat of individual nonentity, where in the Romantic period it worked to offset a negative effect in the

25. The conception implied here has been espoused by James Olney in *Metaphors of Self: The Meaning of Autobiography* (Princeton: Princeton Univ. Press, 1972). Various objections to it have already been raised in this essay. One more may be touched on, in the fact that "autobiographical" novelists like Conrad, Wolfe, and Gide have such difficulty coping with the demands of autobiography proper. What one does to express oneself is not tantamount to how one tries to define oneself. The distinction between the autobiographical and autobiography is at once theoretical and real. Instead of a "symbolic autobiography" we should probably speak of an "autobiographical symbol."

environment, a vacancy resulting from the removal of an external cosmos of thought and value. And fourth, perhaps, because critical expectations and endeavors in relation to the black writer seem to be changing for the better. But when all is said and done, it may be only because such factors constellated for a handful of exceptional individual black writers. Autobiography after all calls for the individual who adheres to the category even as he changes its definition.

Index

ROMANTICISM

Designed by R. E. Rosenbaum.
Composed by Vail-Ballou Press, Inc.,
in 11 point linotype Baskerville, 2 points leaded,
with display lines in monotype Baskerville.
Printed letterpress from type by Vail-Ballou Press
on Warren's 1854 text, 60 pound basis,
with the Cornell University Press watermark.
Bound by Vail-Ballou Press.